THE GAMER'S JOURNEY

THE GAMER'S
JOURNEY

DANIEL KAUFMANN, PH.D.

Leyline Publishing, Inc.
Fort Worth, TX

Leyline Publishing, Inc.

léyliné

7801 Oakmont Blvd, Suite 101
Fort Worth, Texas 76132
www.leylinepublishing.com | https://geektherapeutics.com

Printed in the United States of America
10 9 8 7 6 5 4 3 2 1

Library of Congress Cataloging-in-Publication Data is available upon request.
Paperback ISBN: 978-1-955406-23-9
Digital ISBN: 978-1-955406-24-6
Audio ISBN: 978-1-955406-25-3

Editing and Proofreading by Anthony M. Bean
Copyediting by Madeline Jones
Text Design and composition by Asya Blue Design
Cover Design and Illustration by Arianna "Kaz" Unciano

To my amazing wife Julia and our wonderful son Desmond. I look forward to every step of this journey through life because I am able to experience them with both of you. Thank you for always encouraging me and supporting me, no matter how much time it takes to level-up.

A special thanks to my podcast cohosts on The Gaming Persona. Thank you so much Jenny and Gene for being a part of the never-ending quest to explore who we become when we play games.

There are people who I am honored to say are lifelong friends that I would never have met if not for my time spent playing MMO games. Thank you for giving me the confidence to become Dr. Gameology.

To everyone who believes that playing video games distract us from our journey through life – read on.

For every person who sees themselves as a gamer, this book is for you. I hope by reading this you feel empowered by your gaming experiences, and as always, Continue the Journey...

TABLE OF CONTENTS

ACT II
Initiating The Self By Playing Games

ACT III
The Return to Life As the Endgame

EPILOGUE
Freedom to Live The Gamer's Journey

LIST OF FIGURES & TABLES

INTRODUCTION: VIDEO GAMES & THE MONOMYTH

ACT I: THE DEPARTURE INTO PLAYING VIDEO GAMES

ACT II: INITIATING THE GAMER'S JOURNEY

ACT III: THE RETURN TO LIFE AS THE ENDGAME

EPILOGUE: FREEDOM TO LIVE THE GAMER'S JOURNEY

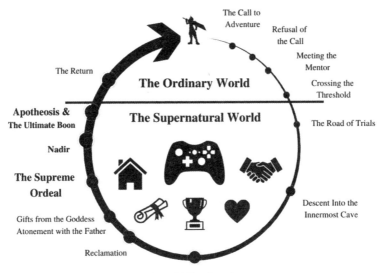

The Call to Adventure

Refusal of the Call

Meeting the Mentor

Crossing the Threshold

The Road of Trials

Descent Into the Innermost Cave

Reward & Transformation

Reclamation

Gifts from the Goddess
Atonement with the Father

The Supreme Ordeal

Nadir

Apotheosis & The Ultimate Boon

The Return

The Ordinary World

The Supernatural World

FOREWORD

HOW WE FIND OUR JOURNEY

Many people identify themselves as gamers. In many arenas, this label is not welcomed as a strength. Instead, gaming often leads to judgment on the person, even to the point of blocking the game player's ability connect and share their passions with others.

When I look back across the stages of my life, I have always been a gamer too. Since the age of four, I remember playing the Nintendo Entertainment System and doing my best to show my family members that I have learned everything it takes to rescue the actual princess from the castle. I was proud of this ability, and it established where I sat in the living room at family gatherings.

I learned to be this way in school too. In fact, the desire to be great at things was born within the screen of my favorite video games, but was a perfect recipe for academic success. If you pay attention to the lesson, study up, and execute the truths of your knowledge well enough, you will win in life too. This lesson has never led me astray, and has worked across childhood, college, grad school, and even professionally.

This book exists because of my passion for all the traits on my character sheet for life. The idea that video games are the modern form of mythological storytelling is something I always remember feeling inside of myself. This became even clearer once games started to play out in 3-D worlds, and even more so with believable action-packed cutscenes to round out the story watching experience. By playing as heroes across an endless list of virtual worlds, I started to see parallels in the challenges I was facing in life. I decided early on that I would do everything in my power to tackle challenges in life with the same effort as I would to complete the quests in my favorite video games.

The desire to level-up whenever possible became a lifelong quest that took me all the way from childhood to becoming a professor who teaches others to find their passions in helping people. I offered counseling for many years through my practice, Area of Effect Counseling, and eventually established my online persona as Dr. Gameology®. Everything about me was meant to let game players know "It is safe to talk with me about how important video games feel to you."

Once I merged my identities as a professor and gamer, my mission expanded to not just help my clients, but to help the clients that will meet with every student who has had the opportunity to learn from me, whether they are gamers themselves or not. At this stage, I found Geek Therapeutics and began my path towards becoming a Certified Geek Therapist. This journey showed me many things about myself that I hoped were true but had not fully realized. I wrote my first published chapter in *The Psychology of Pokémon: The Power to Catch 'Em All*, which showed me that writing was another passion of mine that could make a difference for people I (probably) will never meet.

That idea continues to grow inside of me even to this day.

Around the same time, I shared my presentation entitled *The Quest for Meaning: The Therapeutic Parallels for Journey* with the Geek Therapeutics community. I was so nervous to build a professional presentation around gameplay footage, but I knew this was the only way to let my audience feel the confluence of topics this game revealed to me the first time I had played it. My goal was to share that moment with people in a way that would have meaning for them as well.

To figure out how to do this, I had to reflect on why this game works so well as the canvas for seeing this story within each of us...

I first played the game *Journey* as a doctoral student who was around one month away from completing the Ph.D. journey and defending my dissertation. This short indie title that won Game of the Year from many outlets in 2013 had always interested me, but I had never made the time to play it until one life changing morning in 2016. This game woke up my passion for the monomyth in a way that seemed designed specifically for me. The soaring composition from Austin Wintory paired powerfully with the simple mechanics of the game to bring me a perfected experience of the flow state. By the end of the game, the slow walk into the light at the summit of ultimate fulfillment brought me to tears.

This game impacted me on all levels using my favorite ideas: psychology, flow, challenge, struggle, growth, self-actualization, and the monomyth.

The presentation worked, and everyone that day was able to see my message from slides to game sequences in a way that assembled the story of the monomyth in a way that any mental health professional can enjoy. Just like I had felt when I completed my dissertation defense, I felt a blissful emptiness after this talk that let me know I had accomplished my goal and it was now time to rest until I am ready to choose another one.

I went back to focusing on my work, but I still felt like there was more to this idea that I had not been able to share yet. My entire work identity at this stage became Dr. Gameology, and I hoped more than anything I would be able to make a difference in the way video games are talked about in my field of psychology. The problem is, I have been reading the research since high school, and I know many of the more prolific authors of those studies now in person. I always suspected that these conclusions were being made by non-gamers because the passion for having fun in a digital space was absent in those write-ups. I always felt on the journey to become a researcher that I did not want to be a counseling professional who writes about games, but I actually wanted to be a gamer who was capable of joining the conversation on the psychology of experiencing game play.

The more I have pushed to add my voice to the conversation, the more the conversation has welcomed me. That does not mean it is easy to keep going. In fact, the reason I have not given up so far is largely because of the mindset that is explained in this book.

Yet even though many people would choose to work with me, I have always been shocked at how often video games are discussed by people who have never had a meaningful gaming moment. For me, the mentalities that made the most difference in my life were realized specifically because of my love for playing video games. For many years, I tried to figure out how to explain this to other people, whether it would be my clients, their parents and loved ones, my students, fellow researchers, my own parents, and many other audiences. I often feel like people listen but are lost when it comes to what I am trying to say. This disconnect is because we are not connecting at a cultural level. Since they have never lived this side of life, no matter what language we speak there will continue to be a disconnect between what it means to see the world through the lens of gaming culture.

The Gamer's Journey is my attempt to share this lens in the most powerful way I can imagine so far in this life. The stages of the Hero's Journey became a fascination over 20 years ago when I decided to read the book because it was mentioned in one of my favorite Star Wars documentaries. The stages of this journey are evident over and over when I reflect on my life, meaning they must be an important subject matter if they also are being used to make sure we fall in love with all our most enjoyable forms of fiction. The goal of this book is to use the framework of the Hero's Journey to illuminate the power of video games as a path to finding meaning by mastering our understandings of both story and gameplay.

While you are reading this book, you will notice there are a few different modes I offer you in each chapter. This book is meant to allow the reader to experience the Hero's Journey told through video games. To do this, I have offered every side of my experience as a roadmap for each chapter. There are sections where I select a game that fits the stage and spend time telling the story. If you have played these examples, I hope you relate to my review of the plot. If you have not, I am sharing a new character and their experiences with you the same way Joseph Campbell thoroughly outlined the stories of figures such as the Buddha in *Hero with a Thousand Faces*.

Another mode is when I am relating the topics to the sociological and psychological processes that determine who we are in life. As an instructor, I have taught nearly every class in my university's curriculum for counseling students, and as a result, there are many topics where I see parallels between the concept and what we must find within ourselves as game players to continue overcoming our challenges. These lessons relate to any context where we wish to apply them, not only the classroom, and certainly not only inside our favorite games.

The final mode is in philosophy. Sometimes, we accept limitations by breaking everything down into behavioral measurements and outcomes, and we forget the existential benefits of gaining EXP by enjoying moments. I spend time in this book offering my plea that we should enjoy these moments as an opportunity to practice mindfulness and reconnect with who we are, whether we see ourselves as gamers or not.

The power of the monomyth is that it does not only explain stories, but it is instead used to apply those stories to the way the audience uses the characters and their journeys to understand the modern context for being alive. It becomes a window for stepping from the ordinary world and finding ourselves in the parts of the world that impact us beyond the literal dimensions of ordinary limitations. The power of the journey is that it encourages us to accept ourselves and then become greater.

This book ties together my mission at the levels of past, present, and future. I have always felt the monomyth is being used as a baseline in video games to help us enjoy them and build personal connections. It is my hope that this book will help me connect with more people than I ever could have imagined so in my own way I can help them find that same connection to life wherever possible.

No matter what quests I begin in life, they all come back to being a gamer. I also believe the concepts we use in therapy to help people should focus more on the positive than they do on the negative. Geek Therapeutics and Journey both came into my life at times when I really needed them. They showed me a more positive path than the one I was getting ready for, and helped me preserve my joy for helping people.

Geek therapy is not just a way to make therapy fun. It is a way to translate the ideas of therapy into the same language that the imaginative part of our inner selves is longing to find in the modern world. This language is hard to find in some places, but is made alive when conversations blend with mythology, philosophy, and worlds of fiction. The best source in the world today to find all of these combined is, in my opinion, found in video games.

I truly believe every single thing I have written in this book. I hope that as you work through the pages of the journey, you give yourself permission to agree with ideas that will work for you, and challenge the ideas that will not until they become your own.

It would be impossible to play every game that fits into the concept of the monomyth. Many more games have been released since I started writing this book that definitely belong in the conversation. This reality will always be true, so we might as well consider the discussion to be complete and enjoy adding more to it as society and games continue to walk side-by-side with each other.

I hope every reader is able to find themselves within the stages of this book and can relate to the games that have been chosen. Even more, if you have your own favorite gaming memories, I hope those all come to mind as you read this and help you build your own journey out of the experience in a way that feels perfect for you. The goal of this book was to take the games that I remember playing or using in therapy sessions and translating them into a message that can become useful for more people than I will ever meet. In this way, the mythological influence is built into being a gamer, which helps us level up our life story any time we choose to play a game ourselves.

VIDEO GAMES & THE MONOMYTH

CHAPTER 1

MYTHOLOGY IN VIDEO GAMES

Find something to believe in, and find it for yourself.
When you do, pass it on to the future.

—Solid Snake (Metal Gear Solid 2: Sons of Liberty)

Video games speak to us in meaningful ways. No matter which title started our gaming journey, the experience of controlling each character engages our imaginations in ways many other activities cannot. Whether by exploring the Mushroom Kingdom's vibrant colors or Grand Theft Auto's edgy streets, these worlds resonate for years beyond our final sign-off. We thoughtfully fight through breathtaking virtual worlds while collecting unlimited experience through the joy of play. We are never alone in this feeling. At any moment, countless other players enter the conversation on what our digital stories truly mean. Over time, these stories have become modern mythology.

Humankind has always used the power of storytelling to answer timeless questions in search of a moral compass for each generation. Like mythology, video games allow people to experience ideas that provide insight into the human condition. With so many players sharing in the many journeys found in games, these quests become a valuable foundation for playing through our story in the most fulfilling ways.

For those on the *Gamer's Journey*, there is a deep connection between our favorite games that transforms the meaning of "fun," starting from our first moments of play in these worlds of challenge, skill, and reward. Video games allow us to mentally consider some of the most complicated situations we could ever imagine in a way that encourages us to tap into our strengths, using our problem-solving abilities to become the fulcrum between success and failure in each epic confrontation. We sit in our gaming spaces with the utmost dedication, waiting for each day to sweep us up and carry us toward some form of earned victory.

Just as the mythologies of old have gifted humankind with powerful imagery for centuries, video games have recently provided a magnificent step forward in the evolution of understanding our ourselves. Through this, we see our traits interact with a grand display of digital storytelling as we interact through our skills and choices. We develop these insights across our lifespan each time we play a game and take it to heart. This helps us recognize the modern importance of mythology, philosophy, psychology, and the hope which resonates through each new epic. With every new hero we command, we experience a new interpretation of a familiar journey, which allows the story to achieve a grander purpose. When noticed, this purpose brings the monomyth, as explained by Joseph Campbell in *Hero with a Thousand Faces*, into the modern era, empowering each of us to transform our imagination into understanding how we reach out for the truth in our fiction to understand ourselves better.

Every generation of game innovates beyond its predecessors, resulting in more power to blend story with mechanics for the current player base. It is challenging to choose one exact moment when video games arrived at a point where their storytelling potential rivaled other media. While TV and film are renowned for delivering stories to an audience of passive viewers, video games emphasize reaction time, problem-solving, and agency to achieve their outcomes. This comparison between viewer-based and player-based forms of entertainment has also become more blurred in recent years with the explosive popularity of streaming websites. When followers tune in to watch their favorite streamer regularly, they show the same devotion as those who faithfully watch television shows.

Whether playing or viewing, gamers become fascinated by each new story and gameplay mechanic, allowing us to share our opinions and engage in an endless barrage of community discussion. This enthusiasm reinforces our desire to matter. From this basic need to belong, players often channel their enthusiasm into consuming content as participating members of their cherished communities. We want to know what has happened to our characters and their worlds. This knowledge keeps every player engaged with the endless quest of hoping to understand each new game as they are released. The gap in gaming communities between knowledge gained through playing or viewing is inconsequential when we look at the conversation as belonging. This is why mythology was conceptualized; to share ideas and unify value systems. Whether we play a game or watch it, the stages of the journey each hero walks help us find familiarity in the journey so we can enjoy these worlds every time we think about them in the story of our lives.

FINDING FULFILLMENT THROUGH FUN

With this perspective in mind, it makes sense that video games rapidly became a mainstream hobby for billions of players worldwide. While video games earned an estimated $59 billion in the late 1970s through only arcades and home consoles, the growth in modern times now soars beyond $180 billion annually through the addition of e-sports and mobile game microtransactions. The explosion of popularity for e-sports poses an interesting quandary for parents of game players, as past generations would minimize gaming as a career choice, saying that gaming "will not pay for college." For a small percentage of people, video games can become a career. For others, lessons closely tied to gaming experiences can serve them well in an ever-expanding employment pool founded on technological innovation. Once accepted, this realization pro-vides a massive shift in the cultural awareness of what is viable for developing minds to interact with for skill and entertainment.

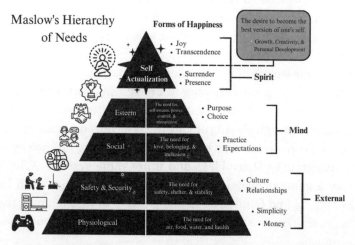

FIGURE 1. *A Hierarchy of Needs and Happiness for Gamers*

As each generation of children experiences rapid advancements in gaming over prior generations, the tendency to pursue monetary forms of happiness to justify the time spent playing these games increases. As e-sports provide an opportunity for society to view gaming as a viable profession, one might be inclined to think that the potential for earning money is a fair exchange for dedicating all one's time to mastering this craft. This view fails to consider the full potential of video games as a tool for pursuing the highest forms of happiness.

Humanistic psychologist, Abraham Maslow, created a theory of psychological wellness known as the Hierarchy of Needs. This explains not just our pursuit of simple reinforcers for basic needs but also knowing how we pursue our needs to achieve our hope of becoming the best version of ourselves. Even when we can focus on becoming better at games such as *League of Legends* or *Street Fighter*, doing so only for money ignores the reality that forming connections with others, learning to accomplish goals, and finding true balance in our lives are all more valuable than what many of us will achieve only by focusing on the monetization of our passions.

Viewing games as a source of modern mythology enhances the possibilities for a person to pursue self-actualization by playing them. Myths are more than just fictional stories. They explain the world and humankind's experience of being alive. The figurative way myths depict character and circumstance allows their lessons to apply timelessly. They become embedded into cultures and generations. They help us form connections and understand the way things ought to be. The heroes found in video games connect our potential to the ever-changing environments around us. They allow us to bond with others, form teams, fall short, and triumph. They help us see the value of time while we decide which version of our story we are motivated to live. When we become the hero of our journey, games show us what self-actualization means using the power of myth. To experience this positive shift, all we need are game experiences that apply to ourselves in the same ways we learn life lessons through the understanding of myth.

 ## MYTHOLOGICAL FIGURES AND THEMES

To begin the discussion of mythological themes in video games, we can start by reviewing one of the earliest mythological figures, King Gilgamesh, and his presence throughout history and video games.

The Epic of Gilgamesh tells the story of the tyrannical king of Uruk, who engages in a contentious feud with the gods and his people. After befriending Enkidu and slaying every combatant sent by the gods, Gilgamesh eventually becomes fixated on eternal life. While the mythological version of Gilgamesh must accept his failure to acquire the power of immortality from the Underworld, contemporary stories from video games offer a fantastic irony. The *Final Fantasy* franchise, beginning with its fifth entry in 1992 and continuing to this day, presents its version of Gilgamesh as a nomadic warrior armed with an impressive array of swords. Being cast in shifting roles of either ally or adversary on a game-to-game basis, Gilgamesh matches his prowess in combat with being eccentric. Unsurprisingly, a renowned warrior, who has journeyed through the world's myths for centuries in search of a haven, would exhibit such behavior. Regardless, the actual ruler who inspired the tale of Gilgamesh has achieved immortality through their use to continue the gaming mythologies thousands of years after accepting their mortal fate.

Ancient mythology influences video games in many ways, from overt to stylistic. Examples like *Final Fantasy* making a new version of Gilgamesh every few years are just the tip of the iceberg. As with the unconscious influences in the theory of psychoanalysis, we must challenge ourselves to push past the surface of what is played to fully realize the extent of mythological symbolism many video games communicate directly through the psyche. To do this, we first start with the conscious level. These takeaways are remembered easily once we play them. As time progresses, gaming stories resonate with us deeper, revealing subconscious themes usually overlooked at first except during focused reflection. This enhances the game's intrigue and gives us a new reason to explore each virtual world again.

More overt examples of noticing the iceberg of consciousness occur in games where dream sequences, flashbacks, or battles with the shadow-self define the story. Consider the experiences of Sora, the perennial hero of the Disney / Square Enix franchise *Kingdom Hearts*. In each new installment, the player has phases of discovery. Sora floats in an unconscious state through the darkness, gliding through the psychic plane that promises new revelations and the certainty of breathtaking battles. Throughout the sprawling narrative of *Kingdom Hearts*, Sora fights versions of his darkness (or his friends) as a foil for the prospect of the darkness taking him over. Sora's journey continues due to his unyielding optimism and the resulting hope he spreads as he wields the Keyblade.

Whether we fixate on the action or delve deeper into our reflections afterward, it is clear that the darkness represents a threat to the core of who we are and aspire to be. We align with Sora and the light because we inherently understand why we would not want to see the darkness succeed. From this internal whisper, we play. We aim to win, to view the next scene, and to see our hero restore the light to *Kingdom Hearts* itself.

When games connect with us this way, they are more than fun challenges we could walk away from. They teach us to speak the language of the psyche. If we were to leave a game without a conclusion, this would be the player experiencing a refusal of the call in which another unfinished game enters the never-ending purgatory of the backlog. When we have completed our games, it means they have spoken to us on a level that encouraged us to pursue the fulfillment of that heroic journey. To get us there, the story appeals to our desire to move through each step in the hero's actions. The engagement we feel is a parallel offering from the game world to ourselves as we experience our state of play.

Just as the hero pursuing their purpose would never give up, we keep pressing on, controller in hand, seeking to triumph over the shadows that threaten to unwind our hero narrative. This helps us align deeper with the hero to ensure the darkness cannot take control of the narrative at any stage in our engagement in play. Like Sora, we, as players, experience an imperative need to win these battles within ourselves. Games empower us to respond as the hero, answering a call with origins from the same language spoken within our psyche.

CHARACTERS, GENRES, & PLAYER CONNECTIONS

The hopes of our gaming heroes rely on our ability to guide them to victory in their quest. If we cannot achieve progress through our gameplay, it is unlikely a given character will positively resonate with our psyche. Video games use genre to construct deliberate challenges that train the player to guide their character through the story. All of these elements rely on each other to create the total experience of a video game.

The character we play as is the key to shaping these experiences. For example, multiple characters in different games can

8

fulfill the same archetype and still impact players differently. An example of this dynamic is seen in the treasure-hunting efforts of Nathan Drake in *Uncharted* and Lara Croft in *Tomb Raider*.

Other games allow the player to establish the hero's identity via character creation. Games with this approach enable players to project their idealized concept for playing the game by creating their avatar hero. Many role-playing games present this structural element as the opening task of the game. Both pathways allow the player to connect with the hero's identity as long as playing the character enhances the integrity of the story to be experienced.

Games from the Massively Multiplayer Online Roleplaying Game (MMORPG) genre are among the most prominent to include avatar creation. Players use their hero through MMOs to complete endless tasks that fulfill their unique motivations for play. Even games outside the role-playing game (RPG) genre generate similar connections with characters by approaching the storytelling of the game's central conflict using a "blank slate" hero concept. This means the player commanding a neutral hero can imagine their voice interacting with the narrative to choose their own heroic actions. Whether across the lands of Azeroth in *World of Warcraft* or playing as Link in *The Legend of Zelda*, heroes can provide a direct connection between our identities when we experience the choices of game structure through the playable character.

For decades, gamers have carried these connections with them in ways that last beyond the literal play of each story. The feeling of empowerment from playing the game fosters a sense of kinship with the experience of life, creating a unique and meaningful connection that persists beyond each adventure. For example, players often list their captivating experiences as Link in *The Legend of Zelda: Breath of the Wild* as life-changing. This game is renowned for gameplay that encourages players to experience the land of Hyrule through mindful presence. At the same time, players tackle quests entirely at their own pace. This creates a different connection between the flow of our day and the play of a game on a cognitive level. Each player is not simply resigned to the same experience by playing the same game. We subconsciously find more of ourselves in how we play games because of how we choose to play. Learning about ourselves through a context of fun is why video games are made, which serves as a continuous rationale for why so many of us will play them.

 ## FROM PSYCHOLOGY TO GAME DESIGN

Projecting our identities into the entertainment we consume is a revealing activity across multiple levels of the psyche. Early psychology, practiced by clinicians such as Sigmund Freud and Carl Jung, explains many concepts that echo our interpretations of various character choices and story turns. Intrapsychic conflict, a foundational concept in the theory of psychoanalysis, is used to describe the interplay between three elements of the mind functioning within all of us at various levels of persuasion. These elements are known as the id, the ego, and the superego. The id within us is a primary process of the unconscious which seeks to obtain pleasure and avoid pain en route to the fulfillment of personal needs and the things we wish for. This principle is balanced out by the superego, which reminds us of concepts of morality and the rules of our society. This leaves the ego to establish the balance, choosing which drive has the more compelling case and allowing us to move to action based on the calculation we make as a person to choose between what is right and what is easy.

Video games can be an exemplar of this effect within the mind of a game player. Returning to the early concept of electronic gaming known as Multi-User Dungeons (MUDS), an online text-based adaptation of Dungeons and Dragons style adventuring, players have been able to exercise the balance in their moral alignment in video game form. Game developers have inherited this innovation across the gaming space, from adventuring to RPG, from story-driven to choice-driven, and everywhere. We no longer have to type our intent into a sea of text on a monitor. In real-time, we can see, hear, and mentally draw feelings from the interactive drama on our screens. Game developers like Bioware, Larian, and Quantic Dream consistently showcase the power of moral decision-making as a method of joining the player's psyche with the game's plot. Playing games such as *Baldur's Gate 3* or *Heavy Rain* embeds the weight of player choice directly into every moment of the game, penalizing foolish decisions and mistakes with a spiraling sense of consequence that resembles life in the physical world. For games in this vein of thought, players cannot just succeed or fail based on the ability to master mechanics, but they also decide to back the forces of good or evil from within the framework of the narrative.

These choices inherently lead to characters becoming a unique mix of the player's self, articulated through the alterations to a template designed originally by the developers. Through decision-making, the player creates the character of each hero beyond the aesthetic sense. The player's ego acts from both the conscious and subconscious, interacting with the game's drama to form the memory of what it means to become each character. This suspension of reality provides a safe method for experimenting with different ego-driven experiences throughout the virtual environment. While shifting from heroic to villainous mindsets could be alarming in reality-based spaces, testing the consequences of these stances in games helps the imagination understand cause and effect in ways that can be valuable in other life settings. All the while, the subconscious observes new examples of courage on the self-level so it will be able to, for each player, explain what it means to go on the hero's mythical journey.

The narrative boon players experience in the avatar connection adds valuable meaning to their time in-game. The insight from this dynamic becomes second nature to a range of player styles. Still, it is challenging to share the experience of the mythological narrative with someone outside of the gaming community. The journey of the hero speaks directly to the subconscious, allowing the player to enjoy a new story while their inner experience unlocks a cathartic joy. This release of energy occurs because the monomyth illuminates the path to understanding how our hero role pushes us from struggle to suffering, and eventually provides the resilience to vanquish the evil hindering our inner world. A triumphant process metaphorically mirrors our hope for what we will accomplish in our journey through life, whether we can explain this well to someone else or not.

Effective communication requires a buy-in from both sides to create understanding. Most people no longer look at the drives of the unconscious as the finish line it once was for self-actualization. The focus now is less concerned with the unknowable within the self but the impact of choices, relationships, our living environment, our career goals, and the obstacles we face. The joy from gaming does little to bridge generational confusion about what video games expose us to unless it is shared from both sides. The question becomes, how can a game player share the revelations they have drawn from their time working through the greatest of their game experiences with someone who does not feel any of this inside of themselves?

For families with game players, the challenge is to navigate these divides with a desire to connect rather than degrade. If we accept the imaginative qualities that help the journey of life speak to us with context, games become an example of how to accomplish each of these things. When we hear the "Hey, listen!" of passion awakening within us, we respond to the same plea we hope others feel when they engage us with curiosity. As this paradigm shift works to illuminate both sides of a conversation, we come to realize that the heroic ordeal is not meant to banish our joys in service of productivity. Instead, they challenge us to experience life through a context that gives us a purpose we are excited to pursue.

Quest chains are a metaphor for the behavioral goals we must endure to reach a desired end. The true boon from games is that we learn how these end goals connect with our efforts using a mix of instant and delayed gratification. When we bring this truth into our awareness, we can connect with our goals using their pro-cesses. We know we can work hard for extended periods to clear out the forced goals while we aim to achieve the milestones that lead to our actualized selves. When we take time to honor the les-sons from both worlds - physical and virtual - using the ideas we have translated from an origin in gaming, we experience our life processes more successfully as game players. When we put this into words, and there is a desire from non-gamers to listen rather than control, we can use concepts like a journey shared in a game space to explain better our problem-solving, sources of self-esteem, and insights for the flow of life with others.

These life areas continuously react to a part of our identities called the persona. The persona is a version of our self-identity designed to shield us from fear by empowering us to focus on our given role. We use these defenses over time to endure tasks that could damage our psyche if we fall short. These personas repre-sent our role for a given job and become increasingly stabilized over time through choice patterns. They could reflect our voca-tion, family role, talents, superior personal qualities, or anything else that can absorb the flow of criticism we may face if judged unfavorably by others.

When personas become permanent elements of ourselves across most contexts, we refer to this full version of self as a personality. Our personality leads to consistency in our decision-making styles. They reduce fluctuation and help us stabilize the values we hold for ourselves in each life area. Personality becomes our character sheet as in a role-playing game, and our situations provide the levels in which we can aim for success, the same as the heroes we play in games.

From this, one could consider what it would mean to start a new game with a fixed choice for character selection. The first *Resident Evil* provides a splendid example of how our personality influences choices of this kind. If we know the goal is to enter the survival horror successfully, would we pick Chris Redfield, the durable male officer who seems destined by the cover art to fulfill the hero role? Would we rather play as Jill Valentine, the female officer who can pick locks while she hopefully avoids becoming a crushed "sandwich?"

While early psychology may quickly relate this to our relationship with our parents (which could be a valuable conversation depending on the player), there is a more nuanced discussion if explored with the right perception stat. As modern psychology expands beyond the psychodynamic, games will also seek to emphasize new features that bridge interactions between players, games, and communities. Inevitably, the player's personality will remain front and center across these innovations as a lynchpin between them and the dynamic connections they form during their play.

The mental realities of these game worlds are deliberately whispered to us through the language of game design. By exploring the structure underneath the surface of a given level, we draw more complete insights into our psyche. When we can see the extent of our ability to dig deep within ourselves, we also successfully continue our growth in the context of our chosen gaming environments. The game gives us the space to explore mentally, but the game's play relies on feeling the push of the design to reveal a new expression of our psychological wants. We are often drawn to new releases because they promise us a new and meaningful experience. Gaming stays appealing because, unfortunately, this need for meaning often goes undiscovered in our daily lives. So we play, focusing on discovering the messages which will inspire our grit and determination.

Successful game design utilizes a perfected learning process by guiding the player through each experience using the basic concepts of psychology. The player feels a constant sense of agency as they build up the control they need to maintain the all-important flow state. Game designers rely on many tried-and-true methods, such as clear goals, simple rules, and feedback loops, to achieve this. The ability to try and try again voluntarily to accomplish each goal is the distinction between what is a game and what can more easily be described as work. While not all games are designed for the same purpose (or even for the same audience), a well-made game will build connections with those who play them. Whether the designer created each mechanic in the game for competitive or cooperative reasons, for casual relaxation, or a display of mastery, a successful game design resonates with us mentally because it shows us that we can accomplish amazing things. A video game with exceptional design becomes a subliminal map of the subconscious that reveals the truths of who we are with each achievement we unlock.

CHAPTER II

MEANING AND
VIRTUAL WORLDS

*We all make choices, but in the end
our choices make us.*

—Andrew Ryan (Bioshock)

As time progresses, the focus of psychology tends to shift with the changing priorities of society. The dynamics used to develop new game experiences change when the elements that define fun change. In this way, psychology forms the link between games and their players.

During the early days of console gaming, genres were easily distinguished by how players were given control to achieve specific objectives. Classic Nintendo characters like Mario and Donkey Kong used to be easily recognized as platforming stars in the 1990s, but now further context is needed to identify their game type. Is the game a platformer or a fighter? A party-style board game or a kart racer? These characters appear in many styles of games, so players can connect through them with whatever genre they feel like at the moment.

The modern game style is more likely to pair hallmarks of multiple game styles together to create a novel experience. By exploring the benefit of hybridization in game design features, a game's appeal expands across player bases to generate a more mainstream appeal. A player may start their game as a first-person shooter, enter into a vehicle, and suddenly be playing an arcade-style racer, only to disembark and find themselves in a third-person action platformer. This is the magic of gaming, the ability to become anyone or anything and play any style within a virtual world, with all activities separated by mere moments.

The connection between a player and the game can be attributed to genre/aesthetics early in the decision to play. Players who stay within their preferred play style experience a synergy between the self and the game's expectations. If a player does not succeed long enough, the stuck feeling of learned helplessness can set in, allowing apathy to occur. The demoralized state saps motivation and leads to hopelessness. An apathetic player will need help believing growth is possible, which hinders their path forward in the game. By comparison, the most dedicated fans embrace these situations as an opportunity to improve (sometimes called 'the grind') rather than giving up. The concept of player types often compares casual and hardcore players, with a key difference being that hardcore players consume multiple types of games with higher frequencies. This form of player achieves need fulfillment from a broader range of in-game activities, so higher genre diversity benefits them more than players with a different style of interest in the games they do play.

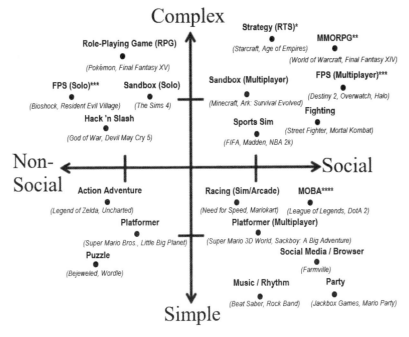

FIGURE 2. *A Conceptual Map of Videogame Genre*
(Updated from original by Granic et al., 2014)

*Real-Time Strategy   **Massively Multiplayer Online Role-Playing Game

***First-Person Shooter   ****Multiplayer Online Battle Arena

To prevent this apathy in the player base, developers package their games as innovative evolutions of multiple game styles in ways that have never been experienced before. Hybridization for game genres has altered the rigid structures which used to allow them to be easily categorized. The *Batman Arkham* series is a notable example of this. This open-world, action/adventure / RPG asks the player to solve puzzles, navigate multiple modes of transportation, and skillfully use a mix of stealth and combat to achieve the identity of the Dark Knight. Online features have pushed the games into the social arenas of team-based PVE (player versus environment) and competitive-based PVP (player versus player). As a result, players inherit a deep well of content from the developers to meet their needs across various motivations for play, all within the same franchise. Players would start, finish, and move on if this game were simply one structural style. The interconnection between hybrid features extends a player's time interacting with the online world. This helps players experience a greater breadth of personal connection within each game, provided the game delivers high-quality, compelling gameplay within each feature.

On the other hand, certain games appeal to specifically hardcore audiences who enjoy learning through defeat. As a result of this shift in desired difficulty for many players, the 'Soulsborne' genre was created. The genre originated with *Demon's Souls* from FromSoftware and has gained more popularity with games like *Sekiro: Shadows Die Twice* and *Elden Ring*. Each of these titles is highly challenging but captivates players through a relentless approach to difficulty.

The most complex of these, *Elden Ring*, is an open-world, third-person action RPG with online features that allow PVE and PVP incursions. The gameplay for this title appeals to a unique group of hardcore gamers drawn by the promise of dark fantasy lore, which the player can only learn through fighting past relentless challenges. To play *Elden Ring* successfully, a player will become known for their skill, as they must master not only the mechanics and strategies required to complete the game's most challenging encounters but also their own digital dexterity and reaction time. For these dedicated players, games of this style represent an ongoing test of their abilities. While playing other video games, one might expect to lose five times per hour on average; in a game like Elden Ring, the most experienced players may be defeated five times across mere minutes of gameplay and in rapid succession. This constant cycle of victory and defeat helps players learn from their mistakes and grow as gamers. Thus, for those who crave truly challenging gaming experiences, *Elden Ring* is a strong example of a game that allows the player to inhabit a deep virtual world and compete for every little bit of success while experiencing a unique spin on storytelling, open-world exploration, and player challenges.

Players must choose difficulty levels when starting a new game, allowing them to play according to their values while enjoying the story. It is rare for games to appeal only to hardcore audiences if it means locking the world's deeper mythology behind a relentless use of skill. Most games come packaged with a more forgiving approach, sometimes even offering a "story-only" option for players to experiment with on their path to enjoyment. In these cases, the ability of a player to enjoy themselves in the game is still important. However, the suspension of ability thresholds allows a player with a lower level of skill to enjoy the story and internally experience a feeling of success.

Take the example of Kratos from the *God of War* series. As a hero (or anti-hero), the exploits of the Ghost of Sparta in the original game tell the story of a man who loses everything from his family to his purpose, primarily by his own doing. In his time of self-loathing, his grief leads him to make a so-called "deal with the devil." Ares sends Kratos out as his enforcer, which eventually turns into an epic quest of vengeance against the entire pantheon of Greek Gods. While fighting a god in any video game would be expected to be quite the undertaking, *God of War* features a range of difficulty levels that the player can toggle. This quest can be story-driven alone or contain the most dangerous challenges. A player must conserve energy and react to opposition with a more strategically punishing melee approach. The world to explore remains the same regardless. However, as the player develops in level and skill, the game introduces new systems and mechanics at a steady pace. The story reward is equally available for lower difficulties, leaving it up to the player to internally decide how skilled they must be to earn the title of 'God of War' for the Kratos they command.

 VIDEO GAME MOTIVATION

Pursuing mastery is not the only experience that can inspire a person to play a game. Gaming motivation is a psychological concept that has been explored in various structures since the explosion of gaming as an industry decades ago. According to Nick Yee from Quantic Foundry, players ascribe three primary motivations to their gaming habits: Achievement, Social, and Immersion. Each of these motivations contains several other categories as well. Achievement has the desire for Advancement, Competition, and Mechanics. Social motives include Socialization, Relationships, and Teamwork. Immersion covers the drive for Discovery, Role-Playing, Customization, and Escape.

These reasons can inspire a person to play, and often we see more than one motive at play during any session. For example, an individual playing a game to relax may also be looking to escape the stresses of their day-to-day life. If someone games for competition, few gameplay elements are as critical as the desire to win and defeat others. However, in many games, there are varied ways to "win." A player can be looking to achieve a high score or collect every item. Some want to see the game through to its completion. This variety keeps people returning for more; all playing styles can find something new and exciting to explore. Each type of player can experience a purpose behind how they choose to play.

Yee himself comments on the misconception about players all being the same.

"Often, the media and researchers collapse video gamers into one simplistic archetype. While this facilitates sweeping generalizations about deviant behaviors and consequences, this strategy inevitably ignores the important fact that different people choose to play games for very different reasons, and thus, the same video game may have very different meanings or consequences for different players."

Yee also goes on to explain his connection with games in similar respects.

"When people play games, they are really playing out their personalities. I am analytical, so I like analytic games like Civilization 6, which seems to be the connection. So people who are more extroverted tend to be the ones who enjoy more of the social aspects of games. They can be more competitive. They are more likely to get involved in raiding guilds. So, early on when I started studying EverQuest, I would get asked "When people play MMO's are they a danger?" Those are the kinds of questions I would get early on. "Don't people lose themselves when they play as a Night Elf and forget who they really are?" And the data turned out to be the exact opposite. The same way that we choose news sources that confirm our biases and beliefs about the world, for the most part people seem to be playing games that reinforce their personalities and who they are. It makes a lot of sense when you say it out loud, but it was not a commonsense position decades ago."

Our early experiences are critical in how we approach and remember our games. The motivations we discover in video games often reflect the reason for playing them in the first place. It is important to remember that only some people who play games will play for the same reasons, and the same game can mean different things to different people. With this in mind, it becomes easier to see how gaming can be a personal experience that connects us with the virtual world.

The story is one of the cardinal places where these connections begin for many. Stories play a significant role in games, more so than many people realize. They can serve as a gateway to the game world, immersing players into the experience and giving them a reason to continue playing. Often, a story engages players emotionally, evoking a wide range of responses from happiness and excitement to sadness and anger. They can touch on our experience of fear but also lend us a taste of victory.

Take this example from a game streamer who connected with the stories of two particular games in the RPG genre on the Sony PlayStation early in her life:

"I had a rough childhood. Stories were a way for me from a young age to escape into another world. I've been playing video games since I was five years old. So when I was a little older and able to understand the stories, I fell in love with Final Fantasy. The first one I played was Final Fantasy VII, and even though I was too young to understand the themes, I was fascinated by games with plots I could immerse myself in. I remember playing Final Fantasy X when it came out when I was around fourteen and not wanting to properly level up for bosses because I wanted to know more about the plot and the world. To this day, if a game does not have an interesting story, it doesn't draw me in. While I don't need escapism as much now as an adult, I like to have a purpose. Why is my character in this world? Why am I making these choices? Does this game have an overall theme it wants to get across to players? My need for story has changed as I've gotten older because my needs in life changed."

Video games often elicit a stronger reaction than other forms of media due to the interactivity of the experience. Game players have a sense of control over their in-game surroundings, unlike those who are only listeners or viewers of a story shared by other means. This level of engagement also allows for a deeper connection with the material. The tales in each *Final Fantasy* entry exemplify how a modern mythology narrative may be constructed. This results in deep ripples of awareness that illustrate the longevity of these games in the consciousness of gaming culture. Whenever a story's impact becomes elevated in our awareness, the praise emanates between two sides of the narrative; the characters involved and the world they inhabit.

 ## WORLDS & CHARACTERS

One of the most elaborate fictional worlds to be created as the setting of a mythical gaming story is Gaia in *Final Fantasy VII*. This planet, brought into existence by the Lifestream, is dying due to corporate greed at the hands of the Shinra Electric Power Company. The story of *Final Fantasy VII* introduces us to this world through the central city of Midgar. Starting on the street level, the camera pans out to show a full view of the impressive city, the many factories siphoning the Lifestream to power each of the eight industrial sectors. As we explore the city as a player, it is revealed that there is a separation between socioeconomic classes across the city, illustrated across three levels. People are partitioned throughout Midgar in the form of those fortunate enough to live on the upper plate and the unfortunate living in the slums and the underworld.

Above all stands Shinra. This corporation reinforces this design for society as a method of control. To profit, Shinra harvests the Lifestream for an energy source called mako, a metaphor for the efforts of humanity to acquire oil or electrical energies. The Lifestream in *Final Fantasy VII* serves as the world navel concept from the monomyth. Shinra's effort to corrupt the flow of nature forms a conflict seen across many tales as a recognizable pattern. This offense, known as *Edenism*, occurs in mythology any time living beings seek out the existence of paradise, and come to believe humanity is the origin of the corruption that causes that very paradise to be out of reach. This belief is what drives many of the conflicts in Final Fantasy VII, from the revenge plot of Sephiroth, to the bonds formed between the party of heroes seeking to save the planet.

The game's opening places the player in control of Cloud Strife, a spiky-haired mercenary recruited for a dangerous mission by a sect of freedom fighters known as Avalanche. Cloud brings the iconic buster sword as a merc-for-hire who cares little for his Avalanche teammates. Led by the gun-powered arm of Barrett Wallace, Avalanche hopes to save the planet by leading a terrorist attack on a Shinra mako reactor in Sector 1 of Midgar. This struggle could have been experienced as unextraordinary by any given player if it is viewed only as a humdrum mercenary mission. If that were the case, it would only justify acts of violence because that is the easiest path for games to encourage their gameplay. In execution, *Final Fantasy VII* creates one of the most memorable opening missions of the first PlayStation era by establishing memorable characters at each pause between turn-based skirmishes. We get to know the members of Avalanche (Biggs, Wedge, Jessie, and eventually Tifa Lockhart) and familiarize ourselves with the turned-based combat of Active-Time Battle (ATB). We begin to experience flashbacks of vague memories as our SOLDIER (Cloud) battles toward the climactic explosion that marks the success of this first mission.

This timeless gaming classic utilizes every interactive feature to its fullest potential; story, setting, gameplay, and characters. Midgar needs a compelling hero. Cloud needs to piece together his past. This synergy elevates the story to achicve a powerful mythical impact. Everyone who plays through the mako reactor sequence bridges their experience with the characters' motivations to reveal insights later in the story. Nearly every narrative game seeks this mix of elements for their players. Still, *Final Fantasy VII* is a game that provides the ideal balance across each of these elements. By doing this, Cloud and Avalanche continue to introduce new minds to the greatest aspirations of video game storytelling generation by generation, all through a compelling experience introducing us to new heroes in a limitless world.

No hero can vanquish absolute evil by themselves. Despite how true this is, heroes often are alone in some way early in their journey, leaving them vulnerable until they accept the needed forms of support from the world around them. This isolation is a defining element of the journey across many soon-to-be heroes' quests.

Using *The Legend of Zelda* series as an example, we see a young boy named Link wake up one morning expecting nothing more than a regular day to happen. The quest is forced on Link in numerous ways depending on the series entry, but they all follow a similar script. A mundane day surprisingly offers a curiosity to solve. Before you know it, Link is solving puzzle after puzzle on his way to eventually finding the courage to take the ultimate quest upon himself to save the land of Hyrule.

By exploring numerous dungeons with the goal of rescuing Princess Zelda from the evil Ganondorf (or Ganon in his true form), Link builds momentum with each small step forward across the map. Mistakes can cause players to miss details and get lost, disrupting the game's challenges. At these times, it is only natural for Link, as the player, to feel discouraged, lost, and even helpless at various points throughout his adventure. These feelings make up the psychological underpinnings of the story, mirroring our own experiences that give us strength. When Link succeeds, it shines through as a metaphor for our success as well. The solutions, however, are often hinted at in the form of Link's interactions with other people in Hyrule. Along the way, he receives help from a diverse cast of friends, including the wise magician Saria, the brave soldier Impa, and the kind-hearted Goron chief Darunia. Perhaps the most foundational guide for support Link receives comes in the frequent chants of "Hey, listen!" coming from his fairy Navi in the version of this story told in *Ocarina of Time*. Without these supports, Link would have been unable to defeat Ganondorf, relegating the fates of both Zelda and Hyrule to the path of ruin. This story highlights, among many other things, the importance of having friends to rely on. After all:

"It's dangerous to go alone! Take this."
— Unnamed Old Man (The Legend of Zelda, 1986)

Heroism is not a solitary endeavor; it requires the help of others. In our lives, we may not be called upon to save a princess from an evil sorcerer, but we often have to rely on the help of our friends to get through tough times. This lesson is not isolated only to the Zelda series. It echoes across most games' stories, especially adventure or RPG-style games. The ability to draw strength from our allies and form friendships is just one principle showing how video games establish strategies for healthy psychology across our many life areas if we consciously apply their lessons. The power of support is only received when we know whom to turn to when we need an extra item, strategy, or the confidence to keep pushing toward the goal. Our quest to discover these truths is one of our best assurances that games can become mythology on their merit.

That makes their power extend long after we have put down the controller to signal the end of each play session.

 ## METAPHORS & ARCHETYPES

The power of metaphor has been relied upon to connect the flow of our ideas with the happenings of reality for as long as humankind became aware of cognition. As such, metaphors become a creative way to understand the world around us. They take ideas on a journey from unspeakable to relatable. They connect our experiences to the mythological and convert them into meanings we can apply. Metaphors allow us to notice the workings of the monomyth around us, from our lives to the events that effect our world. Any journey we go on can use the power of analogy to lend us a sense of importance, normalize the challenges we endure, and help us believe in ourselves as we keep moving forward.

Stories delivered as video games are no exception to this idea. Understanding the metaphorical meaning of video games can deepen our comprehension and reveal the potential for players to form strong connections with their environment. For example, consider the experience of playing the original *Super Mario Bros.* from the Nintendo Entertainment System (NES) era. The game's setup is simple, allowing the central metaphor to vary among players. While modern stories have provided the context to consider the proper archetypes for Mario as a mixture, including the Everyman or the Hero, earlier games only offered a challenge, rules, and a character for players to control as they hop across pipes and use their power star or fire flower to complete each stage.

Archetype	Key phrase and traits
The Innocent	"We are free to be ourselves." – Openness, trust, honesty. Character Example: Sackboy (LittleBigPlanet)
The Sage	"The truth shall set you free." – Wisdom, intelligence, rational decisions. Character Example: Geralt (The Witcher)
The Explorer	"Let's push the boundaries." – Independence, testing limits, bravery. Character Example: Lara Croft (Tomb Raider)
The Outlaw	"Rules are made to be broken." – Risk, individuality, bravery, honesty. Character Example: Joker (Persona 5)
The Magician	"Let's make things happen." – Surprise, perception, intuition, cleverness. Character Example: Bayonetta (Bayonetta)
The Hero	"I can do this." – Strength, courage, faith, hope. Character Example: Link (The Legend of Zelda)
The Lover	"Together, anything is possible." – Belonging, sacrifice for connection. Character Example: Vincent Brooks (Catherine)
The Jester	"You only live once." – Humor, originality, irreverence. Character Example: Dante (Devil May Cry)
The Everyman	"We fight for what's right for all people." – Fairness, justice, equality. Character Example: Sora (Kingdom Hearts)
The Caregiver	"I can help you with that." – Compassion, loyalty, empathy. Character Example: Kara (Detroit: Become Human)
The Ruler	"Power is the best way to make a difference." – Order, control, tradition. Character Example: The Royal Hero (Fable 3)
The Creator	"If you can imagine it, it can be done." – Imagination, design, aesthetic. Character Example: Maxwell (Scribblenauts)

* Note: Certain characters fit the selected archetype based on specific character choices made throughout their games.

TABLE 1. *Chart of Jungian Archetypes with key phrases and character traits*

On the surface, it is easy to see this game as a simple story of a plumber saving a princess. Upon further exploration of the game, it becomes apparent that metaphors help to reveal several archetypes. For example, Princess Peach (or Princess Toadstool) can be seen as a symbol of purity or innocence. In contrast, King Koopa (aka Bowser) shows us the horror of our id choosing the pleasures of evil over respecting the boundaries of others. He seeks to control others and strip them of their autonomy, causing chaos and conflict throughout the kingdom. Playing as Mario, indulging in reckless behavior without control can be harmful, leading to more errors and delaying success. By mindfully navigating each stage of pipes and blocks, the ego establishes a mindful opportunity to move successfully until the flag of victory is claimed. The balance between our need for instant success and paying attention lets us overcome Bowser. This balance proves to be a lesson in understanding the healthy psyche. By staying consistent, Mario eventually reaches the moment of fulfillment where the castle holds the princess, waiting for her rescue.

The achievement of finally traversing the right castle is a play-defining win that only occurs after a series of minor victories. This progression forms an essential parallel for using mindfulness in our own lives. Our biggest goals are not usually one focused effort but are a series of smaller goals accomplished in sequence. This process is reflected in Mario rescuing Toad many times over. He sticks with it and eventually celebrates the triumph of rescuing the princess in the castle he has been aiming for all along.

The connections between Mario and how we understand our lives do not end simply by knowing the stages in the game. The way we play reflects the way we choose to live. For example, the player's choices when controlling Mario (like leaning over to jump farther) are a projection of their inner world. You can play at a strenuous pace, leaning over the edge of recklessness, or you can play cautiously, taking your time to view every level pattern and moving only when the path offers a sense of certainty. The timer on the levels presents a psychological choice as well. While the comfort zone for careful players may be the best way to stay calm, too much hesitation will result in failing to complete the level quickly enough. Again, the player must choose.

When we view game levels as a comparison to the hurdles we face in life, we gain a more profound comprehension of the game and how it can boost our self-confidence when we require motivation. The best way to notice the path towards insight is to identify what choices we can make in our present that reflect the courage of characters like Mario. When we do this, we power up our lives into an endless opportunity to discover what our best selves can look like. This new outlook gives us the transformative ability to realize we can do remarkable things in every phase of life, just like in games.

 ## PLAYING THROUGH DEATH & LIFE

Video games use epic design to have us wrestle with new ideas using scenarios that seem beyond imagination. Going beyond this, we hope we never have to experience many of these situations the same way we see them in games. For one, people generally fear the concept of death. Whenever the drive for self-preservation encounters a perceived crisis, the tension inside each of us generates a response to our environment ranging from stress to anxiety without the actual risk of a life-threatening outcome. One of the defining elements of this dread is our perceived need to control a situation and avoid unfortunate events. When we enter this struggle prematurely, we begin fighting these difficulties as if the continuation of ourselves depends on the outcome. While not the most efficient use of our energy, we justify the struggle by believing we are fighting to prevent a long-term wound to our identity. Whether this response is an overreaction or is absolutely in line with the circumstances, the mind is biologically programmed to pursue life and prevent discomforts from occurring whenever possible.

This general drive to overcome nihilistic despair is one that video games harness to perfection. While gamers appreciate success as a motivator, failures (or non-successes) operate as learning mechanisms. Our creative talents encourage experimentation, and this helps us overcome the despair of being stuck. We want to succeed; likewise, we are playing to be successful in the world we are experiencing. However, we do not lose when our character dies in video games. We lose when we give up. Biologically, this idea only translates into other life settings if the metaphor of gaming remains a source of inspiration, a mythos for life.

Some mistakes we must avoid, and some failures have severe implications. When we approach learning with a growth mindset, we gain valuable creative insights that help us improve our circumstances. This mindset allows our focus to expand and find solutions to our challenges. Video games offer a safer space to experiment with our problem-solving, even if we must translate from the metaphorical into the realistic afterward. This creative space serves as a primary playground for the ideal self to be discovered as we search for ways to reinforce the drives governing the perceived and actual portions of ourselves in reality. We tap into this space whenever our opportunity to try again shows us how to resume from the most recent respawn point.

The balance between life and death is one that video games give us ample opportunity to explore. The classic first-person shooter by 2k and Irrational Games, *Bioshock*, dives through our expectations for control as a player by having us experience a plane crash in the first seconds of the game. The anxiety caused by this could make certain players feel uneasy about using this mode of transportation in real life for a time following gameplay. For others, this becomes another iconic initiation phase to enter into a new game. Taking control of our first-person protagonist, our only option is to navigate through the wreckage of our plane. This brief swim leads us to discover a clandestine mid-ocean lighthouse leading to our descent into the ocean's depths. After receiving the "elevator pitch" on politics, religion, and industry from the founder of our destination city, Andrew Ryan, the true nightmare begins as we take our first steps into the underwater city of Rapture.

As in many gaming narratives, the events in *Bioshock* coalesce to form the same monomyth structures described by Campbell. The opening phases of a story guided by this structure often begin with a character in a place of comfort who ponders the chance to become something more significant. However, for a story to reach mythical levels of influence, the player must be pushed out of the confines of safe imagination. They must face the terrible challenge, and realize what they must transcend. One of the most effective ways to prompt this evolution is to contrast the game's world early on with the understanding that the player is in a game. This means that their "ordinary world" as a player does not fully prepare them for the shock of what lies ahead.

In *Bioshock*, the airplane scene is an unremarkable opening with vague allusions to ideas for consideration later in the game. The player understands what it means to sit in an airplane and does not need mental flexibility when asked, "Would you kindly…" attempt to play through this part of the game. The plane crash begins the shift to leaving ordinary expectations behind. Following the swim into the lighthouse, tension builds. The descent is a visceral submersion into the world of the id, and mentally lets us know this world is no longer safe.

Without a gaming challenge, there would be no threat, making the wreckage ordinary. The horrifying imagery the player is moving through tells the entire story as we await the challenge's true beginning. The player sees this new world purely within their understanding of what is ordinary. This quickly gives way to a sense of unease as the player completes the descent into the depths of Rapture's dangerous world.

"Is a man not entitled to the sweat of his brow? "No," says the man in Washington, "it belongs to the poor." "No," says the man in the Vatican, "it belongs to God." "No," says the man in Moscow, "it belongs to everyone." I rejected those answers; instead, I chose something different. I chose the impossible. I chose... Rapture. A city where the artist would not fear the censor, where the scientist would not be bound by petty morality, where the great would not be constrained by the small! And with the sweat of your brow, Rapture can become your city as well."

— Andrew Ryan (Bioshock, 2007)

These words herald an immediate shift from a world we understand to one we could not have imagined before our time playing this game. Life has changed, and the player has plunged into the depths of Rapture. Seeing a metropolis under the ocean provides a supernatural contradiction to the world we know above the surface. Analyzing the descent to Rapture through a Jungian lens provides bounding implications. In becoming aware of what is possible in a world without sanctions, we begin to see the costs, one by one revealing more horrors. The order of the superego above fades to the reckless id on the ocean floor, and it appears all of Rapture's people are paying the price for their priorities.

In this case, Andrew Ryan is the herald of change. In myth, these characters signal the realization for the monomythical hero that impossible things are possible, and they are meant to be part of the story. In *BioShock*, Ryan shares his conviction to shepherd us to a grander creation. The bathysphere transporting us through his narration of the glory found in Rapture brings an end to the comfort of knowing what the world is and lets us know in our fleeting time in the game so far that our experiences can be so much more. Even the name of the city, Rapture, echoes this calling. We, as players, are the chosen heroes of this story. We are meant to fight through the ocean depths by learning to be a part of this world, yet we still need to find new ways to survive at each turn to keep moving forward.

As a video game, *Bioshock* achieves excellence as a postmodern example of the symbolic separation phase we expect in our myths. It speaks the language of the psyche from the moment we wade through the waters and cross each threshold into the deeper dark of the ocean world. Rapture is impossible, and yet we can see it, hear it, explore it, and even die in it (if only to become reanimated in our vita-chamber seconds later). The ideologies we are exposed to with each new revelation in our character establish the importance of ethics in scientific curiosity. Without the structures of society meant to preserve life through restricting chaos, who knows what monstrosities humankind could unleash on existence?

Rapture shows us the unfathomable depths of our subconscious, unshackling us from the limitations of reality and exposing our darkest fears in the corruption of religion, mysticism, sexuality, and sanity. Sometimes, light entering the room reveals a magnificent sight prompting our applause. Other times, the same light reveals the terror of a broken world and imminent death. Ultimately, we are meant to fear the aftermath of a society that rejects limits and gods.

We experience the terror in Rapture through our sense of ego. Although we understand the importance of maintaining the balance between our ego and reality when we reflect, the concept of

Rapture represents the dominant id destroying the superego. This dynamic is felt through our powers of conscience. As we move the story forward, we face our inner selves, deciding what to become in a world without consequences. Whether we embrace or oppose this chaos, Rapture forces us to choose. Our destructive potential grows each time we save or harvest the Little Sisters, with us being morally exempt while the choice happens inside a video game. The Little Sisters are powerless but represent our path to power. What will we sacrifice to achieve greatness? This gambit answers a primordial "what if?" inside of us and offers encouragement that, if we had to, we could also achieve the impossible. By playing a game, we can save the ordinary world we know and the world of the depths, but only if we choose to take on otherworldly challenges.

 ## EXPANDING BEYOND THE ORDINARY

From the mystical worlds of *Final Fantasy* to the mythology of *God of War*, the hope of the Mushroom Kingdom to the despair of Rapture, video games take inspiration from the monomyth to encourage each player to surpass their limitations and connect with something greater. While heroes typically require a world to rescue and villains to defeat, the significance of their stories goes beyond mere combat and resonates with us on a deeper level. The journey lives on each time we expand our potential using lessons from our favorite gaming worlds. We understand the concept of living in the ordinary world, yet our natural inclination to seek out the extraordinary persists. Video games empower us to believe in ourselves in memorable ways.

Playing games allows us to unleash our imagination and delve into experiences that push the boundaries of meaning and purpose. As our heroes meet each challenge, games let us unlock each achievement with them, through them, and as them. The symbolism becomes a metaphor, and every game offers new possibilities to explain our reality better. When we ask a friend, *"Have you ever played...?"* we ask which heroes they connect with personally. As human beings, our sense of connection arises through shared experiences and the exchange of our ideas. Video games provide this context in the same way as our hometown, systems of faith, culture, and so many other details of how we have reached the moment we call "now."

The journey for gamers provides a thought-provoking energy when we recognize the presence of the monomyth within games and ourselves. It gives us meaning and insight while encouraging gaming culture to embrace itself as a bastion of mythology. By embarking on this journey, we become the chosen hero in our own story. As we advance through each phase of life, these ideas keep this truth alive in a world that often forgets that imagination is among our most extraordinary abilities. When we take the time to remember this superpower, discovering our best selves in-game and without becomes the most fulfilling quest we can ever hope to complete.

CHAPTER III

DESPAIR &

DESTINY

I've struggled a long time with survivin',
but no matter what you have to find something to fight for.

—Joel Miller (The Last of Us)

T he concept of family provides us with a meaningful direction in each phase of life. Every relationship has an origin story, and the same is true in the connections we form with our favorite game titles. When we succeed at an important task, those we consider family will be the first to congratulate us. When we fall into the depths of despair, for many of us, family is where the caring voice will come from to assure us everything will be okay.

Video games provide a safe space to explore the emotional struggle with family as well. In *The Last of Us*, the player seeks to survive a post-apocalyptic version of our world brought to its knees by a sporous infection. One by one, billions of people breathe in the airborne toxins, descending into crazed mindlessness. As each soul drifts into their undead existence, becoming an organism living in a visionless stupor, humanity struggles to keep hold of its nature. The need to connect with our environment has become a liability for those surviving in a world where society has died along with the social contract of right and wrong. This game is yet another example of the modern world wrestling with the fear of death, illustrating the despair we would face by losing the very source for our sense of self, our minds.

As we play *The Last of Us*, we become the audience to a grand process that sees humanity recede while the new status quo favors the rise of nature across each cinematic. The conflict of this world emanates from the global infection that leaves society powerless to do anything beyond simple survival. Among the most notable takeaways from this franchise is the realization that humans, even in a backdrop of horror, still provide the most significant source of terror.

As a family, we witness the world's demise, starting with the confusion of the first night of the outbreak. The characters are a father named Joel and his daughter Sarah. The game's opening minutes are spent with this father-daughter relationship at the forefront. Displaying archetypal innocence, Sarah draws us in with her thoughtfulness and humor as she offers an expensive watch to her father as a birthday gift. The relaxed tone of this opening scene shifts mere minutes later as we are awoken to play Sarah. We wander in a sleepy stupor through an empty house in the middle of the night, each new item we interact with (or window we peer through) slowly assembling our awareness that the world has fallen into a state of nightmares.

Being a survival horror game, *The Last of Us* challenges the player to differentiate between situations where it is possible to fight or more prudent to run and hide. In this opening, there is no combat from either Joel or Sarah. The only goal is to flee their hometown of Austin, Texas. Fighting back is not an option. Controlling Sarah, you witness your father kill his first person, a crazed neighbor who invades your home. Realizing the danger, Joel and Sarah get in the car, hoping to find safety elsewhere. However, the family's "zombie plan" will not work due to traffic. The attempt at an easy getaway is decimated when an out-of-control car collides with your vehicle at an intersection, injuring Sarah and leaving the family grounded in their attempt to escape on foot.

Taking flight on foot is only reasonable if a person can stand. The frenetic immediacy of this encounter comes from realizing Joel Miller is the father of a young girl in a city gone to hell, and he has to try despite being powerless. Responding to his basic instinct as a parent, the player (through Joel) looks to carry Sarah to safety. The player is incapable of fighting, exposed at every exchange as they endure their vulnerability to offer Sarah her only chance to survive. This family could have only a few more minutes; car crashes, explosions, dead ends, and witnessing the hysteria from every angle as more and more runners (as they are called) come at you.

The goal is to reach the edge of town on foot, weaving in and out of buildings until you make it. Just as you escape, an armed soldier greets you, firearm raised and light shining in your face. The order comes over comms to prevent anyone from leaving the city as part of the containment protocol for biological threats. As the player, our hopes are bound to these two characters. The shots are fired as our characters roll away. We are meant to feel the confusion of the scene, knowing that we guided the characters successfully to what was meant to be their point of survival. Joel rolls over, mildly injured, instantly realizing Sarah was not so fortunate. The bullets did not hit Joel because they hit Sarah. We recognize the escape attempt was in vain, and fate has decided the characters we bonded with are not continuing the way we met them.

Our time with this family is now defined by the misplaced logic of a soldier and a father who will never be the same. Despite the "greater good" prevailing, we are sent on to play even deeper into a feeling of crisis. Sarah dies in your arms, crying for life until death brings about her final silence. The separation for the father and his daughter is life and death, and the ordinary world for happier stories is now gone until Joel learns how to survive without his daughter.

The story resumes 20 years later. The world, like Joel, continues forward while memories remind both of a world they will never see again. As the player, we are tasked with guiding Joel through a life defined by this loss, hoping to find a way to reconnect with something worthwhile. The profound personal loss Joel experiences is too devastating for anyone to want to explore in reality. Using narrative elements in video games, such as cutscenes, we can experience tragedies intimately without living them ourselves. *The Last of Us* accomplishes this masterfully as it deploys psychological overture in its characters to define resilience against a backdrop of near-total loss.

This loss has broken Joel. He no longer sees a real purpose for himself. As a hunter, Joel tracks down supplies and delivers goods for those in charge without worrying about any moral compass. This helps him score his rations as a form of currency and maintain credibility across the Boston QZ (Quarantine Zone). In terms of his grieving, Joel suffers in silence, embracing apathy and surviving. He acts in a way that covers up the pain of being the Joel who used to be a father.

Healing has not occurred because Joel has not allowed himself to accept his loss. Denial has mutated into despair. In this way, Joel's inner world has become infected in a way that metaphorically mirrors the world's downfall. His callous temperament is a defense mechanism designed to identify the best method of completing the next delivery. He uses his sense of fear to exercise caution in the field. This helps him survive and avoid being cornered by runners (and more advanced mutations known as clickers). When engaging with others, a stance of intimidation grants him subconscious permission to complete any acts of violence required by the work. This Joel is lost, but the story of *The Last of Us* uses that truth to develop a lasting commentary on humankind's ability to find hope, albeit a subjective one that favors some people over others.

Our time in the Boston QZ allows *The Last of Us* to familiarize us with a desperate version of "martial law." On an equally desperate level, Joel receives his next mission; to deliver a package to a freedom faction known as the Fireflies. The success of this mission is believed to be able to save the future of humanity. Joel becomes the courier for this hope, despite his indifference early on. The package happens to be a girl named Ellie, who had been bitten by a runner three weeks earlier and inexplicably does not turn into one of the undead. Joel and Ellie become partners on this trip across the country to reach Salt Lake City, Utah. From city to wilderness, the plan is lofty throughout.

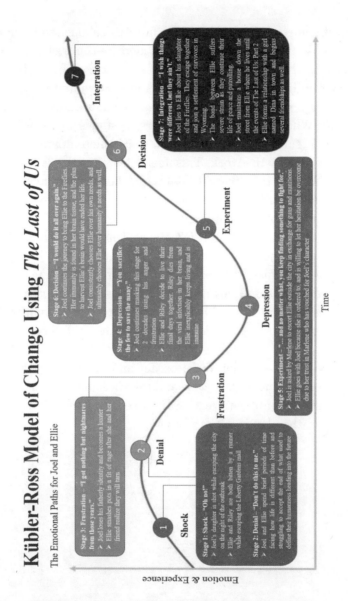

FIGURE 3. *Stages of Grief and Loss as Experienced by Joel and Ellie in The Last of Us*

Together, the two escape several life-threatening ordeals (mostly from sentient humans) in each locale the player guides them through. Their trials result in an eventual bond that proves to alter the flow of fate itself. The parental instincts, which previously represented despair for Joel, reawaken throughout the story. As this happens, Joel subconsciously projects these instincts into the goal of delivering Ellie to the Fireflies. He cares about her despite becoming vulnerable to emotion again, a risk to his priorities for self-preservation. Ellie returns this sentiment when the player assumes control of her after a would-be-fatal fall Joel incurs midway through the story. Ellie's ability to endure is tested beyond any reasonable expectation for a teenage girl, even one born after a world-ending pandemic. Eventually, Joel returns to consciousness, owing his life to the courageous choices of Ellie, who did not give up on his fading ties to life.

The decision to not give up on Joel is part of Ellie's resolution that hope can persevere over death. This is revealed through the memory of her final days with her friend Riley, which occurred three weeks before embarking on her journey with Joel:

"The way I see it, we got two options. Option one...We take the easy way out. It's quick and painless. I'm not a fan of option one. Two... We fight. There's a million ways we should've died before today. And a million ways we can die before tomorrow. But we fight... for every second we get to spend with each other. Whether it's two minutes, or two days, we don't give that up. I don't want to give that up."

— Riley Abel (The Last of Us: Left Behind [DLC], 2014)

Throughout the story, Ellie's idealistic nature serves as a counterargument to the evil deeds happening around her. However, from Joel's perspective, ambiguity in these same situations can lead to tragic death.

In the climax of this game, the concept of absolute good is challenged by the subjectivity of our perceptions. This raises the question of whether good truly exists or is doomed to be a matter of personal interpretation. Joel chooses to save Ellie at the cost of giving the Firefly doctors a chance to study her immunity. He chooses this because the operation requires the sacrifice of Ellie by harvesting her brain and effectively ending her life. The idea of losing Ellie in any way threatens Joel's progress through the stages of loss, and he cannot fathom having to re-experience these phases. Due to his emotional attachment to Ellie, Joel kills every doctor in the room (as well as the Fireflies leader) in cold blood. When Ellie awakens, she is in the getaway car. When she asks what happened, Joel is too ashamed to tell the truth. With the weakest of explanations, Joel tells the lie that there is no hope for a cure, depriving Ellie of her destined purpose. They drive into their future, surviving together until the eroding lie reveals the remaining truth.

Since this lie carries over into *The Last of Us: Part 2*, this journey ends ironically. The protagonists are both alive, but humanity has unknowingly fallen from the potential path of redemption. The chance for our species to actualize is beyond lost. Instead, the dark ages continue, limiting everyone to a world where making it through one day without bite marks becomes the highest of achievements. Anything beyond this is an easily discarded luxury, with the balance of good and evil being hardly more than the distinction between alive and not alive. Any cost to stay on the side of living becomes acceptable as the fall of morality yields to the will to survive. This sounds tragic under normal circumstances, but in this world, it simply means the story continues.

As players, we return to our headspace, wondering what this all means. The despair sets in as we are reminded that *The Last of Us* is fiction, yet we want so deeply to enjoy the ending despite our superego screaming that this desire is unacceptable. We spent time with the characters, and the finale frustrates the expectation of seeing hope prevail. The bleak world of our game influences what wc know we hope to be. We wrestle with things that hopefully will never occur in reality, wishing to be enlightened by what is unreal. Games like *The Last of Us* remind us how fragile life is and why hope is worth holding onto.

 ## FROM DESPAIR TO THE SOURCE OF HOPE

Regardless of how much time each person is granted, the proposition of death ominously moves closer with each passing day. Since it is unknown how much time we receive in our lives, the unknown can be a powerful source of either dread or motivation. It can encourage our pursuit of a lofty goal, convince us to make amends in a strained relationship or build our drive towards noble ideals. The uncertain timeline creates the need to start our journey before we miss the opportunity to pursue destiny.

For the less virtuous, these wants (or needs) could be what encourages us to "go for it." We may take advantage of a situation to achieve these successes no matter the cost (or whom we alienate) because "the ends justify the means." Or we could live a life of virtue, supporting others and creating a positive area of effect for those around us. Value systems are vital in deciding which is ideal on the personal and communal levels.

Ever since societies began sharing thoughts, the mythological concept of the underworld has tied humankind to a collective purpose focused on living a virtuous life and avoiding the gods' displeasure. While early mythology looked at the underworld as an equitable gathering of all fallen souls for a post-mortem existence, later mythologies and religions added the idea of judgment to the process of death. From this, we gradually arrive at the concepts of heaven and hell.

While the original *The Last of Us* game is presented to us without the influence of an afterlife philosophy, the world does contain this concept in *Part Two* in the Seraphite cult. This cult is a reference to the common elements of collective groupthink, but with a nihilistic lens that matches the environs of the game. This fear takes is easy to project in a setting like *The Last of Us*, as society is constantly shifting with a desire to control the trends of thought processes instead of the abstract process of a flowing existence in harmony with our surroundings. This conflict goes back thousands of years in human history, even to the times of those who worship gods or follow prophets being at odds with those who worship the powers of nature itself.

Games expand this commentary all the time, with many great examples coming from the *souls-style* genre. In their punishing mechanics, these games also occur in worlds that embrace a nihilistic philosophy. This genre embraces the loss experience through gameplay mechanics and the ideology of the realms on display. Narratively speaking, the world in each of these games has abandoned hope, and rightfully so. In each case, the balance between heaven and hell has shifted towards the rite of suffering for all people, whether alive or dead.

The player tends to be the one random participant in a fight that has long been conceded for defeat in these worlds. This foundation adds a depressing shade of darkness to each playthrough, and falls painfully short (in an ideological sense) of the inspiring potential a hero's journey usually generates. Stories rooted in darkness lament the cosmic failure of humankind, while video games generally rejoice in a mode of inspiration by the time we finish them. The complete legend of gaming requires both the aspirations of the light and the threat of looming darkness to reflect how we can overcome our own dark times.

Since video games operate through a state of imagination, it is possible to wrestle with our existential worries without plunging into permanent distress. This safe space lets us explore our reactions to things that make us feel powerless while offering a spark of inspiration to make it through tough times. Events of war or pandemic crises put us in a place where we watch in horror as the drama plays out, often without warning. This is how many begin to consider mortality on a personal level. The more tragic the circumstances, the more normal it is to wonder how fragile life is and how to value the time we are given. In a mythological sense, waiting for entry into the afterlife without a sense of agency is among the most terrifying ways to exist, especially as we are constantly reminded that our value relies on how well we accomplish our goals. In a therapeutic sense, externalizing the fears that leave us powerless allows us to refocus the narrative to create opportunities for courage.

Video games often use their ability as a medium to let us explore our worries by using both characterization and narrative flow. One of the quickest ways to identify a villain character is in their motives since our subconscious correlates the lust for power with corruption. Villains such as Ganondorf from *The Legend of Zelda* series represent the power portion of the Triforce. His goal is to plunge Hyrule into a subservient position that props up his dominion for all time. He seeks to become a dark champion of control, lording over all of existence.

In the *Zelda* series, heroes represent the qualities of wisdom and courage. Link, the hero of time, fights Ganon in each telling of their myth to restore freedom to Hyrule and overcome evil. Princess Zelda also manifests in different ways to aid Link at critical moments throughout his endeavors. In doing so, and infuses the narrative with a much-needed portrayal of a heroine wielding the ultimate wisdom of the Sage archetype. She consistently steps into the more modern versions of this tale to restore the forces for good during the direst moments. Her guidance shifts the tides of doom into opportunities for hope. Likewise, her knowledge of the overall mythos opens up critical opportunities for Link's acts of resilience. When we pick up the controller to play as Link, we are choosing to champion the side of life through action. The video games we play cast us as the hero, and each new achievement we unlock exemplifies seizing the joy of life in an ambiguous world.

While it is true that games can tell stories in ways that make them beholden to the world-defeating narrative of the villain, this perspective is not a complete truth on its own. Wherever hope appears futile, the hero reminds us that there are different archetypes that all believe hope has a place in every story. Gaming does not have to be a mirror for despair. Instead, each video game can be a place for new heroes to make their mark and show how creative life can be when we find the path to victory.

The balance between a thriving existence (Heaven) and permanent suffering (Hell) in games is often decided in an epic confrontation between the principal villain and the protagonist. The villain commonly seeks to control the powers of existence that would send the living prematurely into their afterlife. Likewise, our heroes naturally represent the influences of destiny, reminding their world (and us as the player) that life will triumph over death. The ease with which the story delivers these ultimate successes leads directly to the player's attachment to the hero and their accomplishments.

Many people outside of gaming communities assume that video games are only for children and that they involve simple fairytales with happy endings that can be completed by anyone holding a game controller. If accepted as truth, the comedy of this assumption would remove any value from the mythological connection these stories give us. The benefits of narratives featuring the battle of good versus evil can come from many mediums. Still, we seek them out not only because of a need for an entertaining escape but also because our connection with games validates our belief that we could be heroic too. It encourages our lifelong resolve to matter, even if this encouragement echoes in phases of life that sound more powerful on the subconscious plane.

The perception that games amount to valueless play for children limits the experience of any hero story in this space to being a distraction rather than a strength. The implications of this societal value repeatedly cause play, a foundational element of childhood and flourishing mental health, to be forgotten as a meaningful element of growth. The reality is that games tell stories where the influences of good (and sometimes the very heavens themselves) must struggle for the hero to overcome death. The war between good and evil translates into purpose, where the player takes action to play a part in the outcome. Every success is earned by playing through them, despite those lessons emanating from the subconscious first for the audience.

Even stories experienced in childhood can echo into later phases of life, coming to matter even more. Children are hopefully less concerned with dire worries such as despair and the dominion of evil forces. The struggle against despair emerges later in life. Moreso, when introduced in-game, eternal threats such as Hell use inherent understandings from larger belief systems to emphasize this struggle. Without grand stories, we have no place in the battle between angels and demons. Video games that illustrate our place in the mythological realms help us learn the deeper importance of considering our potential for good in the face of evil in our ordinary existence. Play allows us to grow successfully while learning to believe that even the most devastating forces of evil can be overcome.

 ## THE DESTINY OF HEAVEN OR HELL

The result of this dissonance – that play is designed for children, but our purpose is discovered through life experience – is the inception of a different kind of hero; One who relies on satire to juxtapose the struggle between the very Heaven and Hell that determines the differences between good and evil. The Jester archetype helps us cope with the heavy weight of the comedy between hope and despair. Just because a hero might make light of the epic conflict does not mean their status as a hero becomes any less potent when compared with other archetypes.

As storytellers, game developers use this type of character to provide the audience with a hero who brings humor to each encounter, even in the face of despair and potential failure. One enduring example of this hero archetype is Dante from Capcom's *Devil May Cry* series. Named after Dante Alighieri, the author of the *Divine Comedy*, this Dante exemplifies the concept of comedic rebellion in the face of eternal defeat. Many of the levels traversed in this series reflect the imagery of the original narrative poem from Alighieri, referencing the phases of Hell, Purgatory, and Paradise. The story of Dante, the renowned devil hunter, begins in his youth and progresses as he uncovers his true origins. As the son of the demon named Sparda, Dante works to gather information about the growing demonic threats in each game so he can defeat them before ultimate doom sets in. Each time Dante intervenes, the danger intensifies, allowing the forces of evil to move closer to establishing dominion over reality.

Dante has developed a range of defense mechanisms to maintain his positive attitude and effortless style during intense battles. This helps him survive while constantly battling on the brink of fate. Each escalating enemy, from lesser Baphomet to King Cerberus, is met with quips and gestures of boredom from Dante before he unleashes the range of his demon powers to save the day. Even as the cast of DMC face-off against the most formidable of hell spawns, Dante is prone to draw energy hearts in the sky, pose for selfies snapped only in his imagination, and even perform a full rendition of the timeless Michael Jackson moonwalk dance the first time he dons the hat of Dr. Faust. Dante cannot be bothered to worry about the imminent future where he fails and humankind ceases to exist. He steps into every battle unencumbered by dread, which passes on to the player as we laugh our way to defeating every creature found in the encyclopedia of demonology. As a result of the lightheartedness, our jester emerges as a victorious archetype every time the demonic danger is pushed back.

The typical structure of each Devil May Cry game features Dante going straight to the source of the rising devil problem, traversing the descent (the Greek *kathodos*) before he is ready. On this attempt, the powers of darkness always shut him down, relegating him to attempt the climb again once he is equipped with more understanding of what it will take to be victorious. Dante (or the hero selected by the player) must then journey through an ascent (the Greek *anodos*) to find his inner power at the source of the demonic invasion. Every weapon Dante collects on these journeys reflects a form of his subconscious desire to demolish his opponents in battle with a creative flair. This segment of the game can be seen as his banishment to the depths of hell, with the ensuing struggle to return being either a climb through purgatory or an embracing of his punishment for failing to defeat the threats of reality earlier. Staying with the structure of the game, the most common outcome for Dante in these moments is to find out that the actual threat is his family in the form of his ever-adversarial brother, Vergil.

The history of Dante's eternal struggle with his older twin Vergil also draws inspiration from their namesakes, sharing an origin in *Dante's Inferno*. While the literary version of Virgil is known for guiding Dante Alighieri through the nine circles of Hell, the twin sons of Sparda see the same Hell in this series with dramatically different interpretations. Across the history of DMC games, Vergil and Dante repeatedly engage in combat on an equally physical and philosophical basis and do so across locales reflecting a hell that is moving ever closer to eternal victory over the earth. Both resist mortal death, inheriting their core duality for life and death with their pedigree from the pairing between their demon father and a human mother.

Following the death of their mother early in life, Vergil embraced his devil heritage while Dante embraced his humanity. The battle continues with more clarity in each game as the player learns more clearly what Vergil is willing to do to achieve his view of destiny. As Vergil illustrates during their battle in the moment of Kathodos atop the unholy tower Temen-ni-gru:

"Why do you refuse to gain power? The power of our father, Sparda? ... Foolishness, Dante. Foolishness. Might controls everything - and without strength, you cannot protect anything, let alone yourself."

— Vergil (Devil May Cry 3: Dante's Awakening, 2005)

Vergil's chastising of Dante reveals the innate abilities coursing through both of their veins. While the brothers in this particular installment are identical on screen, save for color and weapon choice, they are anything but identical in their ideology.

Dante awakens from the verge of death, ready to tear through the gates of Hell itself to stop Vergil.

In this instance, the battle deciding the fate of life itself has transformed into a personal crusade to proclaim superiority across the chiaroscuro of the family tapestry. Dante is empowered by his terrifying nature and pure resolve all at once. These dual energies are shown off in the battle lyrics from Devil May Cry 4, which opens with a call to intimidate:

The time has come, and so have I. I'll laugh last 'cause you came to die. The damage done, the pain subsides, And I can see the fear clear when I look in your eye.

I'll never kneel, and I'll never rest. You can tear the heart from my chest. I'll make you see what I do best. I'll succeed as you breathe your very last breath.

Now I know how the angel fell. I know the tale, and I know it too well. I'll make you wish you had a soul to sell when I strike you down and send you straight to hell.

My army comes from deep within, beneath my soul, beneath my skin. As you are ending, I'm about to begin. My strength is pain, and I will never give in.

I'll tell you now I'm the one to survive. You'll never break my faith or my stride. I'll have you choke on your own demise. I make the angel scream and the devil cry.

This acclamation of confidence shifts in tone for the refrain. The final aria reflects the pure resolve to choose life and claim oneness with the sides of destiny and light as new voices join each progressing repeat:

They will see; we'll fight until eternity. Come with me; we'll stand and fight together. Through our strength, we'll make a better day tomorrow. We shall never surrender.

— Jason Arnold (Musical Artist for Devil May Cry 4, 2008)

Once Dante chooses the side of destiny, a balance is struck in the family to ensure hope is always possible. This confirms for us as players that life will continue in this universe. The fates of Heaven and Hell profess that Dante must die in these games, and yet he will not allow destiny to take him in this way as we guide him to the end of the tale. With each level, we take the frenetic combat of a hack and slash gameplay, and through our action, we empower the narrative to elevate to mythical levels of story-telling. Games that accomplish this create a sense of mythology, albeit one formed in our awareness as we play the game before us. Once we see beyond each flashy bullet and rebellious melee, the action becomes an epic backdrop of transcendent heroes wrestling against fate. If Dante can choose his destiny, perhaps we can as well?

 ## PURPOSE IN MYTHOLOGY

Mythology strengthens our connection to the unspoken truths that help us persevere through the challenges of our mortal existence. There are countless video games in which we are asked to take on the role of a hero, guiding them through moments of struggle and eventual triumph. With each archetypal hero in the gaming monomyth, activating their traits provides an arsenal they can wield to hold back the forces of evil. This is how they exemplify victory for us as we imagine them.

Video games repeatedly cast us as the overwhelmed protagonist tasked with defying the odds. When the range of these powers seems mortally imaginable, we connect with them in thinking an improbable-but-good outcome just happened in a world that only requires a brief stretch of logic to resemble our own. Even when the abilities bestowed on the hero are otherworldly, we can still appreciate the hero choosing how to address the challenges before them. As their confidence builds, so does ours. They do not approach each challenge nonchalantly because they care less about doing good. The jester archetype embraces the comedy of their goals in this way for a different reason altogether...Because they can.

Both forms of destiny – the improbable and the otherworldly - come in even more diverse ranges of narrative storytelling. Yet they remain triumphs for us as the active audience on a psychological level. We turn to these stories so that destiny can be incorporated into the essence of who we aspire to be. This enables us to use our knowledge through insight to encounter our challenges in life effectively.

The gaming monomyth shows us the truth of our psychological triumph by converting the language of dreams (which rely on the impossible) into potential solutions for our very selves. Characters like Joel and Ellie, or Dante and Vergil, seek harmony in themselves in ways that can only be granted by reconciling their origin. Both examples start with a concept we know as family.

When we connect with the emotional content of a video game and notice a reflection of ourselves in the characters, we see the power of myth front and center. The game is not telling us about the impossible. Instead, it uses the impossible to show us what we can do when we choose the path of destiny. Just as the hero faces fate in each of our myths, we can also expand our perspectives on life by choosing to play and welcoming in another mythical story to our own context. Each time we do this, we experience the thrill of seizing the expressive power of an inner hope that starts in their fictional world, but ultimately resonates throughout our own reality.

CHAPTER IV

THE STAGES OF
THE JOURNEY

Hope is what makes us strong. It is why we are here.
It is what we fight with when all else is lost.

—Pandora (God of War 3)

P laying video games allows players to actively guide their virtual heroes through a grand quest, ultimately experiencing a heroic journey. Consider the challenges faced by heroes such as Aloy in *Horizon Zero* Dawn, Sora in *Kingdom Hearts*, or Link in *The Legend of Zelda* series as we work through setting up the stages in their quests.

For each game, the early stages show the audience a character who, with certainty, possesses courageous potential while still appearing stuck in the throes of ordinary life. Just as the signs of their dissatisfaction come into focus, a catastrophe occurs around the hero. This disrupts the simple choice of staying within the comforts of the known world and prompts the would-be hero to venture into the unknown of the supernatural world. The hero has no choice but to move forward and do whatever it takes to restore the balance of existence in favor of the forces of good. By completing their journey, these protagonists not only surpass the constraints of their mundane reality but also attain legendary levels of influence over their worlds by realizing their potential.

While video games each provide a unique challenge via gameplay, game developers maintain consistency in crafting their story stages, regardless of the genre or play style. For example, Joker and the Phantom Thieves from *Persona 5* enter battle in a Japanese Roleplaying Game (JRPG), while Kratos wreaks havoc using a hack-n-slash RPG progression. Regardless, both heroes experience loss, challenge, growth, and a final showdown to defeat a god so they can restore their lives to a state of normalcy. All these games follow a similar pattern, and our minds enjoy this process because we have been conditioned to see our hopes reflected in these structures in many of our favorite heroic quests.

While it is easy to notice these stages in books, movies, comics, and stage plays, we also see these stages flow to a meaningful impact on our favorite heroes when we play through their tales in video games. The sequence of events for each unique journey can be altered to match the narrative flow required by level design and other influences. Still, the formula that makes any hero narrative resonate with the modern audience often remains intact. We recognize these level structures in ways that range from subliminal to obvious. Even though we can identify the framework, the game will continue to do what it was created for; to entertain.

This recognizable flow is referred to by Joseph Campbell as the nuclear formula. This progression includes three overarching stages which compel the hero to move forward and aim to fulfill their destiny. These stages are separation → initiation → return.

This storytelling process is cyclical, ideally suited for video games since the most popular stories are continued through sequels.

Within each significant journey arc, the hero character and their party will often work to move from the problem of the separation towards restoring what they feel is the proper state for their world. The goal is for everyone to live in the world they had always hoped for, and then the hero party can enjoy a hard-fought peace once the struggle is finished. Even after this peaceful resolution is experienced, it is always possible for a revived threat to prompt a new separation following the first endpoint. When this occurs, the next game is added to the mythos for players to enjoy. The hero then experiences a new initiation, and the virtual characters work towards yet another return until their victory can usher in the desired status quo once more.

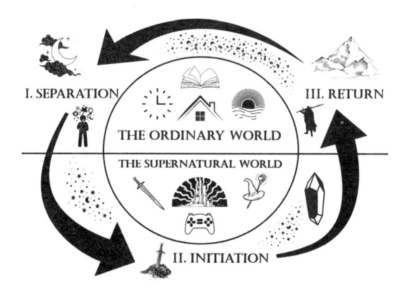

FIGURE 4. *The Monomyth Formula (as described by Joseph Campbell in The Hero with a Thousand Faces)*

As players, we want to experience new challenges with compelling stories accompanied by heroic characters. This symbiosis creates a powerful starting point, provoking a sense of anticipation for each challenge on the path toward narrative resolution. The monomyth, therefore, provides the underlying structure for a video game's moving narrative that can tug at our heartstrings and capture our imagination. Through this formulaic journey, we guide countless virtual heroes toward existential fulfillment in the world around them. Through this achievement, they help us believe in ourselves even more.

 ## JOURNEY: BEING THE HEROIC TRAVELER

Among the purest representations of the difficulties faced during the hero task in modern video games is the pursuit of growth and fulfillment experienced by the robed traveler in the game *Journey*. The gameplay opens with the flowing of sand across a vast desert just waiting to be explored. This imagery gently initiates the player into the quest without needing narration or a tutorial. This game focuses on the path ahead rather than the conventions of combat or leveling up. Players can relax while their mind works through the solutions for each area at their own pace.

The goals for the traveler remain largely the same as the heroes of other games, but pursuing goals this way allows the player to exercise their mindfulness abilities. We can be present even as we utilize the "doing stance" through our actions. This contrast allows the quest to be achieved in a way that perfectly matches whatever inner world the player is experiencing when they sit down to add this game to their day. These elements make

Journey an optimized experience for a personal connection with the monomyth.

Upon taking our first steps forward, our attention is instantly drawn to the many tombstones scattered across the desert landscape. These stones serve as reminders of other travelers and their unfulfilled journeys. As our awakened character moves forward, each labored step helps us make our way up the looming slope ahead of us. Upon reaching the top of the hill, we set our eyes for the first time on a majestic mountain. Resting far off in the distance, this destination feels impossible from our starting point. Instead, it serves as the manifestation of our ultimate potential. This motivation helps the traveler keep going at every phase of the long, life-changing journey.

The traveler then decides to press onward. Moving past the hundreds of tombstones lying in the sand, we quickly come to our first site of power. The modest structure stands as a ruin in this fallen world. The curiosity at this site comes from a glowing light emanating from a knowledge long forgotten. By approaching the light, the traveler absorbs the flow of energy. The change from traveler to hero begins subliminally as the robe-like garment extends to reveal a scarf that will trail joyously behind the character for the rest of the game.

The scarf tells the player how much power they have for taking flight. The more energy the traveler discovers, the more enlightened they become. The scarf begins as a minor attribute that allows us to float in spurts but eventually develops the ability for our travel to soar through the sky by the journey's end. By starting small, *Journey* tells us a story about how we build our most extraordinary talents. Every experience we gain is an opportunity to learn more about ourselves. With each discovery comes steady growth in our ability to symbolically soar to incredible heights when we pursue our full potential.

The world-building in *Journey* continuously shows us signs of what the world once was. This helps the game resonate with the player, as the understanding of the world is collected simultaneously as we experience it. From an ego perspective, our actions in life connect us with a timeline for humanity that has been recording its history for around 5,000 years, starting with cuneiform, and arriving at our current state. Like us, the traveler is working to achieve something that would create a sense of purpose. To do this, they decide to fly forward whenever possible, collecting knowledge and experiences. Each stage provides a new challenge, but the growth from the last challenge provides new building blocks to address what needs to be done to continue the journey.

In every new phase, the traveler learns more about the ancient people of their world and the wonders accomplished through their gifts. From the first meditation stone, the traveler sees the history of their calling through an animated hieroglyph that calls for the gate ahead to open. Passing through this gate leads to the first of many challenges. This threshold moment also introduces the mentor, a spiritual embodiment of guidance who interacts with the traveler at each confluence.

From the moment the calling ability is used on the ancient stone, the mentor appears within the consciousness of the traveler to provide a foundation for understanding the grand purpose of the path ahead. In doing so, the mentor figure represents the passing down of the old teachings to the traveler. This informs the player of the upcoming dangers through images of foreshadowing and encourages us to keep moving towards the next revelation to further develop of their gifts.

From the starting desert to the darkness underground, the traveler and their ability scarf continue to chant their truth as they float together through each challenge. Every puzzle the player completes enhances their ability to fly and spread the light onto the ancient structures that line the road to the mountain of fulfillment. They eventually face the fears of the fallen people directly, dodging the assault of the same flying machines who conquered the ancient ones shown in the glyphic stories on the ruin walls. To survive these depths, the traveler relies several times on the reprieve granted by allies of different shapes and sizes, each time learning more about themselves until the time comes to ascend back to the world's surface.

The traveler rejoins the surface world only to find it covered in snow. This hindrance goes well beyond an aesthetic shift as it also includes new game mechanics to overcome. The cold silences the flowing warmth of the scarf, leaving the wandering hero unable to take flight. They can jump but will be quickly grounded. They can sing, but the notes will fall silent as they fight for expression in an endlessly bitter wind. Considering the gifts this traveler was granted in the heat of a desert, the frigid temperatures represent a final separation from abilities that made the earlier challenges of the journey easy to overcome.

The traveler's plight at this stage mirrors the life of the game player when things feel too overwhelming to move forward. We know in ourselves what it would look like to take the right path, yet in many circumstances, we cannot seem to take those steps in a way we think would make any difference. When we play games in moments like this, we witness the Supreme Ordeal. The traveler's version of this experience comes in the climb through the ruins on the snowy mountains, the piercing wind knocking them back, and the cold preventing the simple solution of flight. Timing becomes everything as the player maneuvers slowly through every glacial obstacle.

In our physical world as players, most of us can pick a moment when life knocked us back from something we thought we needed.

While the best game strategy often leads to an anticipation of success, there are exceptions to this hopeful logic. It is possible in certain circumstances to commit zero errors and still not experience success. We can have the right plan, but it doesn't work out at the speed we hoped. For those who turn to games to relieve this disappointment, coping and escape can offer emotional benefits while they get ready subconsciously to make another effort soon.

Coping skills can come from any activity that helps a person recover this energy. The trial and error of playing games can comfort the psyche as we reflect on our situations to discover the proper path. As our traveler works through the icy path to move past their supreme ordeal, they also show us the resolve we need to work through our own. By finding the best path forward at the right moment, we achieve a reclamation of our talents so that we can use them once more when it matters most.

This pattern of learning and moving forward alternates across our gaming experiences to teach us how to play better than we ever considered during the opening stages of each game. The crescendo through the most significant challenges tests our dedication and pushes our abilities to their limit. Still, some obstacles are designed to break the player. When this occurs, the player and character create a synergy, both stuck in a moment where success feels impossible.

This greatest challenge is known as the *nadir*. This occurs when the character has experienced the darkest depths of despair and questions whether they could take another step forward. In this story, the traveler is hindered by a fierce blizzard, loss of sight, thunder, lightning, and total disorientation as they struggle to hold faith that their steps are even heading toward the mountain of purpose. The relentless assault of the snowstorm eventually conquers the traveler on their final approach to begin the path upward. This defeat expresses the suffering of the hero in their darkest moment. At this moment, the game's climax seems to signal a conclusion to a promising journey that was ultimately not meant to be realized. The traveler succumbs to the nadir of the snow, their final moment of life floating away as their near lifeless body falls to the ground.

As with many heroes who face defeat at a critical stage in their quest, the traveler's story continues into a subconscious realm. The fading traveler opens their eyes to see the mentors of past journeys surrounding them, looking on with support emanating through their voiceless expressions. Clothed in the white robes symbolizing mastery, the council of those who came before now look on to either welcome the traveler to the afterlife or to urge them forward for one last push for the goal. The next choice will determine if this journey will be remembered as another calling left unfulfilled or as a great triumph in the eternal history of the mountain.

The questions occurring for viewers now can also point in many directions since the narrative style of *Journey* is, at specific points, a projective test. Did the traveler die? Are they being resurrected by an even more mystical power? Or even more empowering, is the traveler unlocking a dormant potential that comes from the crossing paths of self-actualization, purpose, and the meaning of life?

In these moments, our unknowable strengths help us rise to the greatest of heights. The scarf of the traveler awakens with a brilliant light that tears through the fog of nadir. As the scarf lifts the traveler back to their feet, the traveler becomes instantly different. They are finally connected with the great mysteries of ancient knowledge. The powers of the ancestors are no longer olden legends but are present truths the traveler has formed an intimate connection with. Like that, the traveler launches in full force through all opposition, achieving their ascent. The apotheosis has granted the traveler the power to soar with limitless possibility. Profound revelation occurs as the magical flight redefines everything this hero can be. The traveler leaves every defeat behind in a brilliant display of mastery over song and flight. They move through the light of the highest skies to reach the desired summit and complete the journey. Reaching the summit, the traveler calmly walks forward into the light, realizing they have made it to their purpose, and enjoying whatever lies beyond.

This euphoric achievement reveals our traveler as a form of monomythical hero. From the first steps in the desert, we have seen the range of adversities our character faces. The lessons learned provide the assurances needed to meet every future obstacle with confidence. This allows the hero to transform into one who has claimed the ultimate boon. The final level of universal power fills them so they may join the legacy of the grand quest like those who came before. At this point, they can finally take the gentle walk into their actualized experience, waiting to join in the light so they may guide the next generation. Every step the traveler has taken has led them to this very moment.

PLAYING THE STAGES OF THE GAMING JOURNEY

The nuclear formula of the monomyth is not limited only to games like *Journey*. In fact, signs of the formula become noticeable any time the narrative of the game pushes the characters to step forward and accept their challenges. Aloy, Sora, Link, and countless others begin their quest in a place that is relatively known and comfortable to them. We see them start in their ordinary worlds, each feeling a powerful desire to achieve more than the typical life their world expects.

To review these scenarios more specifically, Aloy must venture away from her tribe of Nora to understand the truths of her origin. Sora is thrust into the epic quest with Donald Duck and Goofy as he struggles to reunite with his friends after the Heartless consume Destiny Island. In *Ocarina of Time*, Link has no choice but to head toward Hyrule Castle after the Great Deku Tree gives him the Kokiri Emerald and, by extension, a greater calling to assemble the Triforce and defeat Ganondorf. These are just three prominent examples from a games industry that provides us new examples of human aspiration each year to play our heroes and achieve their purpose. Likewise, the experience of playing games helps us craft meaningful experiences by interacting with this depth of narrative power, combined with the elements of gameplay, in masterful ways.

The stages experienced in video games mirror the design of the monomythical structure itself. The hero's journey enhances our experience of these stories (and characters) by drawing us in with each victory as the player.

ACT I: THE DEPARTURE INTO PLAYING VIDEO GAMES

Just as the monomyth is partitioned into three acts, so too are the phases of the gamer's journey. These phases will be explored over the course of this book, starting with Act I and covering the following four stages:

I.   The Game Begins

II.   The Call to Adventure

III.   Meeting the Mentor

IV.   Crossing the Threshold

The first act of the journey focuses on the player and how they build their connection with the game and the quest of the central protagonist. Video game narratives use a variety of tactics to deliver the *separation* phase to the player in the early phases of a game. The player could be dropped straight into moments of action via the tutorial or eased into the conflict by experiencing the calming homeostasis of the ordinary world for a period of time. By introducing characters and tensions at a rate that matches the developers' intentions, the game becomes a unique reflection of these early journey tropes. When the hero meets the mentor, this is in parallel with the player gaining their first impressions of this guiding force in the game as well. Finally, the hero of the game, guided by the player's control, will enter the main quest at a certain point by departing the ordinary world. Crossing this threshold signals the beginning of the path that eventually leads to the true battle over destiny. Once this line is crossed, the player is rapidly drawn into the full challenge of the game that the guidance of the intro stages was preparing us for.

ACT II: INITIATING THE SELF BY PLAYING GAMES

The second act, known as the *initiation*, will cover how the player experiences the challenges of their games as a metaphor for personal growth and self-discovery. These processes play out in the journey narrative across six stages:

V.   The Road of Trials

VI.   Approaching the Innermost Cave

VII.   Reward & Transformation

VIII.   The Moment of Atonement

IX.   Enduring the Supreme Ordeal

X.   Apotheosis and the Ultimate Boon

The second phase of the journey involves the greatest test for the hero. This phase is also the longest portion of the narrative. By advancing on the road of trials, the hero understands the purpose of the quest they started in the initiation phase. Isolation leads the hero to feel more alone than they were when they could rely on the guiding influences of the mentor. Support in these phases still appears as the character levels up and acquires new abilities for their quests. Non-Playable Characters (NPCs) add to the contextual life of the story by delivering these boons to the hero and illuminating the knowledge of the story. These allies appear to support the hero in their greatest moments of need, and often in ways that advance the plot in meaningful ways.

Nonetheless, the hero must enter their deepest trials alone and learn to believe in themselves if they are ever to fulfill a larger purpose. Eventually, the time will come when all of the leveling up has been achieved, and it is time to engage in the final challenges in the push toward the endgame. This realization in the player is accompanied by the reality that the game is nearing its end. This completes the metaphorical bridge of what the game is for the player. The reward of knowing the game can be won creates an understanding that the player will go from playing the game in the present to being a person who has played the game in the past. This knowledge triggers the final portions of the playthrough and defines what the gaming experience will mean for the player moving forward.

ACT III: THE RETURN TO LIFE AS THE ENDGAME

The final phase, known as the *return*, involves the player using the memories from being the gaming hero to enrich their lives. This occurs creatively across all the essential life areas until the player's life reflects the preferred narrative that contains the same sense of fulfillment that was journeyed after by the hero. This section of the book will explore the following topics across three chapters.

XI.   Crossing the Return Threshold

XII.   The Master of Both Worlds

XIII.   Freedom to Live the Gamer's Journey

The player discovers the final takeaways from the gaming experience in these stages. The hero is required in the final battles to emerge victorious in a way that reflects the total growth from their journey. They must summon all of their abilities to complete the pivotal confrontation successfully.

When a person plays these moments, they see the metaphor of resilience play out from within themselves as they channel that instinct into the characters they control. The process at play shows each character in their story arc taking inventory of their strengths and, just as we notice our skills when we experience self-esteem, digging deeper into their skill tree to reach the end-game.

The ability to achieve the final victory with these gifts is an experiential power that game players can learn from, but only after they start seeing themselves as the hero of their own story. Once this realization occurs, the stages of the monomyth illuminate our lives the same way they guide our favorite games. This achievement unlocks more profound questions, such as "Where does the heroic power come from?" By recognizing the stages of the monomyth in our lives, any gamer can use the metaphorical journey to realize the answers have been within us all along.

CHAPTER V

FLOW AND THE

HEROIC SELF

Time passes, people move... Like a river's flow, it never ends.
A childish mind will turn to noble ambition.

—Sheik (The Legend of Zelda: Ocarina of Time)

S ince the nuclear structure guides most major video game experiences through a monomythical bent, it has helped the gaming activity over time to become the modern experience of mythology. When a story from the past is labeled as a myth, it is often because it portrays the relationship between gods and humans in a significant way for the people living during that era of world history. An excellent gaming example of this is *God of War*, in which Zeus and the entire pantheon of Greek Gods serve as the boss characters hindering the journey of Kratos. These games use a mixture of combo-linking and reaction time to create awe-inspiring displays of power for each victory. This allows fans of this franchise to believe in the ability of Kratos not only to defeat gods but to end them decisively. As the story progresses, the malevolent gods intensify the conflict, adding to the epic narrative with each achievement.

However, not all sources of power in games originate from a malevolent god. The cosmic center of the universe is often emblematic of grace, allowing mortal life to exist. This happens to occur in several entries of the *Final Fantasy* franchise. In particular, *Final Fantasy XIV Online* features the Mother Crystal, Hydaelyn, and the bestowing of a power called the Echo. Sometimes, this force is personified in a character the hero meets in their journe~ Other times, the bounds of existence empower the hero to find their inspiration. This is similar to the influence of Triforce or the Lifestream as well.

Regardless of the source, the hero takes their cues from characters who hold the profound knowledge until they become ready to wield the power of light on their own. By considering the personal connection the hero often inherits from these forces of dominion, the character we see as our hero receives a power that sets them apart from other characters. Usually, this separation comes with titles such as Warrior of Light or Hero of Time. Regardless of the nature of these abilities, the hero embarks on a quest where they receive ordaining power, identifying them as a "chosen one" to receive the quest and restore natural order by the end of their journey.

Understanding how a hero enters the grand conflict can do a lot to establish the stakes for the coming battle. The balance between storytelling and compelling gameplay can be the difference between regular game releases and those that stand the test of time in the zeitgeist of gaming awareness. The most effective games allow the player to feel a seamless flow across every phase of a game's presentation.

Mihalyi Csikszentmihalyi established the concept of *psychological flow* in 1975. Flow is "an optimal state of consciousness in which people experience deep focus and immersion." This phenomenon can be used to explain many aspects of the most enjoyable game-playing experiences, from the transformation of time to the fulfilling sensation of finding success when we act through our favorite play styles. Video games provide a perfect feedback loop for player performance, making them an optimized behavioral training activity. When we play games, the connection we form with our goals and reactions during play allows us to feel the sensation of flow. This led to Csikszentmihalyi's writing, "Games are an obvious source of flow, and play is the flow experience par excellence." Flow allows our essence as game players to drift into a sense of purpose toward the end goal of a game.

Letting go of ourselves helps us fully embrace the state of play. When this happens, we psychologically merge with every element of the game. The flow experience leads to a deeper connection with the style of play we are engaged in. This helps us experience the hero's identity, fully understanding every ability they possess to achieve victory. Through gameplay, we can think and act as the character on screen. Through this level of engagement, we form enduring connections with the characters we play.

Flow enables a video game to achieve a sense of value, even when playing is solely for enjoyment or to disconnect from stress. The benefits of an epic story only sometimes become apparent at the time of play. Instead, these implications ripple across the oceanscape of our consciousness for years after the experience.

Imagine the most complicated gaming challenge you have ever attempted and what it took to reach the moment of success. Every mistake took minutes at most to send you back to the most recent checkpoint. You try repeatedly to find the one slight improvement that changes the outcome. After hours of attempts, you may be on the verge of giving up and never playing this particular game again. At that final moment, before surrendering to defeat, you notice something new. One tiny detail in the virtual room moves on the screen differently than you had assumed during all those mistaken attempts. Just like that, you walk into the boss room with a new idea, which works. You may need only a few more tries, and then – Eureka! – the boss is defeated.

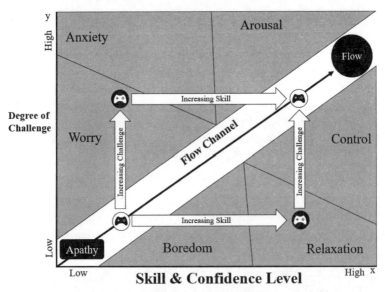

FIGURE 5. *Experiencing Challenge & Skill via the Flow Channel* (Csikszentmihalyi, 2008).

This scenario showcases many of the most valuable game-playing experiences for players starting at any skill level. In situations where every nuanced choice impacts the outcome, games teach players to become more comfortable with their flaws than many similar challenges in our non-digital reality. Despite this truth, we cannot be perfect, yet we want more than anything to succeed in our tasks. As a result, it becomes impossible to tap into our flow state because we are too busy worrying that our outcomes will not be successful.

The purpose of flow begins with addressing the gap between skill and the depth of the challenge. Instead of ending with success, flow extends into the total experience keeping us focused beyond each of the smaller moves we make. Flow propels us into our challenges. It illuminates the chain of causation between player input and gaming output. Once a player can establish tunnel vision, their skills emanate outward from them in perfect time with the gameplay. This experience is the total purpose in psychological flow. It mimics the power of the hero, but not at the moment of discovery. Rather, it is the singular purpose in moments of meaningful victories (known as fiero) that flow pushes us towards.

The enlightened player guides the hero with a nearly omniscient vision earned by increasing skill over time through trial and error. Despite repeatedly falling to mechanics, the player returns for the next attempt. By focusing their awareness through the flow channel, the challenge escalates to its highest point. All these factors come together, requiring the ability to be equal to the task. When the skill is balanced with the challenge, the actualized potential of the game to provide thought-free enjoyment for players manifests across story, mechanics, and player performance.

The elements of flow open the door for many systems inside the game to deepen the player connections that allow the story to matter. Role-playing is one motivation that helps players express themselves beyond the presented confines of a game. When people role-play at different levels, they decide how much of themselves to pour into a character. This helps them achieve a balance between escape and transference into the character's identity.

Many narrative-focused games enhance the mythical sense of importance in their narratives by embracing the concept of moral storytelling. While gameplay and skill create the dynamic of challenge in the gaming journey, the decisions of right and wrong allow the player to decide their level of connection with the tale they are weaving through their choices. Games like *Dragon Age: Inquisition* or *The Witcher 3: Wild Hunt* emphasize the importance of choice. By maintaining a fantasy world backdrop, players experience a sense of history in the quarrels between races and kingdoms. While the setup is the same player-to-player, the experience shifts based on the desires of players to enact their fantasies for the world. The balance between combat and decision-making combines to make the player feel ownership towards the character. This enables the game to provide new levels of immersion while the perception of a uniquely personal experience is created.

The ability to have that deeply rooted self-experience adds to the feeling of flow by enhancing player agency and providing a sense of control which directly fits in with the design of the gameplay. Players slowly work through the repercussions of choosing between good and evil when their choices carry consequences. This level of influence, for example, is less clearly felt when the game provides a character that is automatically scripted for good.

In video games, influence over events creates a flow connection that intensifies as the character progresses toward complete influence on the narrative. By giving the player creative power, games offer a space where moral duality adds to our ability to make a difference. This belief is tied to our basic needs and is something people worldwide hope to feel in one form or another every day. We want to succeed, so we hope our choices matter. Video games provide this feeling within the scope of an entertaining story. By merging elements of story, choice, skill, and challenge, the video game offers a problem that needs a hero and tasks us with making that difference.

When every element of flow and game design merges with our identity, a magical transformation occurs in the psyche is experienced. The game becomes a roleplay for meaning, which, similar to therapeutic interventions, opens us up to the possibility of understanding ourselves as we imagine being in virtual spaces where we have made a difference. This entire dynamic begins with storytelling through game design. When every element perfectly aligns with the player's specific needs, that is when video games unlock the experience of the heroic identity.

 ## GAME DESIGN & MEANINGFUL STORIES

Feeling like our choices matter is no mere coincidence. This experience is created deliberately. The entire purpose of creating a video game is to happily deliver this to the player's mind when they experience the game. In her book *Reality is Broken: Why Games Make Us Better and How They Can Change the World*, Jane McGonigal identifies the four required elements for something to be considered a game. These elements explain the fundamental structures of how we engage the environment of the gaming world successfully over time. Consider each element of the image below:

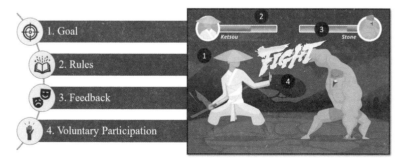

FIGURE 6. *Parts of a Video Game Applied to a Fighting Game Example* (As described by McGonigal, 2011).

The game in the image is reminiscent of many of the most famous fighting games across the history of gaming. Consider entries such as *Mortal Kombat, Street Fighter*, or *Tekken*. The goal of these games is to achieve victory by defeating your adversary before they defeat you. The basic rules include choosing a fighter, waiting for the ominous voice to declare the word "FIGHT," and executing a better balance of offensive and defensive techniques to reduce your opponent's health bar to zero. When successful, the player has been able to "Finish Him" (or "Finish Her"), a symbol of domination for a fight well played. The feedback system occurs in the form of a health meter which reduces each time a fighter takes damage. Animations such as being knocked down or juggled across the screen by incoming attacks also serve as feedback for the player.

The final requirement for something to be a game; it must be voluntary. This requirement preserves the sense of entertainment by reminding us that we do not have to play. We can continue if we want to (or, in the arcade days, until our coins run out). We do not have to keep going. Typically, video games are not considered a profession, and there are no inherent requirements to complete specific goals or engage more than we want to. All of those expectations are decided by the player voluntarily.

These four essential elements combine to form the kind of play we expect in video games. They do not, however, guarantee that a game will provide an epic narrative. A game can only elevate itself into the upper echelon of humankind's most memorable adventures by forming a symbiotic relationship between solid gameplay and exceptional storytelling.

The Legend of Zelda: Breath of the Wild is an exceptional example of primary game elements combining into an epic narrative experience. Following a three-act structure, Link emerges from the Temple of Resurrection one millennium after the heroes of Hyrule were defeated in the critical battle against Calamity Ganon. With the kingdom in shambles, Link hears the voice of Zelda, asking him to answer the calling to become the Hero of Time and restore freedom to the realm of Hyrule. Link starts by completing smaller tasks offered to him by various guides like the ghostly King Rhoam. Gradually, Link is made aware of his real challenge to defeat Ganon. Each shrine he completes brings him closer to reuniting with Zelda, who sacrificed herself to give Link this chance to explore the wilds of Hyrule.

The second act of this story revolves around Link restoring each of the Champions of Hyrule by defeating the four Divine Beasts spread across the map. Link follows the nuclear formula of the monomyth directly, even to the point of claiming the Master Sword as his ultimate boon as a final push to challenge Ganon in the climactic battle. Once Link regains his memory of the past, the battle through Hyrule Castle ensues. Even in final form, Ganon is no match for the growth of a prepared hero in the critical moment. Equipped with every lesson learned along the way, the player ushers Link through the Supreme Ordeal and into the denouement phase.

By completing the challenges of the third act, the player has saved the kingdom from the dominion of evil and successfully deployed the powers of a heroic Link with inspiring resolve. This allows the narrative of the monomyth to be fulfilled. In this reality, the victorious player has led Link and Zelda to a place where together they can reflect on what has happened in their story. The triumphant player reflects in parallel with their heroes, with both deciding the best way to preserve the insights from victory as they move forward to the next challenge in their lives.

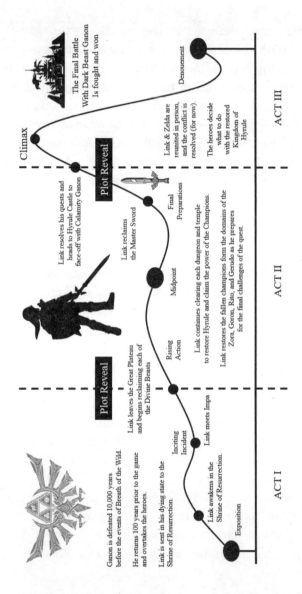

FIGURE 7. *Using a 3-Act Structure to Review*
"The Legend of Zelda: Breath of the Wild" (2017)

Using the Three-Act Structure, video games can masterfully guide their narratives into alignment with the nuclear formula. Countless games depict hero characters awakening in a world that feels normal to them, only to be thrust into adversity against their will. Since these are video games, the player faces a problem to solve through gameplay. They must overcome each adversity by assuming the hero's responsibility to make a difference in their world. Games like these often draw from mythology and ancient storytelling forms to expose the player to new ideas and ways of thinking about life.

In some cases, the chosen settings for the in-game events are used to tackle serious topics that might be difficult to explore in a real-world context. The acts of the monomyth ease us past these divisions in our thinking. In Act I, we gradually immerse ourselves in the world to understand the context of the problem. Act II gives the hero a quest that helps them become more formidable as a champion in the impending conflict. In Act III, the player faces the ultimate challenge of demonstrating mastery in the final conflict. The conclusion of all three acts allows the hero to understand their role in the balance between order and chaos.

For the return phase, the emphasis on gameplay now yields to storytelling. The hero and their companions are tasked with returning to their starting location, but this time equipped with all the knowledge from every previous battle. Reintegration into the ordinary role is only sometimes depicted. Still, when it is, this can be used as a setup for the next adventure and show the extra challenges to be considered when extraordinary gifts are available to people driven to accomplish heroic journeys.

For the player, this phase comes with a different set of challenges. Do we begin a new playthrough? Is there a different ending we can aim for next? Do I have the time and desire to do this all again? These questions often combine into "Would it be worth it to keep playing this game?" As we find solace in the idea that we have led the hero and their world back to a peaceful existence, the reality is that there are always additional challenges in maintaining what has been earned. Even more daunting is the fact that the hero does not always win. This lesson shines through in stories aiming to set up a more sprawling narrative where worlds come to life as connections into new chapters for the next heroes to travel through.

Some of the most renowned franchises feature stories showcasing the failed hero. *Crisis Core: Final Fantasy VII* is a prequel to the original quest depicted in *Final Fantasy VII*. While still featuring favorites such as Cloud, Aerith, and Sephiroth, this game focuses on the hijinks of an up-and-coming SOLDIER named Zack Fair. *Crisis Core* tells the story of Zack's rise in the ranks of SOLDIER until Shinra decides to terminate him as a cover-up for their lies to the world. By meeting a background character from the main title this way, the story is already set up for Act I. Typically, this context is revealed gradually. However, building off the prequel story helps create a greater depth of exposition to enhance future playthroughs of both the main game and the spinoff story. Furthermore, by expanding the universe, lesser-known characters can gain popularity among players, thereby increasing the franchise's longevity.

Another critical difference in this style of hero narrative is that it provides context for the ultimate defeat of any prequel heroes who impacted the setup phase of the main story. When we witness a hero dying in their conclusion phase, this creates a path of redemption for the main hero and their party when it is their time to set things right. We are often already aware of the main story when we finally witness this clarifying moment. This out-of-order storytelling practice also increases intrigue for many properties that have remained in the gaming zeitgeist.

Even if death is not the characters' ultimate fate, the unfulfilled path to victory creates many possibilities for the main story to be replayed with enhanced context. Whether this occurs in a *Nier* title, *Kingdom Hearts*, or *Final Fantasy*, the prequel heroes answer lingering questions while creating more unanswered mysteries to be answered in the climax. As a result, future challenges experience a feeling of increased stakes. This helps maintain anticipation for future additions to the story, keeping the player base interested in the incomplete journey of the hero in a way that can only occur through the expansion of an untold (yet elaborate) backstory.

The ebb and flow of gaming storylines (or any form of long-form storytelling) set themselves up to be ripe for sequels and spinoffs if they are deemed successful in one way or another by the mainstream game audience. In the case above, *Crisis Core* features the original hero, Zack, and shows us how he saves Cloud from certain death in his final act of life.

"You'll be my living legacy."

— Zack Fair

This story was only seen via flashback in the original entry of Final Fantasy VII, so the opportunity to play it is a powerful moment. This prequel expands the franchise meaningfully but in a backward direction for the timeline.

Other games move the story forward in their timeline as sequels, picking up from the events previously played. Applying the word sequel to *Kingdom Hearts*, on the other hand, is complicated due to all the twists and turns this philosophical gaming narrative takes to tell the story of the chosen Keyblade heroes across time. This ever-expanding story features characters from *Disney* and *Final Fantasy*, weaving through a somewhat non-linear timeline to provide Sora with the needed context for the battles ahead.

Games such as *Birth by Sleep* or *358/2 Days* introduce important characters and new mysteries in the lore of *Kingdom Hearts* while players wait for Sora, Donald Duck, and Goofy to stumble upon the truth. Every title in this franchise either results in a conclusive victory or the tease of the subsequent struggle. Sometimes, the denouement phase reveals both. Each story contains a hero; being Sora in the present or a Keyblade wielder from varying points in the past or future of the timeline. By connecting these stories, every game explains why the hero is chosen, and their experiences alter the flow of events in *Kingdom Hearts* mythology. In the end, the Keyblade Master has conquered evil, fulfilled their destiny, and returned in some way to their original state (or one of stasis that connects them back to the primary *Kingdom Hearts* narrative).

The stages of *Separation → Initiation → Return* help stories create intrigue for both virtual worlds and their heroes as they iterate across each new entry. By exposing each generation of players to new situations, game mechanics, and technological advancements in a familiar game context, long-form franchises generate engagement in their stories, allowing their epic tales to become a mythological approach to storytelling in that they now span across time.

 ## NOTICING THE COSMOGONIC CYCLE

The monomythical cycle blends with other storytelling sequences to captivate the audience's minds. Many games with a fantasy element take the time to establish the origin of life in their game universes. When dealing with infinite sources of power and magical beings to fully explain the narrative, it is common to also include exposition on the genesis of life as a connection for why the hero matters in their presented struggles.

When designing a Massively Multiplayer Online (MMO) game, one challenge developers must consider is how a "chosen one" narrative can feel true to every player at once. There must be a suspension of belief that every player in the game is uniquely the chosen one while they work together. By separating storytelling from online/social elements using what are called "instances," this becomes possible. All players experience the hero narrative on a cosmic scale, separated from each other. Once the exposition ends, all players are again free to pursue victory in the cosmic story [mostly] together.

One example of an MMO game with a visible connection to the cosmogonic cycle is *Final Fantasy XIV Online* (FFXIV). Despite having a complex narrative, applying the themes of the cosmogonic cycle – Emanation, Transformation, and Dissolution - to our interpretation of the events of FFXIV makes it easier to notice the framework of the heroic journey across the cosmic interactions in the story.

The first required element for this cycle is the emanation of life from a knowable source. As mentioned earlier, Hydaelyn, in the form of the Mother Crystal, preserves life in one world to prevent the destruction of all others. The conflict of these worlds emanates from the vile plotting of the followers of Zodiark going against the followers of Hydaelyn. This places the hero character directly into conflict with the Ascians, a cult of near-eternal beings who worship the fallen god Zodiark. This cult constantly politics against those who follow the will of Hydaelyn and walk in the light of the Crystal. Fittingly, the Ascians channel darkness and seek to end the world of the hero for their own purposes.

By delving deeper into the events of cosmic genesis, we realize that games, on occasion, create levels of exposition for their in-game conflicts with an intricacy reminiscent of the mythological tales that develop into world religions. Using deities, their followers, and a backdrop of universal battle across an infinite timeline, games can provide an epic narrative for players to enjoy across many hours of gameplay. In such games, any hero who fulfills their destiny through these eternal overtones instantly becomes recognizable as a vessel for the "chosen one" dynamic.

This universe of FFXIV began as a unified world called Etheirys. Ages before the playable portion of the timeline, Ascians created the dark being Zodiark to rebuild their world. Since this would have relied on sacrificing all lesser life, a sect of the original Ascians formed that desired to preserve life. To do this, they sacrificed themselves. This brought about the birth of Hydaelyn, who could sunder both Zodiark and the world. This act caused the breaking of reality into fourteen separate versions of existence. The mythos of Hydaelyn sealing away Zodiark in the ancient times of the original world spawned a multiverse in which the Ascians must create enough chaos to rejoin the splintered realities and unleash the darkness of Zodiark once more.

The religious overtones of the Ascians, along with their philosophical rift with the Scions of the Seventh Dawn in the main scenario quests of the game, harken the player into a feud for the ages. Any scholar of world history will undoubtedly see similarities between actual events and those demonstrated with a lens of fantasy, like the followers of Zodiark and Hydaelyn. While these details are optional for playing the game, for the lore-focused player, telling this story amplifies the importance of the characters and the history binding the online world together.

The act of character creation for this MMO becomes parallel to the unknowable origin of the protagonist in these stories. The "chosen one" narrative makes an appearance again. In this way, the player is given stages to complete as they work towards the transformation, bringing the created avatar closer to the status of a universal savior. In stories of this kind, only the World Redeemer can achieve victory in the cosmic battle against evil so the world can be restored to the intended path.

The alternating experience of leveling and story guides our created hero - the Warrior of Light – towards a complete understanding of their quest. Each major victory from the player is awarded a new colored crystal, empowering the player on the ethereal plane. Completing the circle in each expansion of the MMO leads to the moment of apotheosis. These final encounters feature a moment of transcendence for the hero as their completed knowledge provides unlimited power to finally overcome their opponents. Each time this occurs, fate rests in the balance. Victory in these moments provides a restoration of order. For a time, chaos is vanquished and order for Eorzea is preserved. That is until another expansion quest is created to extend the life of the MMO and encourage more heroics from the Warrior of Light.

The epic nature of playing through these stories allows the player to eventually reflect on the idea that the character they created is the same one that has become the focal point for all hope in the universe. From meager beginnings, this avatar has been the vehicle for every moment of entertainment since the player first decided to turn on the game and join in the narrative journey.

In this way, when video games utilize the cosmogonic cycle for storytelling, they can engage their players' minds in impactful ways. Games with this approach help players find new metaphors for living that make a difference in how they see themselves in the context of wide-ranging problems. By transferring the confidence of the chosen one into reality-based contexts, the player can infuse the basic challenges of life with an importance that motivates them to create their own ultimate story. This is what we practice through the Warrior of Light and other games. The cosmogonic cycle explains through stages how to take responsibility for impacting the deepest problems of the world for the better.

 ## THE SELF AS THE CHOSEN ONE

One of the easiest ways to appreciate the player role in the battle between mortals and deities is to designate the primary hero as "the chosen one." While it is unimaginable to list every game that uses this player trope, this motif is likely prominent in a few of every gamer's most beloved titles. Even going back to the early life of console gaming, Mario runs from castle to castle, only to find Toad as he exclaims, "Thank you, Mario! But our princess is in another castle." By the player having the sole responsibility to solve this problem, it is as if they are chosen to be the difference maker (unless Luigi is being played more skillfully by Player 2). After all, not a single time does Toad or another member of the Mushroom Kingdom volunteer to form a fellowship to liberate the princess from her captor. The task falls on the player and the player alone.

Modern video games continue this logic of viewing the player as the best possible option. Even in games where a party is formed, a central figure is usually meant to receive the projection directly relating to the player and their decisions. While player agency feels empowering, the concept of the player character versus the non-playable character (NPC) can be correlated directly to our best efforts in physical world contexts to make a difference. How we construct the story of our lives orients us to the challenges we face. Repeatedly watching a problem happen to us makes us wonder whether we see ourselves as the key to the solution (a high locus of control) or if the responsibility falls on a different person to make that difference (a low locus of control). One option is emblematic of the hero, and the other represents the accepting nature of the NPC. While calling someone an NPC in the context of their problem is dehumanizing, a growth mindset encourages us to learn from the past and play a role in our solutions. In this way, the goal of shifting the narrative away from the NPC mentality is meant to activate the heroic persona lying dormant within.

The *Persona* franchise is a series of games known to cast the player as the often-unnamed protagonist who must seize their inner power. The character of Joker in *Persona 5* receives their name from the player at the start of the game. This tactic allows the player to establish the character's identity in a way that creates an automatic opportunity for self-projection. This subconscious opportunity connects the individual player with the codenames of the Phantom Thieves. This way, as they battle through the depths of the collective unconscious, every player is Joker, even though every Joker is named differently by each player.

Being rooted in Jungian psychology, the *Persona* franchise explores the conflicts between humanity and fate but with several systemic backdrops. These include the threat of sociopolitical calamity, the chaos of the Japanese adolescent social calendar, and the psychological projections of each character's dissonance between ideal, perceived, and actual selves. The magical gifts that the hero characters come to exemplify result from the supernatural unleashing of each of their personas in spirit form. The initial release for each persona requires unification between the person and their deepest vulnerability. In *Persona 5 Royal*, the first summoning of Arsène by Joker comes at a critical moment where either all hope will be lost, or the heroes will find a way to reach deep within themselves to rescue their friend and make a difference. The following acceptance by Joker signifies this moment:

*"**Vow to me. I am thou, thou art I**... Thou who art willing to perform all sacrilegious acts for thine own justice! Call upon my name, and release thy rage! Show the strength of thy will to ascertain all on thine own, though thou be chained to Hell itself!"*

This moment of acceptance is replicated for each of the Phantom Thieves as they achieve harmony with their persona. While Joker's persona represents the Fool arcana, each character around him fulfills a different facet of the tarot. By working together and forming effective social bonds, the Phantom Thieves become a force for change powerful enough to affect society's collective unconscious.

While the early phases of the game focus on changing society on a smaller scale (removing abusive teachers from high school), the endgame focuses on eradicating the ideological evils wielded by both political leaders, and in some cases, by deities themselves. The desire to purify reality from corruption leads the Phantom Thieves directly into battle with the god who breathed life into existence – The Holy Grail, Yaldabaoth. At the very least, the heroes must defeat the psychological projection their society has built concerning the forces that allow them to exist. Still, either interpretation shows the significance of being chosen to take on the governing powers of existence. The resolve to be the chosen hero requires us to have the ability to hold our own against forces as powerful as a figurative deity.

The awareness a person forms with their experiences helps them create their subjective reality. Throughout history, societies have frequently utilized the idea of gods to shape socially constructed systems into tangible ideologies. This helps abstract collections of ideas, such as value systems, to become more easily understood by the collective from person to person.

In video games, common enemies provide mild challenges until the hero can challenge the more intimidating god-tier opponents. This level of adversary reflects the cosmic origin and is meant to be an intense challenge for the player. From the narrative, these characters represent how the world came to be as it is. This means that change requires the hero to surpass them in both power and wisdom. The symbiotic relationship between game characters and their gods often represents a cosmological achievement. When the opponent matters, playing the hero who defeated them creates the aura of becoming the chosen hero.

The *Persona* franchise is just one example of this. The words "I am thou, thou art I..." form a bond between mortals and those existing on the spiritual plane. By leveling up their persona, each party member can now walk the path to battle the greater echelon of enemies. This culminates in the great deed of the hero's journey, one in which the hero must complete a feat that would prove impossible with a mentality limited by the ordinary.

The hero becomes capable of the impossible because the godhead is reflected in their growth. By the end of the journey, with a hero receiving the full range of ethereal gifts, they are now contenders to free the world from tyranny borne of gods. In a way, the hero and the final god-boss represent two sides of the same coin. Like the bird and the cage, the player assumed the responsibility to level up the hero in their gameplay to overcome this challenge. In doing so, they acquire the power reflective of the gods they mean to overcome. They complete the circle by elevating themselves to the point of readiness.

By analyzing the narrative from human and eternal perspectives, we assemble the complete view of the game as a metaphor. This mystery is revealed to the character through the stages of the journey. This same revelation comes to us through gameplay. Our awareness builds toward the narrative climax, letting us complete the game with the weight of our achievement in mind.

This analogy holds in many of our most important life decisions. The more we engage in opportunity, the more aware we become. The more aware we become, the more we realize all we do not know. By defeating otherworldly opponents, players achieve a gaming milestone while also gaining insight into the mysteries of life. Becoming a part of these stories provides us with new opportunities for personal growth. How we tell the story of this accomplishment helps us establish ourselves as heroic, mirrored by the experiences we draw from every group of characters that taught us what heroism means. Completing the gaming task can provide a great feeling, but there are other answers for questions extending from the subconscious realm into reality.

There is nothing more heroic than becoming the hero of our own story.

The *Persona* games force us to directly see this balance by having us play the schedule of life while also going into the gamified world of combat in our "free time." As the characters get deeper into the mystery of each game, they spend time in both the physical world and the one constructed by the psyche. The true boon in these games is that we see our hope expand by restructuring our belief of self, unlocking the strength of our own persona in the process.

Our gaming persona continues to evolve as long as we continue being a part of new stories. We will never be able to play everything. As such, we are all limited in what we can share through personal experience. This is what makes each of the gaming stories echo brilliantly across our lifespans. By noticing the structure of video games – separation, initiation, return – we can see the value of the conflict across our life stages as we aim to accomplish the most extraordinary tasks life offers us. This parallel serves as a promise from games that life will change for the better when we decide to challenge the whims of fate and become the "chosen one" who completes each stage of the journey through life.

CHAPTER VI

THE LINKING
OF WORLDS

We need to make the most of the time we have – to live
our lives the way we wanna live.
Every minute... every moment matters.

—Aerith Gainsborough (Final Fantasy VII Remake)

In many ways, the protagonists of video games are the modern-day equivalent of mythological heroes. Every successful hero restores the flow of life in some way or another for the world they are striving to preserve. When this victory occurs, the hero is channeling the universal powers found in nature, similar to what is depicted in other well-known mythologies with symbols such as the Tree of Life or the Cosmic Ocean. Like their counterparts in Greek mythology or ancient folklore, gaming heroes embark on quests to restore balance to the world. The restoration can be anything from the hope of survival (*The Last of Us*), the natural flow of life (*Abzû*), or even the continued existence of the spiritual forces allowing life to remain possible (*Zelda / Final Fantasy*). Players must often defeat powerful villains and overcome seemingly insurmountable odds to accomplish these feats. In the process, these heroes learn important lessons about themselves and what it takes to make a difference on a cosmic scale.

Fantasy stories offer players a way to escape the mundane realities of everyday life. They provide an opportunity to explore new worlds and experience exciting adventures. In a sense, they allow us to tap into our heroic potential through imagination. By spending time in each of these worlds, virtual spaces inspire us to see our world in new ways so that we too can make a difference.

The World Navel is a common motif in fantasy and video games. It typically refers to a mystical object that serves as the source of life, connecting the known world with the infinite powers of existence. These monoliths can be a mountaintop, capital city or religious center, or a symbolic object such as a tree of life. This central location is often the site of important events, such as the world genesis or an ancient battle between good and evil.

In video games, the World Navel can also be a hub world where players can explore different areas, meet characters, and learn about the game's story. This can be done as simply as the world pipes in *Super Mario Bros. 3* or an intricate loading area, as was utilized for the Temple of Tyr in *God of War*. This motif is a popular gaming mainstay because it creates a sense of scale for the world. It also provides a convenient way for storytellers to move the plot forward. By locking specific locations behind the advancement of the story, game developers can craft their myths in stages, giving players deliberate pacing to appreciate the game's narrative.

The energy of life emanates in mythological worlds from the cosmic to the infernal, touching everything in between. The conflicts in video games often explore the disruption of this flow in several ways. The forces of evil often initiate the bending of nature for some devious purpose, while the hero character(s) will seek to restore the natural balance. In a corrupted world, the hero could serve the side of light, restoring the world to its nature by removing the source of corruption.

These energies connect characters to the worlds they are fighting to preserve. Whenever mystical characters are present, they commonly draw connections through the ground to harness powers from the aether for use in the present moment. The use of ley lines by black mages in *Final Fantasy* allows these characters to connect the flow of power between the spiritual plane and the physical world. Game abilities like these hint at an untapped potential where ancient knowledge connects humanity with ephemeral existence. In reality, focusing on the space where you are rather than the destination you have not yet reached reflects mindfulness. This practice is often considered a superpower that more outcome-focused players may overlook. By connecting with forgotten (or overlooked) knowledge, the path forward is revealed to the player, allowing for continuity between their experience and the established mythology to take hold.

When a character taps into the power of their ley lines, they feel a connection with the grander schemes in their universe. These lines provide a sense of connection between life and the universal power. They convince us that there is a power inherent in reality itself. Mythology is one method of explaining these profound revelations, leading to the circulation of religious creed and longstanding cultural systems. Sometimes these connections come from a cosmic being, such as in the interactions with the world serpent Jörmungandr in *God of War*. Other times, the source of all things is glimpsed through the monolithic presence of the Erdtree (Tree of Life) as we see in *Elden Ring*, an homage to the Norse concept of Yggdrasil. Other times games may channel mythological symbolism by instilling the hero with a longing for the cosmic summit, as in *Journey*, mirroring the ascent to the heavens in imagining our most significant achievements. Each iteration of the World Navel stands as a symbol of continuous creation, offering the foundation of life for all inhabitants of the planetary sphere, which serves as the backdrop of the journey.

Many gaming adventures provide an opportunity to explore the cyclical nature of existence in creative ways. Life and death, day and night, struggle to triumph. Whether it is the day-night cycle in *Animal Crossing* or the seasons in *Stardew Valley*, each of these concepts requires the presence of the other to form a complete circuit. Players often have to manage their time to complete tasks within the game, which can lead to a sense of satisfaction as they see their virtual world change and grow around their play.

Video games often revolve around maintaining life as a chance to proceed in the quest. On the other hand, death represents the need to use a new attempt to progress, starting from the most recent save point. In some ways, this metaphorically mirrors our lives as we strive to achieve our goals. Just as video game characters level up and acquire new skills, we also grow through gaining experience. The balance in each paired opposite reveals the organized design of our place in the challenge. Whether through game design or narrative structures, these tropes form the challenge each player faces in their desire to welcome each new myth into their player history.

WORLD MAPS & THE INEXHAUSTIBLE POINT

A common tool for exploring a vast virtual space is found in the world map. By orienting themselves to the map, gamers can chart a course from one location to another and plan their journey accordingly. The desire to understand the layout of a fictional world creates a mythological alternative to our physical reality for us to master. The sense of direction is one facet we must conquer to divine the need to arrive at our destination. The map is the lexicon for the directional language we long to speak. By learning each hidden path in our varied questlines, we better understand character motivations, the nature of the conflict, and the source of power in these fictional locations.

When we zoom out and review these elements from the vantage of the heavens, we become more aware of the different cultures of our quests and the physical barriers that separate them from the central struggle. By the end of the journey, we have often explored each cardinal direction, coming directly into contact with each culture. This establishes the "World Traveler" identity, giving us the sense that we are mastering all phases of the world where we hope to become the hero.

The map serves numerous purposes beyond navigation. It conceals the source of power until we find a path to explore it. One of the best ways to take notice of these subliminal pathways is by considering the four directions of the world horizon. In games featuring an ancient city or sacred space located at the center of the map, the creators subtly establish a subconscious connection with the player. Whatever lies in the central area could be a shrine to a cherished leader, a center of the dominant religion, or even a final haven of rest from the onslaught of the forces of evil.

Other locales may contain an "out of bounds" for the action of the adventure. This "Inexhaustible Point" comes through in games such as *Demon's Souls* or *Elden Ring* in the form of the Nexus or the Roundtable Hold. They can be a safe zone near the center or placed in the "elsewhere," detached from the main path as a place forgotten by time. Being a place where combat is disallowed, players can rest, purchase items, converse with NPCs, or advance quests in various ways. Despite these opportunities, the player does not suffer the same threats here. Only the implication, rather than the reach of evil, exists in this space.

One example is the Temple of Time, which offers Link the chance to shift timelines or alter the lay of the land in some mystical fashion. Again, Link cannot be attacked or suffer death here, despite certain timelines making it seem as if nowhere is safe. The powers connecting the cosmic to the ordinary rely on places such as these. By walking through them, players can witness the spiritual sense of the characters and their beliefs as a reality worth fighting for. Beyond resting, these hub locations can serve as a center for commerce in MMO games. They also can be places where the story occurs in the form of exposition instead of only being delivered through action.

The World Navel uses the four significant directions to reveal the story of the prevailing world to the player. This central area offers a sanctuary for the player to ease their ego-centered urge to rush through each storyline. Instead, it allows them to display a more profound respect for the mythos portrayed along their hero's path.

The history of the hero explains their path through the map, showing where they have been and where they cannot explore yet. When looking at the Inexhaustible Point as a game mechanic, these could be viewed simply as "save points" where a player receives a brief pause in the action before resuming the combat-driven mayhem in their natural play style. From a narrative perspective, these points provide a sense of security for players, allowing them to relax and enjoy the game without fear of unforeseen setbacks. In certain stories, there is a location the hero and their friends have strived to reach for a while, and once you arrive, the true significance is often revealed through the ensuing events.

This place could be used to save the game or to select a chapter by choosing which doorway of the nexus to embark upon. These safe spaces are the Inexhaustible Point, symbolizing hope and safety for all who reach them. They serve as a transition point between past struggles and challenges in the next phase of the journey.

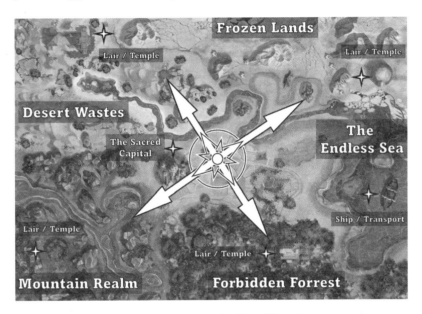

FIGURE 8. *Noticing the Four Directions of the World Horizon on an In-Game Map*

Other times, these locations tap directly into the forces of existence through their function as the peering window into the World Navel itself. This sanctum connects the people to their source(s) of life. In some games, this is a literal location where a character can reach out and touch the primordial stream of life. Such a vortex of energy is often the focus of enmity for the forces of evil. Whenever all aggression becomes fixated on extinguishing (or controlling) this purity of life, it brings the nature of good and evil into more of a focused lesson for the player.

These sentiments are more than virtues. They are the sequences of choice coming from a transcendent state resting inside all of us. Games teach us to revere these locations to allow the game to achieve a sense of wonder as we play them. At first, we might play to complete easy objectives. As our experiences deepen, however, our dedication to exploring every area tells the story of who we strive to be in our lives, both as gamers and as completionists for anything under our control.

The security of these locations is not always certain. If a villain can violate the sacred nature of the Inexhaustible Point, it usually signals an escalation to the intensity of the mythic journey. One principal example of this violation is in the City of the Ancients in *Final Fantasy VII*. For this pivotal scene, Sephiroth (the antagonist) seeks to become a god and end the life of the hero he perceives to be the greatest threat to that goal, Aerith Gainsborough. The player leads Cloud through this abandoned city for minutes, eventually finding Aerith safely praying in an open chamber at the apex of the sacred space. Safety is first shattered when Sephiroth enters the hero's psyche to force him to execute his friend. While Cloud is spared this embarrassment at the last moment by the jarring cries of his friends, Sephiroth descends from the heavens with a killing stab, piercing through Aerith's chest and ending her life. The motive for this traumatic moment is explained later in the game by Sephiroth himself:

> *"All that boundless energy will be mine. By merging with all the energy of the Planet, I will become a new life form, a new existence. Melding with the Planet... I will cease to exist as I am now... Only to be reborn as a 'God' to rule over every soul."*

While Sephiroth soaks in his accomplishment, a distraught Cloud holds onto his friend's lifeless body. He offers this frantic message to his opponent:

"Aerith is gone. Aerith will no longer talk, no longer laugh, cry... or get angry... What about us... what are WE supposed to do? What about my pain? My fingers are tingling. My mouth is dry. My eyes are burning!"

This trauma defines Cloud until his opportunity to save the Lifestream from Sephiroth during the final battle. Sephiroth floats confidently above the conflict with his plans to control existence. By contrast, Cloud must learn to let go of his pain and reconcile with the trauma of his losses. Cloud's journey requires him to reintegrate into acceptance of his past and present. Finding this congruence in his identity will bring back the hope he experienced when Zack and Aerith were both still among the living. This sense of self is ready to confront Sephiroth for his actions. The spirit of Aerith seems to release Cloud from his guilt in the sequel film *Final Fantasy: Advent Children Complete* when she says during her eternity in the Lifestream:

"I never blamed you, not once. You came for me. That's all that matters."

These three points of view complete the vision of life caused by the existence of the Lifestream (and other legendary powers in mythology). Some seek to control life to boost their vitality. Others seek to enjoy the natural flow of reality. For the hero of the ever-repeating journey, however, doing what is right is a way to honor the people who mattered most during their quest. Evil was never meant to step foot on the sacred ground. This is why the heroes often must defend this space at some point in their journeys. By pushing to cleanse the influence of chaos, the hero seeks to share their victory with all points of the map. This restoration honors the essence of the World Navel itself, supporting the harmonious existence of all living things in the past, present, and future.

 ## PERSPECTIVES CREATING REALITY

Constructivism is a philosophical perspective that believes there is no such thing as objective reality. Rather, all knowledge is co-created through shared experiences. This allows for a unique point of view for every player. This can sometimes lead to different people playing the same game in entirely different ways. For example, two people could play the same decision-based game, such as *Detroit: Become Human* or *The Walking Dead*, but have different experiences depending on the choices they make in the game.

How a person experiences a video game is largely subjective, as every game we play achieves different levels of meaning for each player. Subjectivism makes it possible for each player to interpret the exact same events of a game differently. Some people might see a game as too easy, while others might find it a rage-inducing difficulty. Others may see a choice as noble, while others may view it as ridiculous. Ultimately, subjectivism helps gaming become a personal experience for each player on an individual level.

These relative perspectives also allow the player to connect with the motives of both heroes and their nemeses. The objective reality for a game narrative exists only insofar as the storyteller wants it to. This makes video games one of the most ethically safe ways to explore different conceptions of morality without the inherent risks to society. The player can observe how other choices within the game affect not only the protagonist but also the people around them. The unique interactivity of games allows for experimentation with life that is impossible in other forms of entertainment. This aspect of video games enables them to function as modernized parables in a way that encourages personal growth for the player.

Our perspectives shape our reality. This is because subjective truth is formed mainly from our point of view. We see things from our fixed perspective, creating how we see the world. When we play a video game, we are limited to the perspective of the character we are playing (or to those the developers give us access to). You can only see what your character can see and only do what your character can do. This is why video games become immersive. Every time we play, we experience the world from an altered perspective. However, video games are still fiction. They are not reality. By seeing the many narrative ties connected with our decisions, we consider complex lessons, such as how we can do our best and still not succeed while others seemingly achieve what they hope for with less struggle.

FIGURE 9. *Representation of the Axis Mundi and Omphalos Stone As the Essence of Life*

When we recognize our values are personal to ourselves, and hence are decided with equal value when compared to the viewpoints of others, we achieve a clarifying peace many in society have not achieved. While gaming stories offer this path to us by asking, "What will you do next?" life is much less obvious in revealing these options.

The actual "Choose Your Path" game is life itself. By noticing the convergent decisions in our day, we come to see merit in all points of view, not just our own, but those of others, and those we will never meet as well. We can choose to champion the Horde or the Alliance, Red Team, or Blue Team, and even our favorite console from the years when gamers seemed caught up in a war between Nintendo, Microsoft, and Sony (and also the PC Master Race). The clarity to see beyond the pettiness of tribalism becomes the Axis Mundi of gamer culture; a perspective as a gamer where all tasks in life successfully integrate with the passion to play games, while still allowing life to be experienced in perfect balance. The game player, in balance, sees each choice as a step in the sprawling story of what it means to have a plan and use their abilities to move closer to their goal one day at a time.

Our world is designed to capitalize on bitter disagreements. Even with game ratings, for every ten-out-of-ten masterpiece, there will be people trolling in the comments, highlighting every bug they found, and commenting on how much this franchise is a waste of time and hard-earned money. If the purpose of playing is to have fun and experience moments of clarity, these complaints are missing the point. A game can be flawed yet still be a masterpiece in the eyes of those who have played it. Just as a piece of art benefits from errant brushstrokes, so too can a game become greater when it is accepted despite its imperfections. For the worst offenses in the comments, we have Day 1 patches. For everything else, we can simply appreciate that a game studio did its best to provide us with an activity we can enjoy (and, from time to time, learn something from).

The divine comedy is that both perspectives can be correct simultaneously. While other industries need us to be distracted by our squabbling to control our views on life, video games make the experience of thought internal, leaving the possibility for introspection. Once decided, our views help us form bonds with others through discourse. We can still argue, and we can certainly still be objectively wrong. We experience both sides knowing that wins and losses in real life carry consequences. We constantly face high-stakes challenges where we must succeed on our first attempt. While, in some instances, the best chance for therapeutic growth is not to achieve these successes quickly (allowing us to discover our true selves by facing adversity), we can learn these truths in a far less devastating way through video games when we see ourselves through the lens of the hero who is allowed to struggle, and even fail.

Once we embrace the metaphor of a game, every challenge becomes a journey. The map, our guide in the virtual world, becomes the path to every place we encounter in our routine. These represent the achievements we have already met and others we hope to complete one day. In *Man's Search for Meaning*, existential psychologist Viktor Frankl wrote that the meaning of life is something that each individual must find for themselves. He explains that we cannot rely on external factors, such as our careers, relationships, or possessions, to give us a sense of purpose. Instead, it is something that we must discover within ourselves. Frankl argues that the only way to find meaning in life is to develop our sense of meaning free of the influences forced on us by others, regardless of circumstance. By focusing on our meaning, the perspectives of others matter far less, provided we keep hold of our sense of purpose. We cannot simply follow the map. Instead, we must open our minds to discover why we are in this world in the first place.

We constantly test out new points of view when we play video games, enjoying a worry-free trial-and-error across every fantastical situation. Our psyche explores the narrative complexity to find a balance between frustration and satisfaction. The voluntary nature of play helps the game offer intrinsic rewards in a way that other activities often do not. We choose how to interact with the virtual world around us, allowing us to define what is meaningful for ourselves.

Gaming allows the opportunity for self-exploration as we shift through each aspect of our personality to discover new things about ourselves. They teach us how to compete with others and learn from our mistakes. They show us that it is okay to disagree with others peacefully (unless we are purposefully aiming for the "bad ending"). They remind us that it is okay to struggle. Through mindfulness, we can just as easily try again or choose a different path. The full range of experiences in video games help us notice, one level at a time, that each destination on our map plays a role in helping us stay true to our purpose while we follow the path of the gamer's journey.

ACT I

The Departure Into Playing Video Games

CHAPTER VII

THE GAME

BEGINS

You will be the one to open the door.

—The Voice of Calling (Kingdom Hearts)

There was a time for all of us when we had never played a video game before. For some of us, this only describes a matter of years. For others, decades. The moment when we are presented with our first virtual puzzle to solve, we awkwardly press the buttons, experiencing the new processes of cause and effect as we move digital objects across the screen. Once we play a game, we transition from identifying as a "non-gamer" to becoming a gamer ourselves. This memory is what we can call the "nascent moment."

When we take the time to reflect on this transformation, the reality of how much this challenge changes us is enough to make our heads spin. Whatever our first-game experience, the nascent moment is a departure from the limits of ordinary reality because it engages our mind's ability to imagine. We are sitting in a room, controller in hand, moving a character through a virtual world to live or die, working through the challenge on screen. Behaviorally, we are playing a game with our hands, but our minds can imagine anything within its potential. For this reason, our awakening to video games may eclipse many of the most significant mental shifts we will ever experience because it transforms our connection with what is possible in reality on a foundational level.

From this moment, we have the potential to solve problems as if they are games. We can memorize codes as if they are keys to advance to a later stage. We can respond to rhythms and tones as if they are a memory challenge. Before we had ever played, these sequences of information would have been offered to us with limited context, even to the point of needing a goal matching our talents. Since we have played a game, we understand the challenge. We see the outline of the challenge and can envision using our abilities to form a strategy for success. In this way, each game we play develops our minds further for the many challenges in life. The question is, which games do we need to play to find a purpose, making this passion a path worth experiencing?

We re-experience this question as a microcosm each time we add a new game to our infinite library of quests we hope to complete someday. Feeling overwhelmed by the number of games being released in our favorite genres is a common worry. With so many options, deciding which games to start or which ones to purchase for life in backlog purgatory is difficult. The pressure to play and complete games in the backlog is an anxiety that interacts uniquely with the nascent moment. We survey the time in our lives as an essential resource not to be squandered. We can casually stroll into a new adventure or become paralyzed as we estimate how our cherished time becomes a commitment with each new initiation. The best game experiences are the ones that allow us to enjoy our games the right way, having fun and not holding onto any remnants of self-loathing.

To accomplish this feeling, video game players can implement mindful ideas to help them move through these decisions. Mindfulness is a mental state achieved by focusing our awareness on the present while calmly accepting our feelings, thoughts, bodily feedback, and situational pressures. When enjoying our games (or deciding what to play next), players can use mindfulness to consider what they want in a game. Are we looking for a fast-paced shooter or a slow-burning RPG? Will a game with breathtaking graphics enthrall us, or do we need an engrossing story? Once we have considered our needs, we can narrow our choices and decide. Being mindful of what we want from our games can save us from the paralyzing worry of where to look for our next journey and how to move from nascence to action meaningfully.

 ## GAMES AS A TRANSITION POINT

Certain video games facilitate mindful practices in applied ways. One example of a game that opens us up to our sense of presence is *Spiritfarer*. This game is a sandbox action adventure focusing on resource management. It casts the player as Stella, a girl who inherits the duties of Charon from Greek mythology to usher dead souls to the afterlife by way of the river Styx. The relaxing quality of the music in this game forms a mindful duet with the flowing story to help the player reflect on the meaning of life alongside the characters. While the stories of Greek myth commonly used this river as a confluence between the ordinary and supernatural worlds for heroes such as Heracles and Theseus,

Spiritfarer uses it to share a lesson on finding value in the path we take through life.

Each time Stella ushers a new soul to their time through the Everdoor, she helps them find a final moment of peace in their consciousness. The heroic quest in this game is to guide others towards these last moments, despite the gameplay being about collecting items and building the accompaniments each NPC will need to embark on the ride with you. You get to listen as the characters reflect on their lives, who mattered to them, and even what they regret in their final moments. The legacy we all leave behind enters our minds as we hear the cascading reflections from these fictional lifeforms. In each animal form, from snake to lion, Stella guides these lives to the final bridge between consciousness and peaceful unification with the circle of life. With a final hug, you accept each spirit, helping them accept themselves in their last moment. The light completes the circle as the journey becomes complete. Their spirit bursts in the brightest energy, symbolic of a life well-lived regardless of merit or other external pressures we add to it with our conscious selves. The spirit joins the sky, becoming a constellation of meaning to serve as a memory for those who continue their lives in the ordinary world.

The subjective experience of helping Stella accomplish each of these journeys allows each player to reflect on their progress through life and how far they have made it in each life stage. For those of us who choose to add a game such as this one to our ordinary world, we are met with lessons such as these throughout the time of play:

"Meditation, Stella, is an affair of wholeness. Wholeness, and oneness."

"Leaving what could have been is sometimes harder than leaving what has been."

"The ones who really love you never really leave you, you know."

Perhaps one of the most meaningful exchanges occurs with the mentor, Summer, early on in the game.

"I was looking forward to so many more lessons with you. You've been such a gifted student, Stella. I am so proud of you. So proud of your heart. So proud of your blossoming soul. I'm sorry to leave you. You'll have to learn for yourself. I have no doubt you'll pull through. The only lesson I have left is to show you what you're made of. Of ephemeral starlight. We're but a few particles of thought on the vast stream of consciousness. This is the last thing I can teach you, Stella. That all things change, and all things end."

FIGURE 10. *Big-Five of Mindfulness as identified by Nilsson and Kazemi (2016)*

By accepting our world as it is, we see each day as a mean-ingful addition to our experience. As new challenges come our way, we aim to achieve the mindful essence of games like *Spiritfarer* as we respond. The goal is only sometimes to make our lives reflect the lessons of a game. Instead, we often receive more from our ability to enjoy our experiences when we focus our awareness on the present moment.

By staying in our balanced state moment-by-moment, we unlearn the pressure to overreact to every stimulus. By taking inventory of our values, we learn to embrace our challenges while also taking care of ourselves. This does not mean we are slow to act; instead, we patiently wait for events to come to us. Only then do we mindfully influence our situations.

In games where our life bar depletes to nothingness, we can either throw the controller with rage, cry tears of soul-crushing defeat, or choose to restart from the checkpoint and try again, knowing that defeats are part of the learning process. Mindfulness calls each of us to respond. Practically speaking, we all react to our connections with life. In games, we can become more aware of who we strive to be. We also can accept the truth in our time that these aspirations are a process, and the journey is sometimes more important than the destination.

 ## GAMING MOTIVATIONS & PURPOSEFUL PLAY

Motivation is a subject of study that enhances our under-standing of why we play, what we play, and how we play our chosen video games. In order to appeal to multiple motivations, most games will contain a variety of activities for different player types. The primary motivators for playing video games are sorted into three categories: achievement, social interests, and immersion. Understanding these three motivations allows us to start seeing games as a source of need fulfillment. Using the concept of Csikszentmihalyi's flow, we select different activities throughout our day to experience meaningful work. Generally speaking, we want to do things well. We want to be seen and accepted by others. We also hope for a fulfilling connection with what we are known for. Our motivations represent the ways we pursue meaning.

By choosing games that match our preferences, we maximize our sense of enjoyment in the game itself. One of the most common reasons we play games is to gain a sense of victory in a fair, non-threatening environment that encourages a sense of fun. Those who chase mastery want to prove themselves capable of impressive feats on the highest difficulties. This manifests in games that test our reflexes or memory. It convinces players to create structure in their open-ended sandbox worlds to better experiment with the varied applications of physics and survival. Our hope for mastery propels us towards countless challenges to prove our sense of skill against the gaming environment and other players in innovative ways. Regardless of how these motives manifest, the challenges found in gaming push our cognitive abilities to the limit. When we become impressive in a game of mastery, overcoming the feeling of a challenge where the odds are stacked against us proves immensely satisfying.

Moving beyond achievement, social features dramatically improve our ability to de-stress during gameplay sessions. Besides work situations, it is rare for someone to sit down and engage in a challenge socially for hours. Gaming makes this rarity a common occurrence. While avoiding work is something many of us do when we are off the clock, the difference in gaming is that players have chosen these challenges voluntarily for themselves. Also, the challenges are fun.

Through online connectivity, players team up with each other across any geographical distance to work together. Whether a game offers couch co-op or online pairing, we choose the challenges and type of team. Online chat via Discord or some other VoIP service (Voiceover Internet Protocol) eradicates the limitations of distance and allows us to defeat the most daunting challenges together. By pairing with people repeatedly, we build relationships and engage in team-based strategies similar to playing a sport. The psychological results of these connections are that games become more enjoyable.

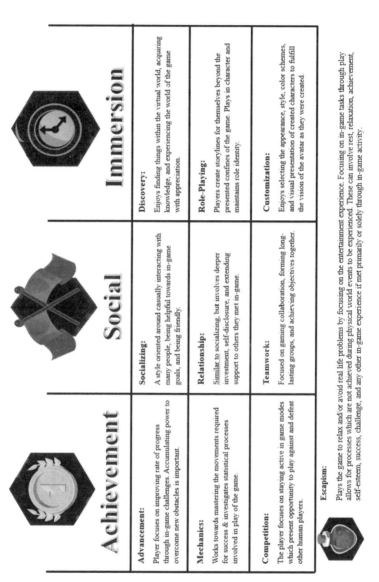

Achievement	Social	Immersion
Advancement: Player focuses on improving rate of progress through in-game challenges. Accumulating power to overcome new obstacles is important.	**Socializing:** A style oriented around casually interacting with many people, being helpful towards in-game goals, and being friendly.	**Discovery:** Enjoys finding things within the virtual world, acquiring knowledge, and experiencing the world of the game with appreciation.
Mechanics: Works towards mastering the movements required for success & investigates statistical processes involved in play of the game.	**Relationship:** Similar to socializing, but involves deeper investment, self-disclosure, and extending support to others they met in-game.	**Role-Playing:** Players create storylines for themselves beyond the presented confines of the game. Plays in character and maintains role identity.
Competition: The player focuses on staying active in game modes which present opportunity to play against and defeat other human players.	**Teamwork:** Focused on gaming collaboration, forming long-lasting groups, and achieving objectives together.	**Customization:** Enjoys selecting the appearance, style, color schemes, and visual presentation of created characters to fulfill the vision of the avatar as they were created.

Escapism:

Plays the game to relax and/or avoid real life problems by focusing on the entertainment experience. Focusing on in-game tasks through play allows for processes which are not achieved during physical world events to be experienced. These can involve rest, relaxation, achievement, self-esteem, success, challenge, and any other in-game experience if met primarily or solely through in-game activity.

TABLE 2. *Motivations for Online Games*
[updated from original by Yee (2006)]

123

The paradigm shifts of seeing games as social rather than solitary extend to other assumptions about games which have been largely debunked over the years. The process of learning is often increased by including other people in the activities we engage in. Since many online games require players to cooperate to find success, the ability to lay out a multistep process strategically across multiple people is challenged by many online games. This extends beyond genres as well. A match in *Call of Duty* will test these abilities in a Player-versus-Player (PVP) warzone, while a raid boss in *World of Warcraft* will tax similar droves of teammates in a Player-versus-Environment (PVE) format. In both cases, the best chance for success comes through knowledge of game mechanics and the coordinated strategy between teammates. As a result, relationships form between players, often extending into real-world connections. Players often absorb an understanding of whom they play with beyond the simple knowledge of what they aim for as gamers. This form of deep investment brings the team closer together. While this process is not involved in every game we might play, many games promote communication between players as a path to in-game success. The image of a player alone in a basement for days is a misnomer. Instead, many games wield power to transport us to be whoever (and play with whomever) we want to have our perfect gaming experience.

The immersion elements of the game are the ones that engage our imagination the most. They transport our minds into the wondrous realities of the virtual world that we cannot experience in our physical context. Nature can expand beyond the places we know, signified by new color schemes and secret alcoves to discover. Neighboring characters can have different dialects and come from other planets (or realms). We create our character concept from scratch rather than being bound by the personalities and limitations already identified for us by our society. Many players feel the most relaxation during the creative aspects of gaming. It allows them to channel their stress and transform it into a vision of their ideal creation.

While many of these motivations fall under the simple categories of achievement, socialization, and immersion, one element connects with each in a more subversive way. This motive is called escape.

Video games are a powerful tool for escapism. In a virtual world, players can leave behind the stress of their everyday lives and immerse themselves in a new environment. For many people, this is a welcome respite from the challenges of reality. However, what starts as an occasional diversion can quickly become an unhealthy obsession. When video games are used as a way to cope with long term stress, they make problems worse. Instead of providing a release from anxiety, video games have become the source of distress.

Knowing how to meet our needs is essential, but fulfilling them in ways that cause other needs to be neglected becomes risky. To truly enjoy a video game, it is crucial to remember how it impacts your mental health. If you need to achieve great things to maintain self-esteem, games often provide a quicker path than a physical-world goal. However, the game only sometimes offers an opportunity for change in the actual world. If you play to find friends, it is vital to make efforts to pursue this support in your overall life. If not, you may feel alone in every situation except when playing in your team.

If you only find ways to love your avatar but not yourself, the damage to your self-esteem will only fade during gaming sessions. Escape is an excellent tool for relieving stress, but it needs to be done strategically, just like the other motivations. By finding the right games for our situations, we can make the nascent moment transformative for the right reasons. We just need to remember what our true journey is so that we can experience it successfully. When we strike a healthy balance with our priorities in life, video games become a delightful part of our lives, evoking a sense of enjoyment for all the right reasons.

 ## THE PLAYER-AVATAR RELATIONSHIP

Many games require character creation as their initiating activity, even before starting the game. The chance to create the ideal hero taps directly into the deepest motivations of our minds. This helps the player project their vision for a preferred identity into their gameplay. A player's basic choices in this activity are to select their hero's name, race, gender, and other defining characteristics. Players even alter their characters' physical appearance to match their actual physiology or an idealized image. As a result, the player-avatar relationship becomes the foundation for playing the game itself for many people.

One of the first games to offer player customization was *Pool of Radiance* for the Commodore 64. Released in 1988, players were able to create a band of adventurers by choosing their stats, race, and class. The options for each were limited compared to modern games, but the ability to select from pre-determined choices was groundbreaking for its time. This game combined many emergent ideas from the Advanced Dungeons and Dragons rulebook to enhance the legitimacy of the gaming adventure for many players. By matching different combinations of head and body images, *Pool of Radiance* gave players a questing party that belonged uniquely to them. Players felt more connected to their characters because they had a hand in shaping who they were at the start and who they would become by the end of the quest. The foundation of this relationship between player and avatar has grown stronger over time with technology expanding the range of customization options available in each gaming title.

Placing a projection of ourselves inside our gaming journey is one way to make the experience more personal. By customizing an avatar, we can better feel like the game responds to us as individuals. Playable characters handed to us by the story, such as Mario or Nathan Drake, matter to us in different ways. We must buy into their quests to feel ownership with them.

For player-created characters, we choose our modes of engaging with the game through our avatar, and then we play in a way that maximizes player agency. The character becomes so much more than a meaningless cipher going through the motions of a quest. They become the focal point of our ability to engage in our challenges. The avatar is not just a game piece to be moved around in the virtual world, but rather an extension of the self, allowing us to explore it. Each success feels earned by the player when our sense of identity experiences this anchor point. Games that begin with character creation send a message from the onset of play that the game is designed for us to project who we become into the game world. This player-avatar relationship becomes the central element in the player's experience every time they begin a new journey.

Understanding the Player-Avatar Relationship Based on work of Banks & Bowman (2013)	Avatar as an Object	Avatar as The Self	Avatar as a Symbiote	Avatar as a Social Other
Personal Identification "I am the character"	**Mild** The avatar is a fictional virtual character.	**Intense** The avatar is a virtual version of me in this fictional world.	**Moderate** The avatar is a part of my experience I connect to this virtual world.	**Mild** I control this character in the virtual world, but they are their own entity altogether.
Suspension of Belief "Game World is an Actual Reality"	**Mild** The gaming environment is a place where a game happens.	**Moderate** The virtual world adapts to become what I need it to be to fulfill expectations.	**Moderate** This world is a space where my avatar belongs, and I can visit it during play.	**Intense** My avatar lives in a separate world that becomes its own fictional reality.
Locus of Control "I relate to my character"	**Intense** The avatar is a tool I can use to sow my abilities and overcome challenges.	**Moderate** My avatar is an extension of me that grows towards social and mastery goals.	**Moderate** My avatar and I mutually require each other to accomplish our goals.	**Intense** My avatar has a separate identity that I assist in goal fulfillment as it requires.
Responsibility to Progress "I emotionally connect with my character"	**Mild** My avatar has no required needs. I play when I want to play.	**Moderate** I am my avatar, so our needs are identical.	**Moderate** I am always aware of my avatar's needs, as it is aware of mine.	**Intense** I am the apparatus for my avatar fulfilling their needs in the virtual world.

TABLE 3. *The Four Player-Avatar Relationships*

The characters we design become our representatives inside the virtual world. The player-avatar relationship in role-playing games can be psychologically experienced in four ways: avatar as an object, avatar as the self, avatar as a symbiote, and avatar as a social other. In the first case, the avatar is seen as an object the player uses to interact with the game world. The creation is designed to experience game features or impact challenges in specific ways. They are not specifically made to reflect the player's personality, as in other creation styles. The second case, avatar as self, considers the avatar an extension of the player's identity but residing inside the virtual environment. This creation is the player, and they can be regarded as one entity. The third option sees the avatar as a separate entity that helps the player navigate the game. The player can make specific choices that disengage from being an adaptation of their actual self in the game world. Instead, the character displays deliberate differences from their creator, but they are presented in meaningful ways that make the game enjoyable for the player. The last connection enables the player to disconnect from limitations within their psyche to experience the new individual they have created inside their gaming space. The character has detached from the actual self of the player. However, the player still can experience relief from limitations as they embrace a different self when seated inside the gameplay. Each of these relationships has a unique balance of traits for how they affect the flow of play from the player to the avatar.

Depending on how we identify with our character idea before starting the journey, we will grow to see these connections play out in different ways. When we objectify our avatars, we are more likely to see them as tools that help us achieve specific goals inside the game world. This could be using an avatar with particular strengths to buff up a party for combat encounters or selecting a specific role for different boss mechanics. We can also experiment with new classes, roles, or abilities defined by a player's stats. The way a character plays is often separated from their visual aesthetic in modern games, allowing for more player expressiveness. For example, an MMO game such as *World of Warcraft* will focus on choosing a class and player role, then designing the character. Specific classes will be restricted from certain player roles. After these play-oriented choices have been made, the game sends you to character design.

Other games use a stat-oriented approach to customizing the character's uniqueness. For example, *Cyberpunk 2077* has every player customize a character named V. This creation process still allows players to form their own identities. After selecting a difficulty level and general path for V's programming, you move on to visuals and stats. The *Cyberpunk 2077* creation suite focuses on allowing the new player to visually customize the protagonist's character to their liking via sliders and toggles for almost any visual aspect of the character's body. After the appearance has been completed, the player assigns stats. This character design style is repeated across many RPG games, including *Elden Ring / Dark Souls, The Elder Scrolls, Mass Effect,* etc.

Taking cues from tabletop games, this character design process allows players to select their character's capabilities based on how they plan to approach solutions for in-game challenges. While the assumption is that any composition of stats can still lead to success, the player's instincts to use their created character can amplify their chances of success dramatically.

The avatar also represents our extension of self when we choose to role-play. This is done by envisioning them with our own personality traits or by exploring game worlds with our values and morals in mind.

Suppose we are feeling limited by our actual selves. In that case, we can create avatars with different characteristics to feel a sense of power or control that we might not otherwise experience. If we want to explore parts of ourselves that we do not understand, we can choose an avatar based on a different set of values than our own. How we explore through this avatar creates further opportunities to benefit from developing our in-game strengths. These choices help us understand how someone with different motivations might think or feel in specific situations.

Overall, our goal is to see our identity face new challenges in a simulated game environment. When this happens, the journey becomes our own. The player-avatar relationship helps us play uniquely, making the game a canvas for self-expression, and the nascent moment before play becomes a defining transformation. We complete this first step feeling like the quest we accept next will lead us to the inspiration we hope to receive from the game as new players.

SEEING NEW GAME ELEMENTS IN LIFE

One of the most rewarding aspects of video gaming is the movement from a state of nascence to being able to create an identity quest that explains our journey through life. Many therapeutic insights rely on the idea that our thoughts determine our reality. The stories we explore time and again in our own head space help us define the parameters of that internal universe. Whether through books, movies, video games, or even the feeling of escape until we find our deeper meaning, we use these fictional worlds to help our lives shift from the mundane to one with purpose. Imaginary worlds with the most profound personal connections help us create the path toward fulfillment. For countless people around the world at every moment, this occurs through the play of video games.

Life can be considered a series of challenges. These phases can be defined as places we've lived, intimate relationships, additions to our family, career advances, and any other changes we can use to separate one year from the next. While many games will encourage us to focus on the action, our use of mindfulness allows us to cultivate our meaning in the present. This sense of purpose represents the perfect balance between how we have arrived, our present, and our awareness of what we hope to become as we head into the future.

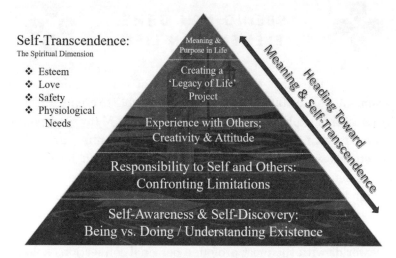

FIGURE 11. *A Stage Approach for Finding Purpose Towards Self-Transcendence*

The lessons from any range of games, from *Spiritfarer* to role-playing games and beyond, can be deeply personal in their abilities to influence meaning. While we may not notice the wonder in each nascent moment early in life, our ability to experience them is limited. The games we play represent our interests as we push through each new phase in our lifespan. We alternate between many different directives in our lives as much as we will in the metaphor of our in-game protagonists and their quest log.

Some missions are essential. They become our "Main Scenario" quest line, the tasks defining our sense of being. Other challenges are whimsical (although their importance is debatably a different kind of significance). Still, others are "busy work" upon reflection. With each opportunity, we decide further what stats to enhance across our character sheet. We choose our class in the form of the talents we offer to share with others. We define our traits in the activities we emphasize in our daily routine. The people we meet along the way help us to expand our creativity and influence.

When we decide to play a new game, we are also choosing to add a new challenge to our ordinary world. This form of play can help us relax as much as it can help us see our everyday situations in new ways. The project we complete in each of life's stages is a legacy that helps us know who we are with greater certainty. While our primary sense of meaning may not come directly from a game, how we find solutions can be traced back to many of our gaming activities.

By demonstrating patience and determination, we can apply the same approach to advancing from one level to the next in a game to our daily lives. As we continue to level up our character, we also remember that at one time, each of our journeys had a nascent moment. We decide how we want to move forward and then make it happen. The quest to find our purpose only resolves when we determine what quests would be the most fulfilling. Once we know this, we move forward.

The search for meaning is more than just in what games we choose to finish, or even to start. It comes from what we take away from the gaming activity itself. When we feel a genuine connection with a game, the story, our characters, and the final goal, we create a meaningful context for our lives through our playtime. The many roles we fulfill in our lives are reflected in how we play games, even if the game is sometimes life and sometimes a video game on a screen.

By assembling this context across our daily routine, we experience a calling to become more significant, pushing for the maximum level-up in our purpose. While games do not grant the path to all our needs, they teach us lessons about all of them. All we need to do to benefit from these lessons is take the time to reflect on how we moved from the nascent moment, never having played, to exploring new perspectives as a person who has finally chosen to play the game.

CHAPTER VIII

THE CALL TO
ADVENTURE

Every journey begins with a choice.

—Professor Oak (Pokémon Red & Blue Versions)

T hroughout life, it is empowering to wonder. Our sense of imagination helps us create context for our random discoveries in life. These ideas become our reality built from both the conscious and subconscious sides of life. When we dream, our minds wander to familiar places while giving us the feeling that the experience is new. We get placed in the middle of bizarre situations with only the psyche to guide us through a whimsical mix of obstacles.

When we choose to play, we let go of the requirement to be productive and are free to explore the next phase of our day focused on enjoyment. Play provides an opportunity to experiment with various aspects of our personality without allowing the stressors of reality to define us. The part of our mind that awakens in these moments is the imagination. When we venture into the unknown, we start to see our self-concept in ways that would never have been possible had we stayed in the ordinary world. This opportunity helps us consider happenings beyond the usual. In these scenarios, only innovative ideas guide us into the unknown future. This is the realm of dreams.

Our dreams have a magical power to connect us to that inner psyche. They inspire us to find meaning inside curiosities, seeking out new interpretations that feel obvious despite never coming to mind in our waking moments. Dreams and video games both help the mind preserve that sense of wonder by providing an outlet for exploration and adventure. In video games, we are presented with an interactive environment in which to play. This digital space is designed for inspiration as we take different personas on a journey through countless game worlds.

Some games initiate this shift to a world of discovery using a dream sequence. When playing the original *Kingdom Hearts*, we open with the main character, Sora, dreaming about adventures in other worlds with his childhood friends Riku and Kairi. This dream sequence shows us a version of reality where Sora stands on the shore as he spots Riku in the water. As Sora steps towards Riku, his friend looks up, holds out a hand, and is swept away by a giant tidal wave. With Sora now in the water, he turns back to the shore, only to see Kairi in the sand, offering an excited wave for him to return. They see a sleeping Sora flying across the ocean as he approaches her. As they meet, the Sora of our perspective faints, falling to the ground as it fades into a sea of darkness. As Sora descends, Kairi and Riku are left to find their own paths through the dream of destiny.

While the imagery of this dream has profound meaning, the next challenge is to guide Sora through the tutorial. As each phase ends, Sora moves across a series of stained-glass windows, each featuring a Disney princess and a valuable lesson for the player. Some of these platforms educate the player on movement. Others offer the first combat with the Heartless, the enemies borne of darkness to hinder Sora as he seeks to unlock hope for each world. One by one, the player overcomes each challenge to move through the phases of the dream. Sora sees his shadow form rise from the floor at the platform. Growing to giant proportions, this shadow shifts from Heartless to becoming The Darkside, the first real combat challenge of this psychological training ground. Once victory is achieved, Sora is dragged down into the pool of shadow again, met with a disembodied voice that reminds him:

"The closer you get to the light, the greater your shadow becomes. But don't be afraid. You hold the mightiest weapon of all. So don't forget: You are the one who will open the door."

As the sun returns to view, Sora awakens on the beach, reunited in the conscious world with Kairi. This is where players are introduced to Destiny Island, the ordinary world of this series. We are casually introduced to the real-world connections between Sora, Riku, and Kairi, along with some other appearances from Final Fantasy characters who also dwell on the same island. While the village appears completely safe, the options for adventure are nonexistent for those who live here. Destiny Island is a limited space designed for a tranquil balance between humans and nature, permanently floating together in an endless ocean. Due to the desire for exploration, the heroes long to build a raft and sail fearlessly into the unknown.

Seeking provisions for the voyage, Sora ventures into the cave at the island's center. Inside, he is met with a vision, replaying a memory of his younger self drawing together with Kairi on the cave walls. Once finished, a robed figure reveals himself, standing beside the unopened door blocking the center wall. The ominous conversation that follows serves as a harbinger of challenges to come. According to the figure, the door connects the island to the rest of existence by channeling the power of darkness. He claims that Sora cannot comprehend what is in store for him. As the message of predestination echoes through the cave, the player is guided by the childlike optimism that defines the temperament of Sora. The quest to learn the truth has commenced as the robed man fades into the shadow.

That evening, the island is attacked by the Heartless Sora first encountered in his dreams. His first frantic thought is to find his friends. Armed only with a wooden sword, Sora runs through each section of Destiny Island, lacking the power to repel his pursuers. The Heartless show no mercy as each area is pulled into the vortex. With the inner cave now blocked by an ethereal white door, Sora strikes a new path to continue the search.

Moving to the small island where he had engaged in play fights each day of his early childhood, Sora finds Riku staring up into the looming vortex of darkness. He turns around, proclaiming to his friend that the door has opened, and it is time to leave Destiny Island together. Sora, however, is concerned about the nature of the dark energy. Not fearing the darkness, Riku raises his hand as an offer of guidance (just as he did in the dream sequence) as the ocean claims his body. This time, the darkness separates the two friends in reality, leaving Sora alone in the light as Riku embraces the path of darkness.

Coming through the light, however, is a power known as the Keyblade. This weapon, shaped as a royal key, works as the sword meant to protect the Keyblade Master from harm as they seek to reconnect each world to the light of *Kingdom Hearts*. While all of this is unknown to Sora for now, he returns to the ethereal door at the cave. This time, the door opens. Running to the end of the cavern path, Sora finds Kairi mesmerized by the old door that connects reality. She turns to face him just as the door erupts with darkness. As she flies with the racing current, her body disappears just as Sora reaches out to save her from harm. Now Sora is alone while the only world he has ever known falls into darkness.

Sora eventually finds himself at the last remaining edge of the island, the endless tide of monsters creeping closer. Equipped with the Keyblade, Sora begins fighting for his life as the edge presses closer. The final space holds a rematch with The Darkside. Our Keyblade Master decides to fight both minions and their master. Emerging victorious, Sora's only resolve is to find his friends despite not knowing how to begin. As Destiny Island succumbs to the darkness, Sora is dragged helplessly into the vortex. With the worlds now connected and Sora deemed the Keyblade wielder by fate itself, a new hero embarks on the journey to find his friends and set reality back in balance for the side of light.

The story of *Kingdom Hearts* uses gameplay and story to illustrate the Call to Adventure in a way that matches the cadence of the monomyth. In games, as in mythological tales, the Call to Adventure symbolizes a push that sends the protagonist out of their everyday life and into new realms of existence. The darkness overtakes the safe world, leaving the hero with no choice but to confront challenges head-on.

These events can come in many forms. Sometimes, they can be a choice the hero casually ponders. Other times, the action rips through everything the hero ever knew, leaving them only with the chance to react or die. For Sora, the call comes in the form of being separated from his friends and having to find them again while simultaneously unlocking the heart of each world from the dominion of the Heartless. He runs selflessly through the darkness to save his friends. When lacking strength, his faith still leads him to do what is right. This is why the Keyblade chose him instead of Riku. The dream sequence has come true, and the plot of the darkness has moved beyond Destiny Island. Sora answered the call, and because of this, he wakes up in a new world on the other side of the darkness, having no choice but to keep moving forward until he finds his friends.

 ## PATHS OF AWAKENING

There are many ways a game can begin. Unlike the stories we read, game narratives make deliberate choices for delivering their stories around (and through) the gameplay experience. Early in the game, players often guide a hero character who has to make choices that will affect the course of the adventure. Sometimes these choices are part of a scene, meaning we are watching and cannot alter the outcome. Other times, the choice is ours. As a result, our options shape the narrative while the story evaluates our attempts to accomplish our goals.

How we arrive at these pivotal moments is unique in how games draw us in as players. The moment of awakening is a recognizable structure, initiating the player with the virtual world and pushing them toward the plot. Games capture this moment in many ways. One possibility is to introduce important concepts to the player using the cutscene as exposition. For example, the opening scene of *Ocarina of Time* has The Great Deku Tree sending Navi to awaken the "boy without a fairy." Once awake, Link quickly receives a quest to fight the growing darkness, which eventually leads him to saving Hyrule.

"The Awakening" opener is replicated in other games such as *Knights of the Old Republic*, *Chrono Trigger*, and *Uncharted 2*. The sleeping player is thrown into the action and must gather information along the way no matter how perilous the scene feels.

This struggle helps establish a mystery for the story, drawing the player in as a hero who knows as much as they do. This creates a synergy of learning together as the story continues. Another approach to initiating the narrative is through a prologue mission. These segments offer backstory or sometimes a glimpse into the actions of different characters. They make the world feel epic by inserting an overpowered character who is primarily off-limits during the main story despite their importance.

Each element of the opening creates the framework for the conflict and the characters once the story continues. Like the human psyche, gaming narratives often contain conscious and subconscious elements. This is important for creating moments that capture the essence of the monomyth, helping video games become a lasting mythology.

According to Carl Jung, the themes we dream through are likely tethered to the complexes we hope to overcome in our conscious existence. These images form a similar repetition through the heroic journey we experience each time we move a character beyond nascence by answering the call to adventure. The cadence of these stories tells us we can make these changes in our lives just as we do when we play. This belief gets lost in translation because we need to connect it with the importance of answering our own calling. Nevertheless, these connections remain intact when we believe in ourselves the way the most pure-hearted heroes demonstrate in our games.

FIGURE 12. *The Steps to the Call in the Original Kingdom Hearts*

The example of *Kingdom Hearts* illustrates this connection exceptionally. Using a story about friendship and fulfilling our destiny, the tale of Sora, Donald, and Goofy begins with an unwanted separation guided by every archetypal image from the monomyth.

First, Sora is introduced to the player as a young boy living on Destiny Island. He is safe but hopes to embark on a grand adventure with his friends.

He experiences a dream that foreshadows an untold destiny to defend the light against the darkness.

Next, Sora wakes up on the beach and meets his friends. They all plan to leave on a raft they have built together.

Unknown forces meet Sora throughout the day. While one voice deems Sora "the one who will open the door," the herald of change arrives as an ominous robed figure (and eventual villain) known as Ansem in the island cave.

That evening, danger is unleashed as the Heartless devour the island.

Sora inherits the power of the Keyblade to save Destiny Island, but it seems to be too late. Sora is separated from everything he holds dear. Sora was separated from the ordinary world before he was ready to face the darkness alone.

Sora wakes up in a far-off world and encounters a new group of fighters eagerly awaiting the arrival of the Keyblade Master. He will become the chosen hero so long as he accepts the mission to save existence. By accepting this calling, Sora sets off on a new mission to find his friends and save Kingdom Hearts. The new party of Sora, Donald, and Goofy begin flying from world to world, battling the forces of darkness. By unlocking each Keyhole, the heroes fight to restore balance to a universe in disarray, one world at a time.

Using the stages this way, many other games enhance their plot and character development to deliver an epic gaming experience. In parallel, *The Witcher 3: Wild Hunt* opens with a series of visions, a dream sequence, and a tutorial.

By witnessing this entire sequence, the player better understands the sequence of events they are interacting with across the early stages of the game. The metaphorical nature of the dream analysis identifies Yennifer of Vengerberg as a critical character in the quest to find Ciri. The arrival of the Wild Hunt and their armored leader shifts the tone of the dream from utopian existence to a nightmare, leaving Geralt to witness the death of everyone in Kaer Morhen. When Geralt awakens, he knows his calling is to find Yennifer (and eventually Ciri) and stop the Wild Hunt from covering the lands in frigid darkness.

The nascence of the dream leads quickly to the call. The tutorial itself demonstrates how players can directly engage in the monomyth phases of the beginning quest. This is how the player quickly moves through the separation until they can join in the later stages of the fantasy epic.

With gaming stories such as these two in mind, discovering our personal separation from the ordinary becomes a tremendous reflection to explore. Once we take the time to recognize our ordinary world, the nascent moments of our dreams crystallize into whatever meaning we assign them. What grand calling would you accept to achieve meaningful change in your journey? Who are the friends and loved ones for whom you are willing to search near and far? What limits will be tested before you decide you cannot keep going?

The heroes in our games often find a respawn point, a second chance whenever they must be better. Can we learn from this and accept our challenges more effectively? If we can see life's challenges the way we view a heroic quest, the only possibilities are that we finish successfully or decide to return to the ordinary of the main menu. The challenge is not what ends our quest. Our choices are. To have a chance, we must find our supernatural world. What allows us to face our fears and confront our most significant challenges the way a Keyblade Master or a Witcher would? What do our games teach us about recognizing the journey? More importantly, what do they teach us about accepting the call to adventure?

 ## REFUSAL OF THE CALL

There are phases in life for all of us where we are left to wonder what might have been. What if we had chosen differently? What if we had tried harder? ... asked differently? ... called for help? Noticed this or that sooner? ... and any number of other things. The call to adventure is a powerful moment where we are faced with a decision that will change the course of our lives— accepting our calling triggers the push to accomplish something more significant than ourselves.

Sometimes we are not listening, and the call comes. We miss it, and the opportunity fades into the aether. These moments can be as simple as starting a new job or expanding your family. Anything that takes work, dedication, and promises an answer for purpose can be the call we are listening for, which becomes inherent to our existence. Just because we do not advance the first time does not mean we never will.

Purpose and meaning are achieved in different ways for everyone. Sometimes we have a choice, and we refuse to step forward. When this happens, we accept our ordinary world and continue to accept the status quo. A gaming example of this comes from the movie tie-in title *The Matrix: Path of Neo*. Replicating the pivotal movie scene between Neo and Morpheus, the player is offered a red pill to learn the truth or a blue pill to wake up tomorrow and never know the reality of humanity's enslavement. If the player chooses the blue pill, the scene completes, and you return to the main menu with a game finished in the most unfulfilling way possible. The player, however, can choose something else to do and never know what the full game was like, or they can restart and choose to be a part of the experience.

When the refusal path is chosen, the story is less about shifting into a heroic quest than about naïve existence. The adventure becomes routine, and repetition slides into the mundane. The tireless efforts of the prevailing culture often result in monotony, where valuable abilities are applied to mundane and unexciting duties. Flow is impossible but also unneeded. Rather than becoming a hero, we resemble a non-playable character (but hope at least to be one of the good ones). While our purpose draws us to accept our quest, the refusal to even begin saps away our intention to live our lives well. We can play a game as a way to forget, but even then, the stories echo the lesson of what it means to step onto the path of the supernatural world and strive for greatness.

The refusal of the call is demonstrated in both linear and open-world game narratives, although this looks different based on game design. For a linear example, we can turn to *Assassin's Creed II*. On the action side of the story, Ezio Auditore da Firenze serves as the flashback hero running throughout the Italian Renaissance to aid the cause of the Assassins against the Templars and gain revenge for the death of his family members. Early in the story, Ezio makes his kill and flees Italy with his mother and sister. They head for Spain, where Ezio's uncle attempts to induct him into the ranks of the Assassins. After a full year of training, Ezio refuses his rightful place as an Assassin. He wants only to preserve his family's safety and does not seek to cause further bloodshed. This decision is only temporary, and eventually Ezio does follow his uncle to the storming of San Gimignano. The hesitation is a refusal of the call, despite circumstances pushing Ezio to accept the call under the right conditions. What he needs for his purpose is more than safety. He is seeking a connection with life and a sense of belonging. The mission and creed of the Assassins are the way Ezio ultimately achieves these things as we continue to play the story.

Open-world games also offer notable examples of how refusing the call can impact gameplay. Any game operating outside the linear approach allows players to explore the virtual world at their own pace. As a result, quests are often differentiated between "main story" and "side quests." When a player chooses to avoid finishing the main quest, this can parallel the hesitation of the hero's journey in places where the refusal is chosen.

Certain games build this into their narratives as well. In *Final Fantasy XIV Online*, the *A Realm Reborn* main scenario offers the player the choice to join the Scions of the Seventh Dawn or reject them. Of course, the narrative requires that you join them. However, the player can deny their membership in the order, leaving them free to wander the open world without a main scenario to complete. This also ends much of the opportunity for the created character since most MMO activities include requirements to advance past certain quest lines to make them available. A player who selects the "refusal of the call" will never become the Warrior of Light. They will struggle to connect with other players and find meaningful activities while traversing Eorzea.

Just as our characters are left directionless when these choices are made, we move through life devoid of purpose when we avoid our path to fulfillment. Despite video games serving primarily as entertainment, the metaphors we build from these virtual worlds generate real meaning across our reality. Through our choices, we are defining what is essential and what is worth working to accomplish.

In reality therapy, William Glasser identifies five basic needs we aim to generate for ourselves through the construct of choice: survival, freedom, love and belonging, power, and fun. We have completed the main quest when we have acquired each of these needs. Once this is done, our choices serve to maintain the accomplishment or to progress to new levels as we do so. The refusal choice comes from an ego that does not believe we can (or should) achieve the required task. Excuses abound in this path when it impacts our choices. "The mission is for someone else." "We can do this later when we are ready?" "I am not the person they think I am." All these excuses get in the way of moving forward and affirming our potential.

This aura of avoidance allows the fear of failure to discourage us from taking the next meaningful step forward on our path of fulfillment. For many, failure sounds like an all-encompassing word that grows to define the entire person. As it relates to the journey of the game player, failure can be recategorized as any effort in which forward progress was not achieved. For the play of video games, the reality is that problem-solving often involves the experience of failed attempts to move forward. However, completing a game is only sometimes the goal. For some, the game is a coping mechanism. This means prolonging the play becomes an opportunity to avoid something elsewhere.

As a result, a person can play a game that could have ended hours (or days) ago. This is the equivalent of a player for a Bethesda title such as *Fallout* (or also The *Elder Scrolls*) choosing to set out from The Vault (or main quest zones of Tamriel) but do everything in the world except complete the main story. While this can appear successful by only examining in-game progress, the actual result brings a non-success sequence in other life areas. This procrastination becomes multifaceted. It involves a shift in personal energy, lack of confidence in a plan moving forward, difficulty organizing information, distraction, and avoidance.

In certain rare cases, video games will include the refusal as a narrative hurdle used to introduce characters to situations with personal stakes in a more delayed fashion. In *Persona 5*, the protagonist you play will eventually become Joker, the leader of the Phantom Thieves. When he first gains the ability to enter the Metaverse Palaces via a mysterious app on his phone, he deletes the app. It reappears later and eventually forces Joker to become a captive in the Palace of his gym teacher Kamoshida, who, it turns out, is abusing students and is heavily implied to be sexually manipulating at least one of your classmates. Learning this, Joker accepts the ability to call for his Persona, which begins the relationship between Joker and Arsène. The refusal has ended. The call is answered. The party has formed, and the mission is clear.

With so many examples in video games, how can we take better notice of our opportunities in life to answer this call ourselves? More importantly, what must we do to knowingly make the tough choice and take the next step forward?

With the Jungian influences of the *Persona* series so entrenched in these narrative choices, the ability to break through the refusal moment can certainly be understood psychoanalytically. When we understand the needs of our inner archetype, we achieve balance between our ego and the forces within us that keep us trapped in the ordinary world, allowing us to finally answer our calling.

The infantile fear that we can never rise to our potential perpetuates the choices that make us stay precisely as we are. This pre-decision state is philosophically relatable to the experience of childhood. When we aim for genuine autonomy, we realize we must accept the risk of failure to move beyond the safety net that keeps us dependent on the ordinary world.

In video games, we experiment with our autonomy in a way that shows us that metaphorical bridge between answering the call, beginning our challenge, and putting in the work for our independence. The things that make us "comfortable but dependent" are the threshold guardians; lair bosses we must overcome to advance in the challenge. Our shadow is the fear that we would fall short if we did try.

Ultimately, we must overcome ourselves if we are ever to pass the thresholds of our ordinary world. The world we call ordinary is only that because of how we accept it on an intrinsic level. The act of tearing away the persona's mask gives us the moment of accepting ourselves and shouting proudly, "I am ready." Whether playing a game or facing a momentous life decision, we answer this call or hesitate the way many of our gaming heroes do. That is until we pick up our controller and move forward in the campaign to achieve greatness.

By unifying our understanding of self with the powers in our gaming stories, we can build successful bridges between ourselves and the stories that influence our ability to hope. So many desires for our present come from how we envision our personality achieving success. If we only find success from external sources, we may struggle with chaos when left to experience our inner selves.

Instead, we must believe in ourselves if we are to answer the call gracefully and begin walking the path of the hero archetypes.

Life as a gamer shows us consistently that even when we team up with others, our ability to perform the task is the only element we genuinely control. Accepting this results in willful introversion, the ability to perceive our own experience as valid and draw value from this realization through the experience alone. Even if others have a hand in the success of the multiplayer team, the only way to move forward is to phase out the worry for others and focus on the personal level of the task. The locus of control falls on each player independently, whether playing a solo or team effort. When we recognize our impact, we keep trying until we make it through. By moving past the judgment of others, we learn to focus on our path mindfully. This is how we move forward. This presence allows us to focus on ourselves, staying patient as we wait for everything to fall into place.

This example applies to any scenario in which our hopes interact with other people providing their own input into the system. We interact with games this way in a rapid-fire stimulus-response model. The game becomes a world of challenge, and we respond. Based on the feedback, we know when we have succeeded and make the next choice.

When we embrace our archetypes, we achieve flow as our reward for pursuing success. Whether it is solving a puzzle, dominating our opponents, mastering mechanics, or planting a radiant garden, we find the games that fulfill us in the best ways, and we play them. We turn our non-successes into lessons. As a result, we transform our punishments into revelations that give us the confidence to move forward on the right path, the one we feel chosen to experience.

Games allow us to relax, feel, balance, and find the flow channel. We unlock our most vital abilities when placed in the right situations. One person cannot become everything. How we play games and choose which calls to answer is reflected in how we live. Once we understand the fear that holds us back, we begin searching for ways to create the counter response for the stimuli that claim we "haven't made it yet."

The call to adventure is not an endlessly repeating offer; refusing it too often will result in it being gone one day. We turn on games to run from this problem until we are ready to embrace it. Once the time for refusal has ended, the feeling inside that "this calling is the right one" becomes impossible to ignore. We find the right situations by becoming aware of what we hope to be in the world. Once we feel this purpose, the call of our potential breaks through, and the time to answer is now.

 ANSWERING THE CALL TO ADVENTURE

To answer our call to adventure, we must first recognize the opportunity for monumental change aligned with our purpose. This recognition occurs through an event that forces us to consider whether we are ready.

In these moments, we must ask ourselves what we are meant for. Considering an example like Destiny Island, our ordinary worlds can be fantastic places to live. Yet, there comes a realization that we want to progress somehow. Like Sora, Riku, and Kairi, we want to set sail and see how far we can go using only our abilities. We want to explore what is beyond the horizon to discover our true purpose.

Like them, we are often stopped by our beliefs surrounding our potential and all the demands of people who rely on us in our present. These people, while intending to keep us safe and happy, instead inadvertently block us from the growth we need to feel complete. The inner conflict of deciding whether to venture out or stay is based on whether we have enough faith in ourselves to strive for growth or to settle for the status quo. The choice of the gaming hero to fight their foes instead of running from them crystallizes when they understand that the world needs them. To fulfill our destinies, we must find it within ourselves to become the person who chooses action when the time comes. These are not easy decisions, but these moments decide the eventual fate of our path through life.

Not every person along our path encourages us to stay "as is." Some push us to see our world clearly from the onset, even if we do not recognize the true purpose behind why they ask us to do so. The herald of change, in the structure of the monomyth, is anyone that appears in a story to signal the start of the hero's journey. In games, these could be an unknown figure, the looming darkness, a beast we have never encountered, a creature who knows more than us, or a whimsical change in our normally mundane perspective. This character typically represents change, and their appearance often prompts the hero to leave their Ordinary World and embark on a quest.

Beyond gaming, the herald of change can be seen as a catalyst for change in our own lives. Many people dream of being something they have not become due to resources, credentials, training, and other thresholds in life. It is easier to focus on whether something is a realistic goal, and those who want us to stay can be the biggest influencers of our decisions in those instances. Whether we hope to be an artist, writer, musician, athlete, college graduate, or anything short of becoming a medical doctor, most people can identify a conversation in their life where the message was "that goal is too far /too hard/irrelevant/silly" and everything in between.

When we feel encouraged to change our path, the relief we feel for those pressures signals the start of our heroic journey. From this experience, we learn to believe in the mission, which starts our transformation into our ideal vision of self. The world we thought was "so far away" is much closer, and we can join it as long as our hopes equal our determination to stay there. The experience of encountering the herald of change is empowering. This meeting gives us the strength to leave our Ordinary World and embark on a quest to find our purpose. In many ways, this experience becomes a turning point in our lives. It is when we finally begin to believe in ourselves, and ultimately, we become the hero of our own story.

With the story of heroes front and center in our minds, the narrative greatly benefits from deciding which form of hero we intend to become. As Professor Oak tells us in *Pokémon Generation I*, "Every journey begins with a choice." While this classic game moment referred to the choice of a starter Pokémon, the meaning relates to leaving our comfort zone when we set out to evolve into something new.

Games typically offer this concept to us in the form of morality and class decisions, character creation, and so much more. We are often challenged to use our personalities to do our best in similar situations. There are vast differences between players of role-playing games, for example, despite many players reaching similar endpoints. The time we take as trainers to explore, train, and finish the path of league champion are all markers of our goals for how we intend to play. Having a plan is the start. Deciding to begin the work is next. How we choose defines the flow of the journey. Despite arguably similar endpoints, there are definite differences between players who complete a story using a lawful/neutral/chaotic approach (or good/neutral/evil). Looking across game genres, it becomes clear that we are the result of our choices, and the first choice is often the decision to set out on the path to becoming something new within ourselves.

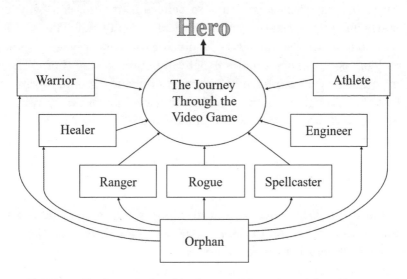

FIGURE 13. *The Seven Paths of Archetypal Valor* (adapted from Bean, 2018)

This understanding of self comes directly from the archetypes we choose for the challenges we accept. Although most stories have identifiable elements of the monomyth present in the telling, heroes can be understood through many compositions. The backstory of how we get to the point of the calling is as diverse as the people who enjoy the narrative tradition of the monomyth.

Are we destined to explore our chosen path, or are we being thrown in by fate against our will? Was power handed to us, or did we grind for every opportunity to discover our herald of change?

The rules that govern our developmental pathways through life are often illuminated in storytelling to help people move across the thresholds of their stages when they recognize the metaphor. Before achieving these benchmarks, we all fill the position of the orphan. In fiction, the orphan hero is a character who has faced adversity but will be tasked with doing heroic things to answer the calling to save their world. This ordeal requires them to discover their strengths as they take each step forward. Challenges of physical acumen are best suited for the warrior, athlete, or rogue. Quests requiring wisdom, knowledge, and range match better with rangers, engineers, and spellcasters. Others seek to support and guide others, such as the healer. All of these hero types fit into their own stories wonderfully. They each carry traits that fill in the gaps of others, just as we do.

When we understand our tendencies, we connect with the world differently. Our talents lead to the quests we are excited to accept. When we see the challenges in life through the metaphor of a game, it does not mean we are taking them less seriously. In fact, by applying the structures of the monomyth to what we attempt in life, we are bestowing the challenge with the most significant importance imaginable.

Like starting a new game, we answer the call to adventure. We inhabit the hero, their abilities, and the drive of their stories. By recognizing the path, we also accept our stake in the journey. This relates directly to the first stage of The Hero's Journey. Like the heroes in our fiction, we embark on a journey to find meaning, purpose, and destiny. The fear that we "might not" finally yields to the hope that we "absolutely will" come through in the end. Even if we do not succeed, it is better to attempt the quest than to realize we never moved beyond the limited experience of the ordinary world. No matter how the story begins for each of us (a random mistake, an epiphany, or a challenge we have been trained for since birth), we can each do meaningful things that affect our ordinary world and leave it changed forever.

This crucial takeaway is echoed in the way we play video games. For those of us who need an extra boost to take that initial step, games can be the herald just as much as anything else. The important thing is that the journey means something to us on a personal level. We cannot continue a journey that only matters to someone else. We would quit at the first convenient opportunity because the consequences would not reach us. If we truly see ourselves in the story, it will affect us. This will encourage us to be resilient and problem-solve with a focus that often leads to lasting change. This is why games matter and why they work as a teaching tool. We choose to play games willingly, as they provide us with inherent learning opportunities, even if the lessons are presented within a fictional setting.

Humanity, as a species, is driven to explain lessons through story. As a result, the opportunities to learn lessons from video games will continue to expand ad infinitum. If developers have a message to pair with a mechanic, characters will continue accepting quests. The point for all of us who play, watch, and listen to gaming stories is that we bring the lessons off the screen and into our lives meaningfully.

It all starts with engaging our world, finding something we hope to become, and then taking hold of the chance to pursue it. Like in games, we may only achieve brilliantly on some first attempts. All the same, we make each attempt so that we can find the right path forward.

The power of the monomyth is that it shows us how to keep our hope strong as we focus on the change we hope to achieve in ourselves. We know that when we see our path as the hero through to the end, we will finally have helped the ordinary world endure the obstacles that give us a need for hope. It all begins with the calling. When we rise to our first challenge, the true story of our growth begins. In games, the path forward begins by pressing 'Start.' It is up to us to take this lesson and apply it. Only then will we set out on the adventure to meet each trial head-on, hoping to one day complete our journey of fulfillment.

CHAPTER IX

MEETING THE
MENTOR

You were always an unruly child. I adored that about you. Now Fly!

—Vesemir (The Witcher 3: Wild Hunt)

E very hero, at some point, will need help understanding the
nature of their challenges. Having a mentor can help reduce
anxiety and ensure enough confidence to keep moving forward through overwhelming obstacles. The mentor figure often
reveals themselves to the hero early on this path to help them
better navigate their uncertainties. Most mentors have faced
the present challenge before or have discovered knowledge the
hero lacks from some point earlier in their lives. Mentors come in
many forms, from supporting characters, guides, or as one who
repeatedly offers the wisdom of the sage to the transitioning hero
as they move from the ordinary to the supernatural phases of the
journey.

There are different types of mentors in video games. Some mentors are supernatural beings, like the fairy Midna in *The Legend of Zelda: Twilight Princess*. When Link awakens in his cell early in the adventure, Midna breaks him free and offers her aid as long as Link behaves. The player guides their animal-form of Link to discover the ways of the wolf. With this new mechanic for the Zelda franchise, Midna becomes the bearer of knowledge for both Link and the player as the tutorial section for wolf mode is completed. This partnership grows throughout the game, and the mechanics of the Twilight realm directly connect to Link using his human and wolf abilities to succeed in his mission. Without Midna, Link would not understand his supernatural powers in this quest to save Hyrule from Ganondorf.

Other mentors, like Auron in *Final Fantasy X*, connect on a more human level. At the start of this game, Tidus has already formed a relationship with Auron. Tidus, a renowned and youthful blitzball athlete, contrasts with Auron's stoic nature as a warrior.

The evening's sporting event in Spira is interrupted by a massive tidal wave and an onslaught of smaller monsters being shed by the colossal whale-like creature known as Sin. During their run for safety, Auron guides the player (Tidus) through the first series of battles. The learning process is front and center for Tidus, whereas Auron knows precisely how to find the best path forward. This guidance helps Tidus survive, although they are separated by time and space at the end of the encounter.

Without Auron's advice at the moment of crisis, Tidus would not have been able to survive long enough even to begin the story. As the mentor, Auron provides advice at each critical moment. His knowledge of Sin and its origin guides the entire party until they eventually have a chance to save the world.

In life, mentors give us the lessons we need so we can overcome obstacles, just as our favorite heroes do in their epic stories.

By finding a mentor like Auron, we can learn where our strengths lie and find a path to take on the most incredible challenges, aiming to bring our dreams into reality.

Many games that endure the test of time use the dynamic of meeting a mentor to help the hero initially awaken to their power, beginning the path to becoming the world savior. For Joker in *Persona 5*, the guidance from new strangers helps him understand the nature of the Velvet Room. Being a transformative space in the subconscious, the Velvet Room is where the contract to survive the story is signed. It is also where the player is introduced to Igor, the master of the Velvet Room, and the bizarre twin wardens, Caroline, and Justine. After signing the contract, Igor enforces the agreement while the twins help the player synthesize new personas to move through the subconscious areas more effectively.

Without these characters, the protagonist would be locked into a permanent "low-power mode." In the narrative side of the game, the player meets a mentor to join their party inside the first dungeon; a cat named Morgana. This talking mascot character appears after a supernatural foe attacks the player and awakens to their latent power; an ability known as the Wild Card. From there, Morgana becomes an invaluable resource in the real world and metaverse as a member of the "Phantom Thieves."

Each mentor plays a role in guiding the protagonist to realizing their potential. Their support allows the protagonist to ascend from being a Fool, incapable of navigating the Metaverse, to being a leader. This cycle of growth, a defining feature of Persona, directly aligns with the cycle found across stories monomythical stories.

Awakening to the spirit of the world is essential to achieving success in any narrative. The forces which govern the game universe function as the rationale behind the in-game mechanics.

Without understanding these dynamics, leveling-up, equipping gear, or fulfilling objectives would become impossible.

In *Elden Ring*, this happens when a player refuses the calling deliberately. At an early campfire in the opening area of the map, a woman named Melina appears to your Tarnished and asks you for aid on her quest. If the player refuses, the game becomes significantly more difficult since they cannot spend runes and increase their abilities. The words "Summon me by grace to turn runes into strength" will never echo across the Lands Between.

In a game defined by intensity, this is quite an ability to forego. The importance of runes in *Elden Ring* lore blends directly into gameplay. As a mentor, Melina serves to empower the character. Without her, there is no connection between the Tarnished and the power of the supernatural world, making survival virtually impossible. For this reason, it is essential to heed the mentor's words, especially when they can guide a newcomer successfully across the threshold of experience.

 ## THE SUPERNATURAL AID

Receiving the power of the supernatural world is a critical element for growth for the fictional hero. Using concepts from mythology, video games introduce characters to various types of leveling-up through these otherworldly abilities. When the mentor in your party is not enough, a guiding force for existence can anoint the hero for their quest. This gift often comes from a supernatural being, such as the mythological figure of the Cosmic Mother (the form of the goddess), who will often bestow the player with the blessing they need to pass through the fields of battle triumphantly.

In Final Fantasy XIV, the Cosmic Mother is represented by Hydaelyn, who repeatedly offers her power to the player by urging them to "Hear, feel, think." While Hydaelyn, in her whole nature, remains a goddess, she intervenes in meaningful ways through members of the hero party many times across the main quest. This happens each time the Warrior of Light collects a new piece of the Mother Crystal. It also occurs every time she resurrects the fallen warrior from certain death to save Eorzea (or another connected realm) from ultimate destruction. Hydaelyn shifts the tide of battle by providing supernatural aid in favor of the Warrior of Light. This further empowers the Warrior of Light to find their moment of destiny to avoid defeat at the hands of the Ascians and the god they worship, Zodiark. In doing so, Hydaelyn allows each member of the Scions to tap into their full potential and become the best version of themselves.

"Supernatural aid" does not always refer to a god-like being. Sometimes, aid is received from sources that directly reflect the world itself. This occurs through tutorials, power upgrades, and quests that extend from the beginning to the end of a game.

For example, *Bioshock* leaves the player bewildered as they stumble aimlessly through Rapture in the opening moments after exiting their bathysphere. The horrors they witness include the mayhem of the splicers, the mysteries of the Little Sisters, and the daunting prospect of being drilled to death by a Big Daddy. The safest path is offered by the mentoring voice of a man named Atlas. In exchange for this aid, the player must 'kindly' promise to save the mentor's lost family. As a supernatural aid, Atlas also leads to the discovery of plasmids, a chemical that rewrites the genetic code of anyone who injects it. This opens the player to the true powers needed to survive the submersible hell of Rapture. Now the player has supernatural abilities. They can shoot fire from their hands, levitate objects, and even use mind control.

Atlas is also a timeless example of the mentorship concept as he is not exactly what he seems, pushing the player even deeper into the backstory of Rapture one step at a time.

Inside each gaming journey is a world with a struggle. We may not always know what is right from the beginning. However, our mentor guides the direction of the journey early on so we can make the right decisions until we are ready to make them on our own.

In this way, our choices become the critical points on which the world's fate hinges. While the narrative gives us non-playable characters (NPCs) who offer this guidance from the start, we learn to embrace our agency. As a result, we can just as well complete a game as we can struggle to the point of avoidance. The heroes we control experience this same dichotomy within the confines of their lore. They can accept the mentor's guidance, embracing the struggle to fulfill a courageous destiny, or they can refuse the call and run away from every voice calling them forward. The best heroes eventually place their faith in the words of their mentors. They receive the blessing of their supernaturally endowed abilities. They become more than they were at the beginning. At least, they discover the potential they had inside them all along to make a difference in their world (and the world of others) forever.

Whether being protected by the Cosmic Mother, a warrior from an older time, or another survivor struggling to make a difference, lessons from the mentor guide the hero through their trials. The supernatural aid they offer is a form of power that helps the hero overcome each obstacle on the way to achieving the final goal. The mentor's role is to help the player unlock the abilities hidden within. Sometimes this requires direct guidance, while others can be more subtle. No matter the approach, the mentor plays a vital role in the gaming journey. While gameplay uses innovation to illustrate this growth, storytelling elements remain relevant by infusing mechanics with meaning. When this is achieved in a game, the moment of meeting the mentor is able to challenge us and build a metaphor that helps us understand ourselves more completely.

 ## BALANCING THE ORDINARY & THE SUPERNATURAL

The mentor is often a catalyst for the hero receiving their calling. In many ways, this is the fulcrum of the mission, a tipping point between whether the hero will accept or refuse the quest. Usually, a hero has a vague awareness about their eventual mentor while still in the ordinary world. Still, the significance of this idea is lost due to their cognitive focus being entrenched in the ordinary world.

Regardless of the looming crisis, the only way a hero can witness the true nature of the mentor is by answering the call to become heroic. This choice continues the cyclical nature of the journey, mirroring the accomplishments of the mentor earlier in life. Their knowledge makes them ideally suited to guide the aspiring hero across the threshold of the supernatural world. The hero often avoids catastrophe by choosing to be courageous. Had they stayed dormant, they would have perished in their ordinary existence. The time for comfort has ended, and the hero has joined the mentor on the path to destiny.

The pairing of the hero and mentor gives every journey a unique aesthetic. Going back to the original use of the word, Mentor was a friend to Odysseus in The Odyssey. This Greek epic establishes several mainstays for a story to feel mythological, including the importance of support characters in the story of a hero. While Mentor promised to raise Odysseus' son during the

Trojan War, Athena was present across the journey to grant aid and complete the concept we come to expect in fiction from the mentor characters. Including a real-life mentor and supernatural aid shows the range of help required to help Odysseus make it home.

Each innovation in the mentor concept expands how the role varies from story to story. The variations in the mentor can be noticed when we look for character dynamics instead of focusing on traits such as gender or character origin.

Take, for example, the very different worlds of game franchises *Horizon Zero Dawn, The Witcher 3: Wild Hunt,* and the *Uncharted* series. Each protagonist in this list has a mentor for realizing the lead character's talents.

In *Horizon Zero Dawn*, Aloy is led through her training for 12 years to win the test called "The Proving" by her caretaker, Rost. He is more intimately aware of the past events of this world and has become an Outcast to keep these secrets from spreading through the Nora tribe.

In *The Witcher*, Geralt of Rivia is a formidable hero in his own right. Still, he receives guidance and camaraderie at several points in his travels from Vesemir, the oldest and most experienced of the witchers across the 13th century.

For *Uncharted*, Nathan Drake completes many of his heists alongside Victor Sullivan (a.k.a. Sully). While the duo began their interactions through a mutual tendency for manipulation, they bonded through similar values and a reciprocated quest for the "perfect steal," as Sully viewed Nathan similarly to how a father looks after his son (and vice-versa).

In each of these examples, the mentor is a character who has lived the life the protagonist longs for, prompting the pupil to want to learn from them. These three characters exemplify how the mentor operates within a gaming narrative. They offer guidance and train the hero, helping them become more aware in a much quicker fashion than perhaps they were able to experience alone. With formidable skills, the playable hero becomes the quintessential lead once they receive this training, ready for the supernatural experiences which they are about to face.

The aid given by those aligned with the goddess motif are often more mystical. Originating from the actions of Athena in the Odyssey, the receipt of this aid tends to empower the hero to understand the magical energies as opportunities for prevailing in the challenges to come.

Many gaming examples use this approach. Mario, in his space-focused adventure *Mario Galaxy*, meets Rosalina.

In *Kid Icarus*, Pit receives the power of flight from Palutena. However, not all aid delivered in this style is mystical.

In *Halo: Combat Evolved*, battle revolves around weapons and technology. As a result, the aid which allows Master Chief to attempt his mission to stop the Flood comes from Cortana, an AI entity designed for complex problem-solving, cloned from the mind of a brilliant scientist named Catherine Halsey. This addition to Master Chief's ability, despite being based on technology, makes him more believably a supernatural hero.

These characters all play an important role in helping players achieve their goals. Each character empowers the player via guided tutorials (training missions) embedded into the game's flow.

Mario would be unable to use lumas, meaning the game would be impossible to navigate. Every sling star would stay out of reach, and Mario would fail to soar beyond his atmosphere.

Similarly, a *Kid Icarus* game in which Pit lacks the powers he receives from Palutena would be entirely different. The ability to fly is a central mechanic to playing Pit, so on the level of being a hero, Pit needs Palutena's aid to be who he is as a character.

Cortana is so renowned as an aid to Master Chief that a personal assistance app in her name began circulating on Microsoft devices in 2014. Without her AI assistance, the legendary exploits of Master Chief would have ended short of the destruction of the Halo installation and the saving of all sentient life.

Each scenario forces the hero to learn from their mentor until they can survive the path on their own to save the world. When this occurs, the relationship between the hero and their path becomes a synergy between what they are capable of and what they are required to do. In essence, both sides of the journey become essential to the world, allowing the hero to actually complete any mission they choose to fight as we play through their games.

 ## TRUST VS. MISTRUST IN MENTOR RELATIONSHIPS

There are also times when a character with a mentor style of influence has ulterior motives. From a developmental perspective, Trust versus Mistrust is considered the first stage of human growth according to the Stages of Psychosocial Development constructed by Erik Erikson. Mentors in games (and reality) often have a different perspective on events than we do until we become mentors ourselves. They benefit from their experience and can objectively evaluate a situation more reliably than a novice. As a learner, the hero character has to grow into this maturity. As a result, the mentor may have goals that only partially align with what the novice understands about the path ahead. Sometimes the mentor means well and has a different perspective on the best path forward. Other times, their intentions are nefarious. We only gain enough information to interpret by playing through and choosing to reflect once we reach the end of the game.

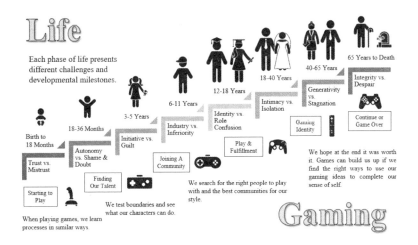

FIGURE 14. *Psychosocial Stages of Development Applied to Gaming Processes*

In *The Prince of Persia: The Sands of Time*, players control Prince Dastan, guiding Princess Farah back to the hourglass holding the Sands of Time. They hope to use the Dagger of Time to undo a mistake that has upset the balance of order in their world. The supernatural aid is the power to rewind time and undo gameplay mistakes. The plot uses timeline manipulation to allow Dastan to change pivotal scenes which define the adventure. At several points in this game, Farah hides her intentions and withholds her knowledge about the nature of the sands. She also helps the Prince learn to navigate battles more effectively, earning her a mentorship status.

As the game progresses, Farah betrays Dastan and steals the dagger while he sleeps. When she dies in this timeline, the Prince has no choice but to reverse time again. This decision saves her life but eradicates their entire bond from across the game. The tragedy of falling in love while saving the city but being the only person who remembers leaves him as a lone traveler for his return journey. While the honesty between mentor and hero could have prevented these setbacks, the perception of trust between the two was enough to propel the Prince forward.

Trust is not a guarantee on every journey. Some stories also explore the idea of a villain posing as a mentor, using the hero's good intentions to ultimately serve an evil purpose in the end. Throughout *Resident Evil 1 and 2*, players are introduced to several mentor characters who seek to capitalize on chaos. The zombie outbreak leading to Raccoon City's downfall is a backdrop for several heroes who battle for their lives while being sabotaged by untrustworthy mentors. The structure of these games involves players exploring horror environments as their characters, interacting with supporting characters, and earning endings that reflect the choices made along the way. Several support characters, namely Albert Wesker and Ada Wong, offer guidance as mentors to the playable characters. However, we eventually learn characters like this should never be fully trusted.

Whether playing the original *Resident Evil* as Chris Redfield or Jill Valentine, the plot turns at the betrayal of your squad leader, Albert Wesker, who was working for the Umbrella Corporation the entire time. Besides being your leader on the Special Tactics and Rescue Service (S.T.A.R.S.), Wesker has a long history developing bioweapons for Umbrella, and is in charge of your group as a way to collect data directly from within the Spencer Mansion. This makes the first game about saving your friends and handling the conspiracy of the outbreak.

The feeling of relief each time you find Wesker clearing a path to safety becomes redacted following the final plot revelations. Rather than hoping you would survive, he was looking to see if you would live long enough for him to unveil his final creation. The

Tyrant, made purely of the T-virus, kills Wesker (supposedly) and then chases you throughout the facility. You may destroy him and escape via chopper or wait too long until the entire estate explodes during the self-destruct sequence. Either way, the conflict with your mentor is left unresolved, and you have learned by playing to the end that the depths of corruption in the Umbrella Corporation has ruined your ability to ever trust your leaders in Raccoon City again.

The sequel features different characters but continues these themes. As a setup, Leon S. Kennedy, the newest member of S.T.A.R.S., is reporting for his first day of service at the Raccoon City Police Department. This day, of course, happens to be the day of the city-wide outbreak set months after the mansion incident. Despite Leon being capable given the circumstances, his first encounters with monsters borne of the virus (colleagues, police dogs, a Tyrant possessing basic intellect known as Mr. X) do not go gracefully.

On one occasion, Leon is saved by a reporter named Ada Wong. At first, she seems to play the hero out of amusement. However, Ada seems more aware of their chemistry as Leon continues forward. She even trusts him with information that leads him into an Umbrella Corporation lab deep beneath the city. The plot reveals that Ada is an agent of someone in the shadows, there only to collect the sample for her employer. Her betrayal cuts deep, and Ada seems to perish when she falls from a catwalk late in the game.

The fluctuating dynamic between Leon and Ada continues across several games. Still, her introduction as a role model for surviving zombie apocalypses has made her an endearing figure in the minds of many game players despite her ambiguous moral compass.

Within each story lies a source of power (the Sands of Time, the T-Virus, etc.) and the threat of danger. By examining each plot through the lens of the monomyth, the hero is cast in a light that encourages us to collect our resources, gain new knowledge, and advance the story as we move closer to the ultimate victory. Seeing the connections between our character and others is one method of better understanding the world. Sometimes, the plot uses a magic dagger. Other times, the threat comes from the outbreak of a deadly virus. Whenever we meet new characters who already understand the situation, they could become a mentor.

While the challenges we face are not often as destructive as what happened in Raccoon City, the metaphor is there for us to see our challenges as a threat we must overcome. The decision to accept the quest is not preparation on its own. It is only a decision.

Like the heroes in our games, we likely have a person to learn from until we rise to the level of making a difference. We must grow to meet the challenge when our abilities advance beyond our natural talent. This is the goal of the mentoring experience. No matter the skill or vocation, there is someone there who plays a role in helping us become the thing we are meant to become. When we connect with positive mentors like Athena or Rosalina, we can move forward while we learn. This allows us to trust the larger view of the world we are becoming more aware of at this opening threshold.

 GUIDANCE AND THE STAGES OF MENTORSHIP

Whatever the calling is from person to person, avoiding the greatest challenges in life often feels easier than facing them. This does not mean avoidance is the right choice. In fact, one of the most fascinating transformations happens for the idea of success in video games when they convince people to fail upward in the face of overwhelming challenges.

The people in our lives who demonstrate the best examples of perseverance are not always more disciplined and focused than those who do not keep going. Instead, they have learned to ignore the message that they are not worthy of making the attempt. We are often taught that free will requires a sense of success to feel satisfied with a performance. If this happens, the shame of not succeeding will promote avoidance from making future attempts.

In video games, we instead learn to accept the fairness in judgment. We can usually sense how close we are to victory. In kind, we seek out the information that makes us feel secure that we are on the right track to complete the task. The guidance of gaming turns success into a recipe. We experience the growth mindset. While this truism requires a more concrete understanding to use it outside of the gaming context, when we use this mindset effectively, it becomes a winning strategy that encourages the next attempt.

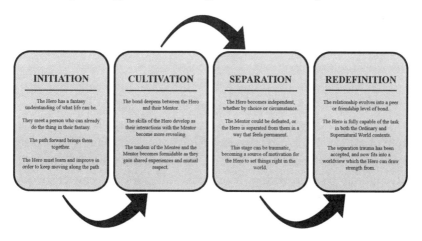

FIGURE 15. *Phases of Mentorship Applied to Video Game Narratives*

While growth can be a solo endeavor when exploring it through the stages of the monomyth, the relationship between the hero and the mentor can also be considered a staged development process.

In the first stage, initiation, the hero might be reluctant to undertake their quest. They may believe it is "just a dream," or they "can never be that great." The mentor interacts with them in a way that forces them to expand their idea of what is possible. When the catastrophe strikes, the hero must accept the call and band with the mentor for their survival needs. The weight of their situation causes them to leave what is ordinary behind. When this occurs, they have been convinced by their new mentor figure to embark on the journey.

The second stage, cultivation, is when the hero begins to develop. They receive guidance from the mentor, learning to utilize their hidden talents. This phase often shows an increase in power and skill as the player progresses through the game. The supernatural world that seemed so out of reach now feels like it is where the hero truly belongs. This stage also encourages the hero to build relationships with the mentor and others who will support them on their journey.

In the separation stage, events force the hero to accept that they must face their final challenges alone. They have gotten so far in their journey with the support of their mentor and the help of others. Now, circumstances have blocked them from these comforts. They must now become the hero they have imagined throughout their training. Moments of separation can occur as the Hero transitions between mythic stages or can be imposed on them as they build towards the climax of any phase in their story. Once this moment has occurred, the Hero must succeed or fail on their own merits. This loss of comfort can be shocking at first. It can also expand the sense of personal conflict between heroes and their villains. When separation is experienced, it convinces the hero that they must see the challenge through to the end for the loss to have a purpose.

In the final stage of mentorship, the continuation of growth relies on the terms of the separation. If the mentor is gone from the physical plane, they could still be communed with on the spiritual plane. The hero and their allies could also memorialize them in some way. If they are still alive, they may have retired from battle but still show pride in what their pupil has brought to the world. In the betrayal style of mentorship, the mentor could have become a central villain or an even more ambiguous wild card in the future exploits of the hero. In any scenario, the bond is transformed beyond what was evident during the early phases of mentorship. The hero can move on to continue using their abilities to preserve good and honor the origins of their learning from across the entire process.

The phases of mentorship are noticeable in our gaming life, but they also occur in the many areas of our personal lives. With separation specifically, we learn in our safe space in gaming what it is like to lose our secure connections. The stages where we think the mentor has been lost can send our hero into a panicked hallucination. Every time Nathan Drake loses the father figure of Sully (or when Batman fears his mentee, Barbara Gordon / Oracle, has been killed in *Batman: Arkham Knight*), the trauma response reminds us that our most valued bonds in life should be appreciated to the fullest whenever possible.

Other times, the loss is permanent, and we feel something deeply, as with Aerith in *Final Fantasy VII* in a shocking example, or B12 sacrificing herself in *Stray* to complete the journey of her cherished cat master. These separations show us that the journey does not end despite our emotional reactions to some of the worst experiences imaginable. The people who show us how to thrive come to matter even more to us once they are gone. We can see small examples of this in games, but it means so much more when we identify the parallel experience in our real-world existence.

As we move through the ranks of life, we often have a vision for what we hope will become our result. When it comes time to participate in the journey, there are usually people we can point to that serve as the launching point for us to learn what it takes to fulfill that dream. We may consult a master of a craft to ask for an apprenticeship. Sometimes, this person may find us and take us under their wing to show us the ropes and help us learn how to turn our raw talent into realized ability. This hierarchy can sometimes be peer-oriented, finding a person who will be our cheerleader motivating us to the very end. We may need someone who finds creative solutions or offers new information when we feel most stuck. For other problems, we may pursue solutions during a lesson, a therapy session, or a role-playing campaign.

From teachers and supervisors, friends, family, and coaches or therapists, these people are all around us, hoping to learn the skills we need in much the same way as the guidance we work through in our games. When we find opportunities to form these bonds, we start to gain the ability to take our talents beyond our ordinary world and grow them into something far more formidable. The knowledge from the mentor is what makes us capable of making a difference in the real challenges of our lives as we step into the unknown of what feels to us as the supernatural world.

CHAPTER X

CROSSING THE THRESHOLD

You know, I was afraid at first, but now I'm ready.

No matter where I go or what I see, I know I can always come back here.

—Kairi (Kingdom Hearts)

The final step before leaving the ordinary world behind happens when the hero moves past the point of no return. While the opening stages of the hero's journey revolve around sensing a need to change, video games prove to be perfectly suited to tell these stories in a way that encourages engagement with this precise moment. By answering the call, the hero of each game sets out to leave the safe space behind, crossing the threshold to experience the path to fulfillment.

As gamers, we familiarize ourselves with the controls for our characters by going through the tutorial and experiencing this stage as a learning process. This links our reactions to the game through the controller as we learn to manage each incoming challenge. Tutorials are perfect ways for players to gain an awareness of every beginning element of the journey: the ordinary world, the quest, player abilities, and the mentor. By battling waves of common enemies, the player overcomes the first challenge of understanding the game. The themes of the journey are established, and the new hero steps forward to claim their next victory.

The threshold to begin the journey, however, is often guarded by more than common enemies. The chance to cross the threshold between simple fun and true test is often moderated by a more formidable adversary, commonly referred to by game players as a boss. These threshold guardians have an inherent connection to the world of the hero. To the player, they represent the source of darkness. They could be relics of an ancient evil. They can represent the Omphalos (or Navel of the Axis Mundi) on which the four directions of the map rely to preserve existence. Deciding to step forward and draw swords is critical for the hero to begin their quest.

Before the crossing, the hypothetical fear was only a psychological barrier for the hero. Now, the danger is real. By breaking through the doorway that shields ordinary life from the threat, the hero unleashes new horizons where they can fail, meaning life would end in a cataclysm.

However, the hero is currently on the path to make their impact on a world they always felt could offer more. This is the only way to bring the world they have been dreaming of into reality. If they can find a way to triumph, they will have to step foot on the path to fulfillment and earn the right to pursue it to the end. If they fall short, they will have to find a way to accept the resulting regret, trauma, and disillusionment with the things they hoped for. Crossing the initial threshold opens the hero to gaining experience, expanding their arsenal, learning new abilities, and becoming the best version of themselves. The risk is worth it, and the fight with the first threshold guardian commences.

FIGURE 16. *Crossing the Threshold Allows the Pursuit of the Hero's Dreams*

Across memorable stories, the hero succeeds in this battle and earns the right to cross into the supernatural world. This side of existence possesses a power the ordinary world cannot offer, unlocked potential. In bypassing the guardian, the hero has entered the larger world where they can level up in unimaginable ways.

This opportunity to cross this threshold makes it possible to understand the ideal self for the first time. The ideal self is the version of our self-concept that can fulfill our potential and achieve our dreams. This actualized version of the hero has reached max-level, accomplished great things, and remained content with who they are. While the subconscious drives may govern the non-playable characters (and also heroes who have not moved forward at this phase of the journey yet), the destudo (destruction drive) and libido (creation drive) have struck a balance in the way they move through their environment. While actualization remains far off in the endgame, it can be imagined as possible by the hero who steps foot onto the true path of the journey.

When players achieve this level of clarity in both life and gaming, they become more aware of their role in choosing their approach to each challenge. This is why the main quest matters in the path of the heroic journey. The outcome of each struggle forces the player to learn more about their environment. This knowledge leads to better fulfillment potential and dramatically increases the likelihood of success.

When we actively pursue our growth, we experience a transformation that Non-Playable Characters (NPCs) do not experience. NPC characters stick to their place in the lore of the world. They do not cross any threshold lines. They stay on a programmed track. They recite their lines eternally, hoping to sell goods to heroes stepping into the unknown. These characters have accepted the status quo of their ordinary world. For some, this is a great way to live. Perhaps they have already fulfilled their journey in the prequel? What if this character was destined for greatness until they took an arrow to their knee? Maybe they get their greatest satisfaction from watching the hero struggle to be heroic?

In any case, once the hero crosses the line and defeats the boss, they break the chains of the programmed routine and become a member of the outgroup (from the perspective of the people they are leaving behind). Once again, the player has moved past the people who offer a message of "stay" and chosen to say, "Let's Go!" while moving towards their greatest aspirations.

GAME DESIGN, BOSS FIGHTS, & THE CROSSING

When experiencing the threshold crossing in a video game, it is awe-inspiring to notice how design decisions create the desired impact on the memories of players across the world. Whether the game genre is action / adventure, role-playing, shooter, or anything in between, the story structures follow a predictable yet flexible sequence. Depending on the player and their skill, these processes illustrate the elements of the journey while also helping the player enjoy the growth of their abilities in turn.

One timeless example of this sequence comes from the original *Super Mario Bros.,* which begins with the characters of Mario and Luigi running through mushroom stages, underground caves, and castles. These stages gradually increase in difficulty. They teach the player a series of rules:

- Do not run into enemy goombas.

- Avoid falling into any spot on the screen where the floor is not visible.

- Progress from left to right until you reach a flag.

- Do not let time expire while still playing through the level.

A new sequence of running and jumping is presented in every level. Eventually, the stage explores a castle. The fire traps are new, coming in stationary and airborne forms. At the end of the first castle, the player meets the threshold guardian: the first version of King Koopa (later known as Bowser). He is literally guarding the threshold at the end of the bridge where a convenient axe sits. This weapon lets Mario cut down the haphazard bridge, dropping Koopa into the lava pit below.

Suppose the player uses every idea from their victories in previous stages. In that case, they dodged the fire, paid attention to the timing of Koopa jumping into the air, and ran under him to claim the axe, crossing that final line between challenge and success. Unfortunately, the princess is not in this castle, meaning this plumber's heroic journey must continue if Mario is to find her true location.

While this serves as an action iteration of crossing the threshold to vanquish a major enemy, other games use this concept as an opportunity to provide a choice to the player. In the first-generation *Pokémon* games, the player character walks around Pallet Town and talks to everyone as they become ready for their training adventure. However, Professor Oak is nowhere to be found. By approaching an invisible line at the edge of town and leading into Viridian Forest, you trigger the guidance of Professor Oak. He ushers you back to the lab, where you must choose your starter Pokémon. After choosing between Bulbasaur, Charmander, or Squirtle (or being given a Pikachu), you are challenged by your rival to your very first Pokémon battle. In this way, the Pokémon series utilizes all of the early stages of the monomyth in a cycle of exploration, battle, and victory. This serves to grow the confidence of the new players who set out and become the very best (like no one ever was).

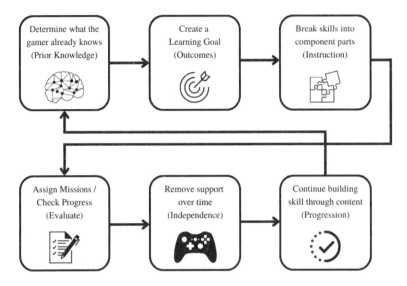

FIGURE 17. *The Scaffolding Process as Applied two Video Game Player*

The mixture of boundary lines, tutorial, and easing the player into the introductory boss mechanics is a tried-and-true method of using the outline from the monomyth to realize educational philosophy. The learning experiment begins by presenting the game player with a new environment for their avatar to explore. Players can interact with NPCs, read signs, interact with random devices, and do many other basic investigations. A well-done tutorial section will teach the player a basic setup for future skirmishes and guide them through their basic abilities. By showing these scenarios to the player, the game helps players assemble a concept of what success requires from their knowledge and understanding.

In this way, crossing the threshold pushes the player to become independent and test their skills in the challenge of the game's environment. This cycle can be repeated as often as necessary to ensure the player eventually learns to link their knowledge and skills together, allowing the further challenges in the game to escalate in intensity.

Boss encounters amplify the intensity of the gaming story by pushing the player to improve the use of their abilities. These challenges present the player with a hint of the total threat they hope to vanquish by completing their journey. Normally, these enemies are larger than the player character, more lethal, and contain imagery commonly associated with an evil nature. While our eyes create this judgment based on appearances, the multimedia nature of video games often deliver the backstory for these characters across the many plot points players engage with.

Sometimes, the threshold guardian is simply an ogre from a long-forgotten myth. This exact concept is portrayed in the early challenges of *Resident Evil 4*. In this game, Leon S. Kennedy, one of the main protagonists from *Resident Evil 2*, is tasked with rescuing the President's daughter by infiltrating a religious cult, the Los Illuminados. By navigating the dangers of a few smaller village areas, Leon has effectively crossed the threshold into the realm of danger. Among his first major challenges is an arena battle against an ogre-like adversary referred to by the locals as El Gigante. Harkening to the cyclops figures in mythological stories such as The Odyssey, the massive stature of this opponent implores the player to dodge attacks at all costs. There is no dialog to explain why the battle will happen. It is apparent from the moment the plagued villagers open the enormous doors that this will be a battle Leon will either survive or replay until he does.

This battle unfolds in a series of steps, creating a scaffolding effect that illuminates the path to victory during an otherwise hectic battle. The player should know the basics, such as aiming, running, knife combat, dodging, and the ability to manage the health meter. The player must successfully link these bits of knowledge together to survive the daunting battle with El Gigante. However, the player needs to learn the cadence of the boss attacks and has yet to see certain mechanics which will make the arena more dangerous than previous enemy mobs. The player will maneuver Leon through trial and error to learn the best places to open fire or run to safety.

A wounded dog mid-way also helps the thoughtful player through the battle, provided they saved them from the bear trap earlier in the game. This distraction buys players precious seconds to recover and freely observe the boss's movements. Eventually, this respite ends, and the boss returns focus to the former S.T.A.R.S. agent, leaving the player with only their poise and execution.

Once the fight ends, players can move Leon deeper into the complex to rescue his target. This is not the end of his challenges. All future challenges build on the abilities established for survival in this specific engagement.

The differing natures between the heroic player-character and the threshold guardians they seek to surpass provide a subliminal commentary on the workings of the game world. The hero's challenge is to become victorious despite overwhelming odds. The threshold bosses are often bigger, faster, or stronger (and any combination therein) than the protagonist. For every colossal strike they land, the player must make twenty (and sometimes fifty) successful attacks to do comparable damage. The player will falter after two or three direct hits in many of the most notorious games regarding player challenge.

The decision to cross the threshold is perilous. The player makes impressive strides toward the iconic expectations from the true hero's journey by achieving victory in these battles. The struggle in the world is revealed through this difference in power as well. The threshold guardian holds a corrupted surplus of the energy the player seeks to emancipate from the darkness. The battle is a fulcrum between the player and the game, with the forces of the Omphalos at the World Navel resting in the balance. The victorious player crosses past the open doorway once guarded by its watcher. However, they are now equipped with a triumphant memory that explains how every single step along the supernatural path will contribute to the fulfillment of their ultimate quest.

 ## ENTERING THE UNKNOWN WORLD

Few people are innately aware of a purpose in their lives from their earliest memories. The guidance we each receive in our upbringing helps us decide what we aspire to be. For some, the chance to become this version of ourselves is easily imagined from the beginning. For others, we begin to see possibilities outside the ordinary trajectory. What if we were somewhere else? What if we could do more? The early stages of the monomyth show the eventual hero coming to grips with these questions and all their possible answers. Whether contemplation is for a game character or an actual person, we learn about the growth process with every hypothetical we consider. After all, even if the possibilities are fictional rather than real, they still exist the same way as the theoretical does at first.

The ability to break through the psychological walls that hold a person in their ordinary world is influenced by many things, from self-esteem to the moral code of our starting society. Some of the most well-known boss battles serve as a metaphorical clash between good and evil. Similarly, societal norms from the world are often imposed on the character as a moral compass to prevent them from crossing the threshold. The player must accept the battle if they are to move forward.

In some games, the walls holding the player captive within the limitations of normalcy are not metaphors but are, in fact, literal structures. This is the case in the *Fallout* series by Bethesda (1997). These games operate as role-playing shooters, with the player controlling a survivor of a nuclear holocaust in the United States during the 21st century. In *Fallout 3* (2008), the player character, the Lone Wanderer, begins as a child born in Vault 101. Early phases of the game feature the player making guided choices during the early childhood development of this wanderer. Your first steps, learning about your deceased mother's favorite Bible verse, your tenth birthday party, your relationship with your father, maneuvering the social structure of Vault 101, teenage aptitude tests, and your final day in The Vault are all moments picked out to show the world you must leave behind when you choose to continue the game.

The society of The Vault is highly organized. From the age of ten, each citizen wears a Pip-Boy 3000 to receive orders (quests), manage their personality (stats), and keep track of their possessions (inventory). The quests start with reporting here or talking to so-and-so over there. The design helps the player feel connected to their role inside The Vault. Even the Generalized Occupational Aptitude Test (G.O.A.T.) teaches survivors to balance creativity with never-ending allegiance to the Overseer. While the structure of each vault is meant to portray the best possible life for survivors of a nuclear attack, many inhabitants are aware of their experimental purpose within the diversion of this supposed safety. The rules in each vault are designed to preserve order and keep experiments progressing at peak efficiency. In each game, this manipulation leads to The Vault's downfall as residents learn to doubt the virtues being espoused within their steel sanctuary.

During the player's final day in Vault 101, the Overseer decides to order the murder of your character. Despite personally committing no act of sedition, the Overseer in *Fallout 3* retaliates against your father, fleeing the vault and joining the outside world. This provides you with motivation for the main quest to leave Vault 101 and discover the truth about your origins.

The combat phase of this early tutorial features important conversations with your childhood best friend as she warns you of the approaching order. This makes you more aware of the looming threat, allowing you to work your way to the gigantic door holding back the all-encompassing radiation of the nuclear wasteland. Once every keycard and password are found, you authorize the door's opening. The decision to become the Lone Wanderer becomes permanent as you lock in every character choice one last time and step into the blinding unknown of this open-world game. As your eyes adjust to sunlight for the "first" time, you are now on the other side of the previously unnavigable line, entering the main adventure for this struggling world.

While the Overseer represents the side of order at the beginning of *Fallout 3*, the idea of staying aligned with this side of the moral continuum would result in a quick death. If this happens, the video game allows you to respawn and attempt your navigation of the hallways again. The martyr's death is not an outcome often rewarded during the play of video games. If it were, there would be no adventure, becoming the refusal of the call.

Video games reinforce the risk of finding a fair path for your character in a way that biased institutions rarely would. In this way, morality becomes increasingly flexible. The choice which saves people (and worlds) is correct, many times without considering the societal mandates which must be suspended to allow this choice to be possible. From the player's vantage point, the only ways to level up come from bold decisions to complete quests and influence change in the world around you.

Crossing the threshold line often results in the discovery of new surroundings along with equally new ways to identify your limitations. The idea of advancing beyond the furthest point gets stretched as the reality of the challenge meets the player front and center. Depending on the game, the player can be eased into the new situation or thrown into overwhelming challenges immediately.

This contrast can be understood by continuing the exploration of threshold lines in both *Fallout 3* and *Elden Ring*. While different in the use of military science versus high fantasy, the setup for both is similar. In each game, a person with unknown ties to the implied backstory of the world becomes aware that they must step into the unknown and accomplish something great. While the Lone Wanderer can casually stroll into the nearby town of Megaton, the Tarnished hero is immediately faced with the patrolling terror of the gold-clad Tree Sentinel. The knowledge of how to move forward in the quest is only sometimes about combat prowess but rather is about the problem-solving ability of the hero player. In this way, gaming reinforces the courage to move forward and the willingness to take risks. While crossing the threshold grants new awareness of how to exist on the other side, the challenge also increases. From this point on, the best hope is to grow in our internal and external selves while we learn to follow the path of vitality in our new challenges.

EPIC CHOICES & UNINTENDED CONSEQUENCES

Sometimes, the problem a hero attempts to set right is their fault. This degree of humanity is relatable and sets the hero up for further adventures. They must correct the epic mistake. The fear of stepping into the unknown often blocks a would-be hero, signaling a refusal and a journey that was not experienced. However, the failure state of an unintended consequence is caused by a hero who did cross the threshold and delved down into the deepest challenges thinking they would emerge victorious. Like many life challenges, things do not always go according to plan.

In the first *God of War* game, for example, Kratos freed himself from servitude to Ares and became the God of War. The following conflicts revolve around Kratos making decisions in this role that insult the egos of the other gods. This angers Zeus, who, after seeing the Spartan army victorious at Rhodes, decides to siphon the last of Kratos' powers using the sword of Olympus and attempts to murder him with it. If Kratos had utilized his ascension to godhood more subserviently, he might not have insulted the traditionally hierarchical pantheon of gods on Olympus. As a result, Kratos is compelled to seek revenge for this attempted murder and galvanizes the Titans to carry out a direct attack on Olympus. Eventually, all of Kratos's mistakes across Greek history end with the bloody end of every god and demi-god imaginable, along with a final one-on-one battle with Zeus himself. The cost of victory is nearly Kratos life, and the puddle of blood left in this space implies either the death of both or the chance for Kratos to leave Greece and live peacefully somewhere else completely.

Returning to the post-apocalyptic setting, the first two entries in the *Borderlands* series show the playable heroes facing a similar dilemma. To complete the first game, your Vault Hunter searches across Pandora for an alien vault filled with Eridium. By opening the vault and defeating the massive threshold guardian called The Destroyer, you have shown the galaxy where Eridium is found while also destroying the Atlas Corporation. This creates a power vacuum while everyone scrambles for the infinite wealth that can be mined on the planet. The sequel explores the ramifications of this choice, as a new entity known as Hyperion, led by Handsome Jack, decides this wealth is rightfully theirs and all Vault Hunters are a liability to this claim.

Each time we are challenged, we experience another threshold guardian we must learn to overcome. Video games depict this through boss battles, amplifying the importance of the main quest while we find new ways to continue. Sometimes, video games (and life) teach us the harsh lesson that challenges cannot (and should not) be cleared on the first try. If we complete our challenges on the first try, it is unlikely we were pushing ourselves to improve. This is acceptable for leisure activities but less ideal when someone must decide to cross the line on a heroic quest where growth is the goal. By openly engaging in the learning process, we are becoming better at moving past the source of our challenges.

When we decide the reward is worth the risk, we become the bridge we must cross to enter the challenge. As we make each attempt, we learn something new, apply it, and eventually get to the point where we become what we hoped for from the beginning. Fictional stories like those found in games allow us to see how long this can take in a less threatening way. In a world where quick success is expected, it can be daunting to envision a challenge we plan to struggle through for decades to acquire the ultimate boon.

There is no way to bypass life's most important growth opportunities, at least on an existential level (microtransactions notwithstanding). The mindful approach to taking each step, one at a time, can be explained using fighting games. While normally, the plot may take a backseat in this genre, the relationships between characters and their factions have always been there. This gives each fight greater context. The original trilogy of *Mortal Kombat* explores the conflict between Earth Realm and Outworld. The victor in each tournament moves their realm closer to permanent peace (Earth Realm) or domination (Outworld). To defeat threshold guardians such as Shao Kahn, Shang Tsung, Goro, and others, the player must learn from their mistakes and execute flawless strategy with their chosen fighter. The beginning of *Mortal Kombat 3* opens with a motivational message designed to show the truest path to "Test Your Might":

"There is no knowledge that is not power."

This line becomes the ultimate lesson in mindfulness for fans of this series. It also reveals the path to wasting fewer quarters in arcades worldwide. By knowing more about the battle, a player can better navigate the challenge on the way to victory. *Mortal Kombat* shares a powerful truth about growing beyond our present self to become something greater. If each fight is a new threshold, our personal best is only accomplished by making it past every challenge and witnessing the story's conclusion, which is only revealed at the end of the final conflict.

The opportunity to choose our destiny is symbolized in the thresholds we cross on our journey. The wall of paradise comes in many forms but serves our mythology in the same ways as in life. We are not gifted access to God-mode like Kratos was, just as we are not anointed as the "chosen one" like Liu Kang. Still, when we are on the path to fulfilling our potential, it feels exactly like we have found these gifts. Every journey begins with a choice, which can only be made when our vision becomes something we believe is possible. This choice initiates the journey and separates us from ordinary life by encouraging us to dream.

When we play games, our character forms a unique confluence between our passion and our dreams. The doorway we envision stepping through represents our decision to pursue our passions. The voice that told Sora, "You are the one who will open the door," is constantly speaking to us. While ancient myths depicted this as the door to the sun, games show us this path across countless conceptualizations for worlds and origins.

The lessons we learn from games all start with our decision to play them and embody the greatest attributes of the heroes we select. We may jump from saving humanity from an apocalypse to the leisurely pursuit of splattering the world in ink. Whatever the case, we continue to learn valuable lessons from each success and failure. Over time, we hopefully transfer these qualities completely into ourselves.

It all begins with choosing to enter the world of supernatural opportunity and face equally impressive challenges. We embrace the fear to take that first step and move forward anyway. We approach every threshold, and we learn. From random mobs to innovative puzzles, we keep moving forward. Games show us that we can accept any challenge, no matter what guardians attempt to hold the line. As long as the future we see ourselves in is still possible, gatekeepers can only stop us when we lose the strength to keep trying. In video games, we can always respawn and do it again. By breaking past the fear of failure, we build a relationship in our cognitive world that applies this power across any context. Once we break through the threshold, we become a part of a world we always hoped to participate in, the world which holds our destiny. When we become the hero in our own story, this step reminds us that our real challenge has begun.

ACT II

INITIATING THE SELF BY PLAYING GAMES

CHAPTER XI

THE ROAD
OF TRIALS

It's a funny thing, ambition. It can take one to sublime heights or harrowing depths. And sometimes they are one and the same.

—Emily Kaldwin (Dishonored)

The moment when the player steps onto the road of trials signifies their accepting the opportunity to further connect with their chosen virtual world by steadily improving their mastery. Once the journey begins, answering the call and crossing the threshold move from accomplishments to being past memories. The true tests require the player to become more effective in their skillset if they are to move deeper into the quest chain.

On the narrative side, the hero often receives aid from other characters to help them through each quest. The completion of one mission leads directly to another. By arranging the main story as a series of smaller game objectives, the game flows into hours of entertainment. In turn, the time spent in the game creates lasting memories for the player. When a game achieves the goal of engagement purely through healthy enjoyment, it also becomes a meaningful part of a player's experience of life.

The road of trials is a critical phase in helping video games ascend to this distinction as a form of entertainment. Games are uniquely designed to offer linked series of challenges to an engaged player. Flowing from one goal to the next creates a constant source of positive reinforcement most players find fulfilling. This stage of the hero's journey, when executed well, is what encourages prolonged engagement in video games for most player types.

From both a narrative and gameplay perspective, the variety of encounters from mission to mission helps the player to understand their influence as they move the character (and their world) closer to reclaiming the disrupted ideal state. The string of quests must make sense in the lore of the game. They must also offer captivating game design to enhance the player's experience. When this is well done, the player will advance their character at an equal pace to the crescendo of the plot points. The benign power of "the chosen one" is progressively realized.

Alongside this growth is the imposing threat of the gaming challenge. The path found in these challenges is referred to in mythology as "The Superhuman Passage." When a hero walks this path, they are in pursuit of their destiny. By succeeding along this quest, this type of hero will endure their trial so they can set things right in a world where special abilities are necessary to make the meaningful difference.

Ideal World — Pushes the World to Destruction

World Detractors
- Problems which must be addressed
- Offers a new quest in the game

Quest Achievements
- Improves an element of the world
- Provides a new step for the hero

Brings the World into Balance — Flawed World

The Road of Trials allows video games to give the player a range of quests that rely on an understanding that without the hero, the world is doomed, but through effective action, the world can be brought back into a natural balance.

World Detractors threaten the world and provide a challenge to be answered. *Quests & Achievements* give the hero something to aim for that often results in improving the world situation for those populating it, including the hero and their party.

By repeating this cycle across the mid portion of the game, the *Road of Trials* is experienced by the player.

FIGURE 18. *The Road of Trials & Impacting the Fate of Existence*

The genre of each game distinctly impacts what players experience as they move along this challenging passage. For action-platformers like *Metroid*, the game quickly introduces players to their challenges, especially in simpler entries on the Nintendo Entertainment System (NES). Making the protagonist run and jump through the countless available rooms until they discover the one open path makes the road of trials an ideal concept for developing a story through gameplay. When Samus Aran first lands on Zebes, she only uses her arm gun while the player jumps and runs past every alien in her path. As a result, certain pathways are only possible to cross later in the game when new weapons and maneuverability skills are added to her repertoire.

Also debuting on the NES was *Castlevania*. This game tells the story of Richter Belmont, a vampire hunter driven to enter the castle of a legendary vampire named Alucard (an anadrome for Dracula) to rid the world of his existence. Following a similar exploration convention as Metroid, this game challenges players to master navigating the castle and taking advantage of newly acquired items. Through their shared characteristics, gamers can develop preferences for which Metroid-Vania aesthetic matches their style.

While Samus and Richter feature in similar style games, they overcome their challenges with different abilities. The female Samus (surprise!) navigates her world with bomb jumps and technological projectiles while Richter battles through each castle hallway with a magicked whip and all forms of medieval weaponry. Both of them, however, must accomplish their task one new room at a time, often backtracking several steps to collect what is needed for a small step forward.

Moving beyond the two-dimensional realm, modernized platformers offer different compositions for heroes while expanding the range of the platforming action genre. Two franchises that exemplify this inverted mirroring of each other come from Naughty Dog's Nathan Drake in *Uncharted* and Crystal Dynamic's iteration of Lara Croft in the 2013 version of *Tomb Raider*. Both games feature thrilling action set pieces, quick-time events (QTEs), and the opportunity to enhance or expand the weapon arsenal of the character to greater levels of lethality as the game progresses.

While *Uncharted* and *Tomb Raider* are not identical games, they have a similar feel, with the key differences coming from the protagonists' characterization and their supporting casts. The middle segment of both games features new locations, seeking out items, and discovering the real threat being hinted at since the separation phase pushed both heroes across their thresholds and into the adventure. The danger becomes personal in both stories, and certain challenges feel insurmountable. Both Nathan and Lara are driven to survive so they can restore the ancient boon to its "rightful" place. In both cases, the relatively believable world merges with supernatural phenomena, validating the hero's passion for archaeology and allowing the player to feel a sense of imagination toward what is possible in the resolution phases of the hero's trials. These similarities occur due to an enjoyable blending of genre, archetypes, and using the monomyth to guide the narrative beats for the quest of each hero.

Completely different expressions of the road of trials can also occur within the same franchise. Take, for example, role-playing titles such as *Final Fantasy XIII* and *Final Fantasy XV*. In the story of FFXIII, the character of Lightning is tasked with saving her sister from the fate of bringing about the coming of a monster known as Ragnarök (referencing Norse mythology). This event would signal devastating consequences for multiple worlds, called Pulse and Cocoon. Players work through narrative-driven scenes to understand Cocoon, interacting with skirmishes and boss encounters to make progress. The true opening of the quest system, however, does not occur until deep into the narrative when the players finally travel to the planet of Pulse. This way, the road of trials is presented as a narrative structure to be experienced at the end of the story, the same for every player.

The setup for *Final Fantasy XV* tells the story of a final road trip between four friends. The central protagonist is Noctis Lucis Caelum, the crown prince of Lucis. His escorts are his friends: a scion named Gladiolus, Ignis, the military savant, and Prompto. The downfall of Lucis becomes the genesis of this quest, as King Regis, Noctis' father, is murdered by the forces of Nilfheim. In this aftermath, Nilfheim has stolen the power known as the Crystal and declared Noctis and his bride-to-be, Lunafreya Nox Fleuret, dead.

The four brothers in arms decide to road trip across Eos on the way to reclaim relic weapons called the Royal Arms, help Noctis marry Lunafreya, and use the relics (and her magical abilities) to reclaim the Crystal and (eventually) restore Lucis to its rightful state. This game allows the player to immediately take control of the royal car, Regalia, and go wherever they want to complete quests and build the story of their royal road trip. In a few places, advancing the story changes the world and makes moving forward too early chronologically impossible. Still, the road here is a source of many emerging quests, allowing Noctis and his friends to feel the agency of aiding their allies in a fully existing world. The amount of discovery makes the player better equipped for the moments of ascension in the story. The presentation of these trials is delivered in a play-driven style, with Noctis being the vehicle for players to establish connections with the world from challenge to challenge.

Video games deliver a unique experience to each player, regardless of the genre or hero aesthetic. Whether through horror or sci-fi, story-driven, or quest-based, the road of trials is an essential aspect of the gaming journey. In this stage, players can demonstrate their mastery over captivating characters in a dynamic world, creating a sense of heroism in a story that feels personal to each individual.

Each trial becomes a space to explore, make mistakes, and grow into the player we want to be within the game. When we step outside of reality, it is easy to forget that our ability to complete these challenges is an important aspect of who we are. The road of trials is designed to give players a sense of agency while teaching valuable lessons. Whether these moments of growth are mechanical, like being stuck until a puzzle is solved, or personal, like guiding your hero to make their final sacrifice during the ultimate battle.

In the face of adversity, our Road of Trials allows us to become the person we want to be. Games give us this opportunity because they are designed to do so. They motivate us to explore the most challenging levels of experience. Moving through the road of trials shows us the fullest measure of what we hope to achieve in a world of challenges. If we understand these parallels well enough, we find a new way to triumph in our most challenging missions, the same as our favorite heroes on their road to transcendence.

 ## TESTS FROM THE ABYSS

One recognizable path in many legendary stories happens when the main quest sends the hero into the Underworld. This experience often involves a near-physical death that pushes the hero to their absolute limit. This challenge also leads to the spiritual death of the hero's old self, so they can gain the growth needed to triumph in the final battles of the quest. This victory can call for invading an enemy stronghold, defeating an army despite insurmountable odds, or surviving the bowels of Hades itself. This phase of the journey is often referred to as the "Belly of the Whale," coming out of myths that depict the hero being swallowed whole, only to emerge with renewed strength and purpose.

The plunge into the insurmountable challenge can occur at any point after the initiation as the hero moves closer to the conclusion of their road of trials. In video games, this structure allows the quest chains to build in intensity as the player moves closer to the climaxes of each phased ending.

The "Underworld" phase changes how the player sees the world around them once they return to the surface. This narrative structure can serve as a transition into the game's final stages, including the path toward the final battle. Every game world has a unique metaphor. As a result, the belly of the whale concept is reflected in any dark abyss where conventional thinking understands that victory comes only through great struggle. As illustrated in segments such as the literal whale stage in *Kingdom Hearts*, or visiting a dungeon where death and shadow reign as in many *Zelda* titles, not just anyone can emerge triumphant. Games present these challenges through complex puzzles, a confusing dungeon, large waves of enemies, and any mechanic that provides an epic feel to the player as they fight through the separated realm. By linking these extremes together in unique sequences, the chosen hero furthers themselves to become capable of solving the major problem being presented in their home reality.

While many games involve a journey through the underworld, a few examples maximize the presentation of this challenge to elevate both their characters and their virtual world. In *Hades*, the challenge to the player is to guide Zagreus, son of Hades, through the many rooms of the underworld in an attempt to escape into the mortal world and find Persephone, his mother. The House of Hades serves as a staging area for each escape attempt. Before departing, the player must optimize their inventory and abilities. Once ready, they must face the challenges of the abyssal realms; Tartarus, Asphodel, Elysium, and the gates of Hell themselves.

In another trial of tribulation for the realms of gods, the *Darksiders* saga casts the player as the Four Horseman of the Apocalypse. Playing as War, the first game focuses on the aftermath of Azrael and Abaddon breaking six of the Seven Seals. These gates were created as a balance point between Heaven and Hell to preserve humanity. Angered by this violation of cosmic order, the

202

Charred Council goes on the offensive. They prematurely blame War for this atrocity, assuming he has gotten tired of waiting for the true Armageddon and is championing the forces of Hell.

The mission of *Darksiders* is to battle across five main zones from Earth to Hell and claim the hearts of "Hell's Chosen," reinstating War's original powers. If successful, War sorts out all the misconceptions of this Apocalypse and reunites with the other Horsemen. The sequel games follow a similar structure, casting the player as a different Horseman of the Apocalypse each time, and sending them to fetch important items in unique apocalyptic settings. Completing each set of tribulations results in a temporary belief that reality is saved.

By finding success at each turn, the player experiences growth in their abilities through what is termed "The Hero's Passage." This sequence involves an escalating degree of challenge with every trial. When this occurs, both natural talent and growth in ability are relied upon to move forward. This helps the trials ascend beyond being only a superficial form of challenge. Instead, the hero is directly forced to notice the parts of themselves where they are not yet ready. In this way, the hero will either evolve toward their potential or they will remain stagnant from their lack of growth.

The majority of gaming stories allow for this growth to occur organically. A player may need to respawn several times to overcome a challenge at the most threatening part of the hero's passage. Still, they will find a flow where they move forward through strategy and perseverance. As with any task worth accomplishing, this pushes the player to sit down and intentionally problem-solve. Once the fear of avoidance is overcome, the player learns what it takes to finish the challenge, adding another game to their internal list of games they are "good enough" to win.

The player can then start the next phase of the challenge, meeting new forms of difficulty to match their improved skills. This growth in ability affects the inward state of the player as well. Like the hero on screen who had to dig deeper into their resolve, the player kept trying and did not give up. Each arcane battle was meant to halt progress. The player who successfully navigates the hero's passage has engaged in a deliberate process to find the relic, amplify their powers, and wield their weapons valiantly in service to the mission of continuing the challenge.

By embracing our challenges at each turn of the road, regardless of how long, our old self, belonging to the ordinary world, experiences a symbolic death. We rise towards the next challenge with each success, collecting new strengths. The deeper we merge with the hero identity, the more we belong on the road of trials. We become congruent in the hero role the more experience we gain. This is why the hero must emerge victorious from the depths of their world. The old self wrestled with the refusal of the call. The new self, marked by heroic qualities, meets their challenges with resolve, no matter how many attempts are needed to rise to the occasion.

 ## THE ROAD TO PURPOSE

The hero's passage provides many points of conflict where a heroic character must intervene. While games often send heroes toward their greatest challenges, the specific destination reveals that world's unique expression of both the power of light and the dominion of darkness. Purpose is created in narratives once the hero understands this duality. Although the external settings involve temples, underground structures, ancient caves, or military complexes, the struggle within the hero's purpose becomes personal in a way that is advanced by the setting rather than defined by it.

When this personal connection is revealed, the road of trials transforms into a spiritual labyrinth of incalculable significance. Our psyche shapes reality, complete with messages echoed from our past that influenced us on the path to getting here, for better or worse. We experience this idea in a subliminal parallel with the heroes on screen as the themes of play purify hurtful thoughts into beliefs of faith in ourselves. This is because we believe, through the hero, we will be able to prevail on this road of purpose. The power inside this psychological maze of ideas occurs in a near dream-like way. The symbolic figures in this phase urge us forward, representing both sides of the chiaroscuro; friends and mentors, but also fiends and villains hoping to block our path to complete enlightenment.

For anyone who has passed through a phase of life like this one from the monomyth, there is a fundamental transformation in how we engage with the world around us. This change comes from a shift in values and an increasing belief in self. This mental wall is present in many seasons of life. It is there when a parent remembers their angst as a child, when a teacher sees the plight of a classroom differently than their student, and when a game player reflects on how they play games in the present compared to the differences of the past. The risk of falling short becomes irrelevant once the path is chosen.

By embracing the core challenge itself, a person gradually evolves into a new solution. The echo chamber of past beliefs fades while we resolve our ageless problem. Everyone along our path with influence plays a role in how we level up. Children grow into healthier adults when they can communicate with their parents effectively. Students want to learn more from instructors who make the effort to connect with them. In the same ways, game players expand their subconscious connection with goal-oriented thinking by engaging with the labyrinthine challenges on the road of trials.

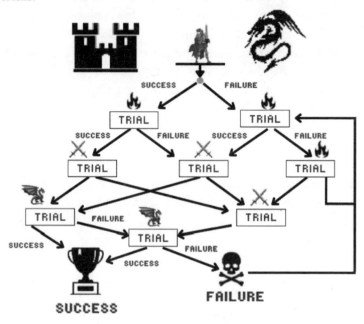

FIGURE 19. *Representation of the Road of Trials as a Video Game Quest Chain*

The mark of a great gaming journey is the ability to explore the thematic needs of a hero while at the same time offering an opportunity to connect with our own greater meaning. When this connection between our perception and experience is linked, the game becomes a clue into what drives us and how our sense of fulfillment is projected throughout the many areas of our lives. Every game has a road of trials in some form or another. As a result, every player who finds joy in their gaming sessions will experience some connection between their drive towards motivation and need fulfillment.

Whenever someone discusses what makes their gaming experiences most passionate, endless examples of these connections can be made. It becomes even more awe-inspiring to reflect with different players on the specific games that help them connect with themselves. We all are unique, and can get this feeling from different games in the same way, vice-versa, and everywhere in between...

One RPG enthusiast points out in their lineage through games, "For me, it all boils down to discovery. In my first *Elden Ring* playthrough, every first time was special. The first time I got wiped out by a Radahn dive bomb, the many revelations in the Ranni questline, winning against Maliketh with a single pixel of health." This player goes on to say, "These memories just could not be matched with any of my New Game + playthroughs."

"I really enjoy playing *Catherine* to overcome my writer's block." This college student explores the way games help him overcome the many hurdles that get in the way of completing research papers on time. He sees how the blocks fit together in the expanding climb through the dreamscape as a way to fit new ideas together in compelling ways.

Another point of view concerns collecting the many items in a game space. "I enjoy *Animal Crossing*," says an aquarium worker, "because it lets me complete collections and decorate my island any way I want. It felt amazing to collect every single fish to have the perfect aquarium to show my visitors." This sense of achievement motivated this player to collect meaningful items until they had built something they could feel proud of.

"I play for the story, but can sometimes blow right past them," shares a military veteran reflecting on *World of Warcraft* and their most influential game experiences. The game provides players with an opportunity to experience flow. This helps the player interact with compelling stories and challenging mechanics for longer periods of focus. For these players, escaping into a game world is a meaningful opportunity for relaxation and introspection using the creative space of the virtual world.

Gaining a certain status while choosing which quests to grind can help people enjoy the thrill of the voyage. "I love the options we get in games like *Sea of Thieves*," coming from a photographer with a strong interest in social games and expressive character design. "Sometimes I feel like battling. Other times I want to enjoy a peaceful sailing across the sea for hours. As long as there is a cute outfit I can earn, I can find a way to enjoy almost anything in a game like this."

"I love first-person shooters and MMOs. This makes *Destiny 2* the ultimate game for me," shares one father who plays games to destress in the evening. "Games like this give you a little bit of everything. I love the lore of the galaxy. There are raids and so many things to do with friends. The loot grind keeps things interesting!" For players like this, the endless trials of a game make leisure time feel exciting in different ways depending on the gaming motivation of the player.

Another player who regularly streams games describes her fun with online gaming as follows: "One thing I've enjoyed about completing tasks in *Final Fantasy XIV Online* is the dopamine boost of a job well done. I have ADHD, so my brain always tries to get this feeling. It's why I find side quests and 'busy work' the most satisfying." She says, "Harder tasks like dungeons I put off because it's not as immediately satisfying. Not to say they're not rewarding, they're even more rewarding because I did something hard and made it through to the other side." There is a built-in prediction for this player about the effort spent mixed with the reward expected. For players like this, the push through the various trials of a massive game world is a deliberate cost versus benefit equation. *Final Fantasy XIV* helps her calculate a positive experience.

Some people play games as a way to interact with novel ideas. From one accountant who has played games since childhood: "I play games to have weird experiences. I am not playing a *Resident Evil* game to have a vanilla struggle. I am going into it because Resident Evil gives you a certain flavor of nonsense." This player chooses survival horror to be presented with a challenge, compelling characters, and ridiculous situations they can discuss with friends later. Games can bring this to people since the developers are more limited by their imaginations than they are bound to practicality.

One mother passionate about fandoms explains their love of *Horizon Zero Dawn:* "I work on leveling and getting points for the skill tree over everything else. It helps you move the story forward and makes you powerful enough to take on bigger machines in that world." When players see an opportunity to expand the abilities of their in-game character, it helps them feel the power of their accomplishments in the game. The positivity around each mission motivates the player to continue for longer play sessions. "There is something incredibly satisfying in that game when you take on the super big bosses, and all the mid-sized machines join in to help you win. This makes the game into a chill and fulfilling experience."

Open-world games offer players an entry and exit point on the road of trials, depending on the player's free will. One passionate *Star Wars: The Old Republic* player states, "No matter how many times I play this game, I need to do every mission. It makes me feel like I'm making a difference in the galaxy and everyday-people's lives. I like delivering hope." While this player completes every quest to improve the game world's state, a *Legend of Zelda: Breath of the Wild* player avoids the end, saying, "One reason I finish side quests is to procrastinate on finishing the game. I often would think, 'No way Ganon, not today! I have to collect some mushrooms.' I also liked that the quests forced you to explore the world in more detail and pay closer attention to everything."

In one example, delivering hope is a process inherent to each destination on the path of the heroic passage. Conversely, the best way to provide hope to the imagined world would be to end the influence of the ultimate evil. For both examples, the time spent inhabiting these worlds feels valuable to the player, and finishing them before the feeling is complete may leave the player wondering what could have been.

Within every game, there is some form of heroic quest to complete. As a result, player interest is limited only by the willingness of the player to accept the myriad of challenges in the heroic passage while connecting with their vision of what is important in their lives.

 ## LEVELING-UP IN OUR OPEN-WORLD

Perhaps the most prudent metaphor to create for an open-world game is life itself. While it is empowering to think we are capable of anything once we put our mind to it, this mindset overlooks the reality that things often occur in stages, one step at a time. The trials and tribulations of development are what make us who we are. In an open-world game, the player chooses their path through the road of trials. There are no right or wrong answers, only decisions that lead to different opportunities. This is much the same in the reality-based side of living as well.

Applying an understanding of the monomyth to psychological well-being through video games requires many of the same philosophical assumptions that allow play therapy and narrative techniques to aid people with their therapeutic journey. While archaic rites and mythological symbols do not apply to our context in a modern system of thought, the projective properties of these methods remain intact when seeking out creative ways for a video game story to achieve meaning for each of us. The expectation to rapidly complete tasks at home, school, and work is a hallmark of modern times, with technology aiding our efficiency while we become more disconnected ourselves than we have ever been.

Despite all of this, play remains a right for all children. Whether physically or technologically driven, the ability to engage in play is a critical and necessary aspect of optimizing child development across all forms of skills; cognitive, physical, social, and emotional.

Game players of all ages interact regularly with bliss as they flow through each quest chain in a risk-free style of fun than they ever would with their tasks of hard work. The lesson also remains that we can choose our leveling path and invest energy into the life areas where we hope to achieve optimal levels of distinctiveness. For this journey to continue despite the constant backdrop of pressures from the serious world, each person must hold onto their intentionality in letting go of the stress from becoming "responsible," and instead believe in the power of approaching all tasks in life the way the hero of our most compelling stories would.

The solution to this challenge comes from the opportunity to complete our trials. Each step we take towards the bigger goal is a small victory. The situations we place ourselves in give us experience. It is no coincidence that experience points (or EXP) are the perpetual measurement of character growth in video games, especially those with a role-playing progression system.

Each threshold we pass in service to our life-defining goals leads to the realization that we also level up in life. After all, every doctor was a student once. Every parent was a child. Every champion was a challenger. On and on, this cycle perpetuates. With each benchmark achievement, we evolve into something more than we were.

The Gates of Metamorphosis originated in Sumerian myth and is repeatedly replicated in games such as *Pokémon* as we push a Charmander to victory in enough battles to become a Charizard. When we find our way to hold firmly to the belief in our journey, we, too, find a way to achieve that mythical status as the dragon who slays the challenge. When this faith in ourselves holds, we eventually walk our own Victory Road.

The leveling-up process was not created specifically to explain fun. In fact, working for experience is a way to pass on an incredibly valuable lesson about life. We must take time to be challenged, to fail, and to solve difficult problems. We also have people to interact with, skills to develop, and areas on our character sheet which begin as weaknesses, but when learned, help us to become impressive in the roleplaying game that is life.

Dungeons and Dragons is one of the earliest examples of adopting the EXP concept. In turn, experience helps create a transference in the tabletop roleplaying game (TTRPG) genre from a social game into a timeless activity with personal connections between created characters who grow across their campaigns. Games of all kinds use this approach to teach a subliminal lesson that effort is required to reach our next level in the many pursuits we are drawn to in life. Even more so, this is true in our life beyond playing games. That very truth is what the EXP system is designed to represent in a gamified way.

The connection we form with our gaming challenges, while feeling fun, are actually low-stakes opportunities to practice becoming mentally ready to put our full effort into leveling up. For many, this lesson stays within the boundaries of playing time.

With guidance and intention, the lesson of leveling up becomes a blueprint for figuring out what version of ourselves we would be proud of, allowing us to form a real strategy for how to conquer our vulnerabilities and maximize our potential.

 ## MAKING THE HEROIC SACRIFICE

Another function of mythology is to explain the nature of the relationship between humanity and their gods, as well as the connection between existence, and the domains of Heaven and Hell.

When battling against the forces of the God or Satan figure, it is important to be able to gain impressive levels of power throughout the story of the game. Building on the mythical themes of the Father and the Goddess, *Bayonetta* is the story of a witch awakened from a 500-year sleep by the war between the Umbra Witches and the Lumen Sages (literally the forces of darkness and light). She possesses a red gem that identifies her as one of two chosen fighters for the side of darkness. With no memories, she battles her way across Paradiso and Purgatorio (borrowed from Dante's Inferno) to clarify her allegiances and set the proper order for all of existence. Her ultimate battle at the end of this journey relies on her defeating Jubileus, the Creator. With her full arsenal of magicked demons and fantastical gunplay, she emerges victorious until the next need to engage in the battle for the heavens.

Meanwhile, a male counterpart to the stylistic combat of Bayonetta comes in the form of Dante from *Devil May Cry*. While many of his battles occur with his brother Vergil, Dante's greatest showdowns are his clashes with the king of evil, Mundus. Adorned with three red eyes, Mundus initially intended to take over the human world, destroying or enslaving all mortal life at his whim.

The first game in this series features Dante moving around a castle, defeating servants and arch-demons to collect new weapons and abilities. This quest chain escalates until Dante must face this parallel version of Satan and banish him to the demon world, mimicking the banishment of a fallen Lucifer in the Christian faith.

While it is unlikely any player will have to engage in a literal swordfight with God or Satan, the idea that, if we had to figure out a way to pull this off, then we could, is a powerful perspective to hold. These heroes grant us a suspension of rational belief to engage with the hypothetically impossible. In a game, the greatest accomplishment we could ever hope for can influence the fate of existence if we fight hard enough. While the mindful path through life guides us to achieve presence and consider letting our attachments float away, the achiever of our gaming side helps us assemble the checklist of goals along the path to triumph on the road of trials. The goal will take time and dedication, but in the words of Emperor Valkorion from *Star Wars: The Old Republic*:

"A man can have anything if he is willing to sacrifice."

The deepest contribution to setting things right in the universe can often be depicted by heroes who give up their entire selves for the greater good of their quest. This is called the Heroic Sacrifice. Another game that shows the weight of dealing with this decision between mortality and the afterlife is the video game rendition of the classic poem *Dante's Inferno*. While the climactic battle in this game is between Dante Alighieri (the original poet) and Lucifer himself, the path through the nine circles of Hell highlights this experience. As a direct adaptation of mythology (or satire) into a gaming experience, this quest challenges the player to wield a scythe and holy energies to reclaim the soul of his fallen lover Beatrice, who was dragged to Hell unjustly by Lucifer.

214

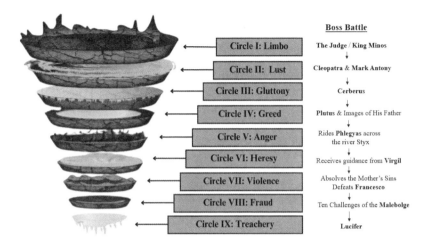

Boss Battle

Circle I: Limbo — The Judge / King Minos
↓
Circle II: Lust — Cleopatra & Mark Antony
↓
Circle III: Gluttony — Cerberus
↓
Circle IV: Greed — Plutus & Images of His Father
↓
Circle V: Anger — Rides **Phlegyas** across the river Styx
↓
Circle VI: Heresy — Receives guidance from **Virgil**
↓
Circle VII: Violence — Absolves the Mother's Sins Defeats **Francesco**
↓
Circle VIII: Fraud — Ten Challenges of the **Malebolge**
↓
Circle IX: Treachery — Lucifer

FIGURE 20. *Overview of Dante's Inferno Using Game Progression and Boss Encounters*

Dante begins his epic descent through the nine circles of Hell hoping to restore the soul of Beatrice to a more peaceful eternity. To succeed in this goal, Dante must suffer through every punishment imaginable and overcome countless tortured souls who reflect the failings of Dante's inner world. Beginning on the shores of Limbo, Dante betrays the help of Charon, seeing him as a threat despite being guided into the Underworld by him. This shows the depths of resolve needed to survive in such a wretched place, as well as the personal inclinations Dante holds inside himself.

The journey Dante experiences on the road of trials through Hell exposes him to many of the milestones inherent to the monomyth.

In the circle of Greed, Dante must atone with his father to set aside his guilt and continue the descent. Moving further along the river Styx, Dante must admit his infidelities in life. His sin is the reason for Beatrice's sentence to the deepest circle of Hell. The suffering of the person he was supposed to love the most was his own doing.

Moving through the circle of Heresy, Virgil offers knowledge as a form of aid, allowing Dante to move forward. He meets with the soul of his mother in the Wood of Suicide, found in the circle of Violence. By absolving her, he overcomes the shame of his family, moving forward with a clear conscience.

By pushing through the challenge of the Malebolge, Dante ensures passage into the deepest areas of Hell, the end of his journey. In the circle of Treachery, he faces Beatrice and claims he has overcome his past sins so she can escape the depths of Hell. Uncertain, Beatrice appeals to all the acts of treachery Dante committed in the Crusades, his infidelity, and cowardice. Dante commits to the ultimate sacrifice when he admits he belongs in Hell and is beyond absolution. This redeems Beatrice completely, and the Archangel Gabriel arrives to liberate her from Hell.

Now clinging to hope, Dante pushes through the frozen surroundings of Lake Cocytus, where Lucifer awaits. The fallen angel hoped to use Dante's soul and the Holy essence from his battle across the underworld to return to Heaven and overthrow God. Knowing this plan would mean eternal doom, Dante absolves himself with a final use of Holy power and strikes Lucifer down in a moment of Apotheosis, chaining him to the lake of ice.

Upon saving all of existence, Dante is granted the right to enter Purgatory. His sacrifice saved all of existence for the greater good. Dante's hope for reuniting with his lost love, Beatrice, has become his eternal bliss in Paradise.

The plight of the inferno requires us to overcome our inadequacies and emerge transformed on the other side. The depth of this struggle gives the experience transformative value. Every person who completes this rite of passage experiences deep personal introspection. By playing this game, a player will likely reflect on their own morality, and either write their thoughts off as the silly aftermath of a playing a game with strong religious themes, or they may realize they have become more aware of why *Dante's Inferno* has been a provocative piece of literature since its writing in the 1300's.

We all have flaws, but some of us use our psychic defenses to pretend these are never a hindrance for our paths. Such perfectionism discourages people from accepting their trials. Embracing our flaws allows us to make the attempt and see what happens next. We overcome Limbo to pursue Paradise, just as Dante did in his quest to overcome the shackles of Hell. By refusing to let the aura of pride dictate our actions, we allow ourselves to embark on the heroic journey.

The road of trials is not meant to reinforce perfection but to unify our sense of self, letting us embrace both our strengths and our weaknesses. In this way, the hero learns to bow amiably to their imperfections. The outward struggle for a gaming hero is to win every trial by combat. On the narrative side, however, the real challenge is finding congruence across our perceptions, beliefs, and reality to form one complete essence by embracing our journey. With each personal challenge, we identify an imperfection, but with each victory, we learn to accept ourselves for who we are. As we become stronger, we are more prepared for the next phase of the journey. In this way, the road of trials teaches us to become aware of our potential so we can find the best path forward in the world around us.

The road of trials guides us to experience a personal ordeal. This is why video games resonate with some and not with others. This is also why we choose different professions, hobbies, talents, and ways of spending our time in meaningful ways moment to moment.

There is never truly a time in life when all challenges cease. Just like there is always another game to play, there are always new challenges in life to accept. We either stay on one road of trials for the length of our journey or stray in new directions to define the next phase of life.

The long path teaches us how to become better. Even though it feels daunting to focus on the big picture, the smaller challenges shape our motivation. We keep moving, solving, and accomplishing in life as in a game.

From the initiate's quest to the transcendent moments of illumination, we grow in experience to become the person we were meant to be. The threshold guardians and daunting dragons along our path evaluate our performance and provide benchmarks as we reach mastery. This road is not defined by the victories we earn but by the defeats we learn from. Each step we take forward becomes our unique journey of discovery. These moments provide joy each time we succeed.

The ecstasy of a victorious moment may be the feeling we try to replicate later in life, but the journey down the road of trials gives that moment substance. When our core beliefs align with our chosen path, we glimpse the hope of what we are working towards. When the call is answered, we extend beyond the reach of our ordinary world. By traveling along the entire road of trials, we become the person who pursues the goal. Yet, by pushing past the familiar, we notice our power to influence reality. Now all we need to do is press on until we transform our world into something wonderful.

CHAPTER XII

APPROACHING THE INNERMOST CAVE

Always fear the flame, lest you be devoured by it and lose yourself.

—Quelana of Izalith (Dark Souls)

The legends that carry on across the centuries proclaim the names of countless heroes who have braved their mono-myth to inspire a timeless audience. These stories inform the values of societies through religion and mythology to define the balance between good and evil for as long as their social structures endure. The exploits of King Arthur, for example, continue to wield a presence in modern storytelling ages beyond the historical periods which inspired them. From the anointing moment of claiming Excalibur to the ongoing quest to collect the Holy Grail, this story has woven itself into the fabric of fantasy narratives at the subconscious level. As an example, Link claiming the Master Sword in any Zelda entry is a moment that resonates because of the value we understand of a hero claiming

THE Legendary Sword. In this way, recognizable themes from fantasy narratives appear symbolically in many video games to ensure we feel the elements of the Hero's Passage in meaningful ways as we play through them.

The opportunity to claim the sacred weapon requires the hero to face their inner demons successfully. In *Kingdom Hearts*, when the Keyblade chooses Sora, he saves Riku from a dark fate instead of becoming a Heartless. In Final Fantasy VII, Cloud must reconcile with the death of the original owner of the Buster Sword, a trauma that resulted in his memories being fractured. Link must defeat his shadow self in the Water Temple, Master Sword versus Master Sword. Countless video games contain examples of these inner battles so the hero can become worthy of wielding the legendary weapon of their world.

Excalibur itself (harkening to the legendary tales of King Arthur) serves as the focus of "a tale of souls and swords, eternally retold" in the fighting game franchise *Soul Calibur*. This game depicts the ageless battle between seekers of the evil sword *Soul Edge* and those who hope to claim the power of the divine to wield Soul Calibur. The elaborate backstory for each fighter brings forth the telling of Siegfried, one of the pivotal characters across the entire game timeline, due to his connections with the mythical swords. Siegfried, running from crippling guilt in the aftermath of battle, slaughters a group of defenseless soldiers. After defeating their commander, Siegfried is devastated to realize he has just slain his father. He loses his mind, running through the forests, convincing himself that someone else committed this atrocity and that only the wielder of *Soul Edge* can defeat such a monster.

The possible fights in the first entry in the series tell the story of Siegfried coming to claim the evil sword for himself. By wielding Soul Edge, Siegfried loses himself in the darkness, becoming a victim of the shadows from his innermost cave. The dark transfor-

mation leads to the reign of *Soul Calibur's* notorious villain, The
Azure Knight, Nightmare.

Both characters maintain a presence in the back-and-forth
battle between good and evil. Siegfried takes the stage when the
divine sword is claimed, while Nightmare brings his inferno to
earth whenever his reign of terror is initiated. Ultimately, they
are the same character, but experiencing different fates. The two
eventually become separate beings, leading to the opportunity to
battle for the fate of existence and redemption at the same time.
Battles of this nature reflect the chance for the inner cave to be
illustrated through the story, blending the psychological weight of
the confrontation with the epic events taking form.

The threats inside the innermost cave push us to our limits
and make us face the most vulnerable parts of ourselves. This
battle can be composed of any threatening feeling: fear, regret,
loneliness, trauma. These feelings push us into a mental state that
aims to convince us that we are not meant for the challenge we
have accepted. Any challenge we have never overcome before can
feel overwhelming. If we have never ascended to the zenith of the
mountaintop, a fear of failure can send many into the refusal to
attempt the climb.

By accepting the call, every hero binds themselves to the difficult realities of their quest. Each challenge seeks to block the
hero's advancement toward fulfillment. When the hero begins
moving past these obstacles, the challenges evolve. What once
felt objectively part of every person's experience can morph into a
challenge specifically crafted to break the hero's resolve.

The encounters fought in the innermost cave push the boundaries of the hero's resilience. The casual battles with each threshold
guardian escalate until the hero must vanquish an opponent who
represents the most personal threat thus far. If unsuccessful, the
hero will be mentally shattered. This challenge often enters the

plot to show what it would take for the adventurer to be brought to their knees. This threat of failure rings true because the hero's schema holds their darkest fears. If brought to fruition, these challenges would isolate each inadequacy of the hero's psyche until all hope is extinguished.

Every type of gaming character will eventually face this level of personal threat. What happens when the warrior is not strong enough to prevail? How can a party progress if the healer cannot outpace the threat of damage? What happens when the rogue is discovered, and the spellcaster lacks the knowledge to channel the right spell? If we turn back from the feeling that we are not good enough to prevail, we never will. In-kind, the heroes of video games, from 8-bit to HD, set an example of learning from past mistakes to improve, pushing through each veil of darkness to progress the journey forward.

 ## PREVAILING THROUGH OUR INNERMOST CAVE

Once the road of trials sends the player into their inner cave, natural talent alone makes each challenge nearly impossible. The element of projection, which many games utilize to create a deeper connection for the player, can be reverse-engineered to reveal what form of challenge will captivate the person playing. Going further, which challenges will break the player and make them rage quit? The translation from mythical challenge to real-world confrontation sends every game player on a path where self-discovery is not only possible but necessary if they are to continue along the Hero's Passage.

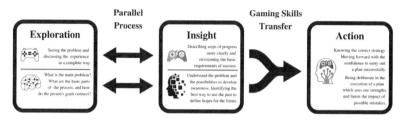

FIGURE 21. *Unified Vision of Problem-Solving in Gaming and Life Contexts*

When a challenge achieves this level of complexity, a player may seek a guide or walkthrough video to make it past the impossible challenge. They could also make several more attempts, choosing to struggle independently to activate their experimental process toward victory. The trial and error found in these personal challenges push the player to see the problem with deeper awareness if they are to be allowed to move on. In this way, the player engages in a parallel therapeutic process to identify the optimized talents for overcoming their difficulties. This is exploration, the first phase of every intervention intended for growth.

The exploration phase exists in both personal and gaming pursuits. It is a critical phase in which the basic situation is identified and reviewed for a complete view of what has occurred. By seeing the challenge with greater detail, the prevailing idea is that a more effective path toward eventual victory can be envisioned. When we review why things are challenging, we learn to see our strengths and limitations more objectively. The fear of vulnerability makes these limits a threat to achieving progress. Ironically, embracing our shortcomings courageously often reveals the path to overcoming them.

Once the basic view of the problem is established, the player moves deeper into the insight-building phase. This phase involves working towards a more developed understanding of the mechanics involved in the problem. We continue to experience certain basic elements from the exploration stage, but also move beyond them towards advanced understanding. Instead of simply describing how a person is challenged, the focus shifts to defining the elements of the challenge until a successful strategy is formed that encourages the next attempt. This requires the person to understand the inner workings of cause and effect that impact them on the path to their outcomes. Whether the challenge resolves itself as a success or failure, the endpoint becomes a calculation between how well the person understands, and their ability to execute a plan that fulfills, the requirements of the challenge. The insight phase allows the person to experiment with the elements of the challenge without feeling like a total failure from every unsuccessful attempt.

By identifying an approach, a person becomes ready to directly confront the challenge to see if they are finally ready. This stage is called the action phase. This stage is about trial and error. If growth is still needed, revisiting the exploration and insight phases allows for a more practical skill transfer while new levels are gained. If the strategy is successful, the person will move on to the next phase of the journey.

This method works across many phases of developmental growth. When we attempt to overcome a challenge in a video game, we engage in an experimental process until we can access further areas of the game. The explore-insight-action model serves as a systematic approach to maintaining positivity while we attempt the challenges we believe are possible.

This strategy exists in both video games and psychotherapy approaches, although the terminology and purpose may diverge in certain situations. The use of exploration-insight-action helps to clarify the things we missed on our first attempts. Once we understand our abilities, any game challenge can be synthesized into a magnificent dance toward triumph. This approach helps us find a path to mastery in everyday challenges. The entire purpose of this strategy is to align the cognitive elements we assign to the situations we are in, refine our actions, then execute the plan.

While games test us on this process using ogres, demons, and nefarious plots, the therapeutic process encourages us to identify which things in our life parallel those adversaries. How do we better provide answers for the enigmas in our humanity? Who are we trying to be, and how do we get there? By seeing the symptoms of our situations, we understand the quest more completely.

As in the road of trials, the missions link together, one after another, until we start to realize we are becoming the ideal we set out to be. With or without therapeutic insight, some of the most advanced problem-solving elements are presented to us symbolically in how we play video games.

Just as past generations could wrestle with the deeper meaning of a dream, a psychoanalyst would provide confidence that these wonderings were on a productive track. The purpose of the great mythical stories was not to convince a person that they are the hero. Instead, it was to help them reflect on their lives as if they were heroes so they would carry these significant life lessons with them. When this occurs across societies, it creates a culture of like-minded people equally capable of believing in similar forms of resilience across their humanity. In these ways, insights from psychotherapy, ludology, and mythical storytelling bind with our struggles as we aspire for self-actualization. Every video game player experiences this same opportunity. We learn to imagine the connection between our lives and scripted games urging us to overcome challenges.

THE CAVE OF THE
PERSONAL ARCHETYPE

Entering a cave symbolizes many things in a game player's mind. Drawing from their physical counterparts, caves represent separation from the open-world sandbox in many games. Entering the tunnel, the player can only progress in one direction. The challenges within must be faced in sequence, with no escape to draw from other than completing the path forward or succumbing to the failure / respawn option. Video games often use these locatio..s to house important boss fights or treasures the player will likely be drawn towards. Unable to escape, the struggling player must accept their inadequacies and rise above them as they endure continued attempts to clear the obstacles within.

Games such as *Elden Ring* or *Breath of the Wild* isolate their challenges from the expansive world by placing these rites within the walls of mountains, tunnels, and other formations across the landscape. To enter a cave symbolizes a subliminal belief from the player that the challenges within should be overcome, and the skill we have developed over time is good enough right now to make the attempt. In this way, the cave structure forces us to overcome our fear of failure in at least a small way. In doing so, we either learn we are good enough or face the reality that we are not ready for certain challenges. By facing these truths, we join with the struggle of our characters in the story, wrestling with inadequacy despite knowing we must continue pushing towards our endgame, no matter the cost.

The challenges faced in the cave reflect the inner workings of the hero, including their strengths and vulnerabilities. Game players witness these struggles in both narratological (story) and ludological ways (gameplay). This reflection pushes the hero to leave the challenges of the past behind so they can work towards fulfilling the Supreme Ordeal. This is the ultimate goal, revealing the hero's greatest fear in a metaphorical way that will only be overcome when the time is right.

A narrative-driven example of this fear is survived in *Resident Evil 4*. Early in his mission to rescue Ashley Graham (daughter of the U.S. President), Leon S. Kennedy is knocked unconscious. When he awakens, he feels a strange sensation in his arms. He looks down to see his infected veins spreading the virus quickly across his body. His face is soon covered with the infection of Las Plagas. He screams in terror, and then the nightmare fades back into consciousness. Leon is infected, but the fear that he has already lost his mind to infection has not come to pass. His mission is now time-limited. Leon must find Ashley, return her to safety, and, if possible, find a cure to this new virus to prevent the world (and himself) from falling victim to another *Biohazard*.

Tapping into the Explorer archetype, Lara Croft exemplifies several playable opportunities to traverse caves to secure access to relics across her adventure. In the *Tomb Raider* rebirth, Lara completes various cave challenges to improve her abilities, discover artifacts, and save her team from danger. Her innermost cave moment happens at the Tomb of the Stormguard General. Lara must avoid detection by guards to navigate the burial chamber. When she finds the skeletal remains of the fated general, she removes his sword and inspects it. Hidden inside the hilt is a scroll revealing the source of the cursed storms ravaging the island. Her friend Sam, a descendant of Queen Himiko and heir to the powers over the island, is now the target of the Solarii cult, who seek to control these powers for their evil purposes.

Lara fears not being able to learn the truth in time. Her deeper fear is that in her haste to explore the island's power, she has not understood the nature of these truths well enough to become worthy of saving her friend. During one of her encounters with Mathias, the cult leader, she is faced with the hypocrisy of assuming the hero role when he says:

"Do you think you're the hero, Lara? Everything I've done, I've done to survive! How many lives have you taken to do the same? There are no heroes here, only survivors!"

If Lara is truly worthy of the title of hero, she will understand the nature of the supernatural well enough to save her friend. This example of the innermost cave places Lara directly on the path to her final test. There is no turning back at this point. There is only the chance to do well enough or fall short. In this way, the challenge within the innermost cave transforms the journey from an unlimited growth process to realizing that the final test, the supreme ordeal, lies ahead.

The supreme ordeal challenges us to overcome an impossible challenge, against all odds, to become the exception. This ordeal in story form is a metaphor for the challenges we face in our own lives. It represents the challenge that was only imagined during the nascent moments before the call to adventure was answered. These challenges are intimidating but represent the greatest opportunity for personal growth and development.

The fact that these stages can be experienced inside the safe space of a video game is a wonderful application for this metaphor. For most people who accept a symbolic challenge this way, the escape of achieving something complex in a game addresses the incongruence between an ideal reality we can only imagine and the actual reality being experienced incongruently. When cast as the hero in a video game, we symbolically fight for this ideal to exist. We share the character's deepest fears when we enter the innermost cave. Yet, we benefit from the chance to experiment with the feelings of pursuing the victory represented by the supreme ordeal before we actually must accomplish this ourselves.

Understanding our personal archetype is a great way to appreciate our connections with certain gaming characters and a shortcut for seeing which threats feel the most significant to overcome. Every type has a set of strengths and weaknesses. Each of these brings about hopes and fears, which define the quest the character must complete. The value of archetypes comes from our connection with them, which grants them a powerful ability to describe the complicated areas of life with simplicity.

Many game characters demonstrate how overcoming a challenge on screen exposes us to a refined value system using archetypes. The Innocent archetype, displayed masterfully in *LittleBigPlanet*, depicts Sackboy in a cardboard utopia enjoying a peaceful existence through endless creativity. His ordinary world is interrupted by the Collector (or Negativitron), threatening to conquer the created space and corrupt reality. While a person in this archetype may fear punishment for an act that relinquishes their innocence, Sackboy unflinchingly presses on to restore the innocence of Craftworld.

Drawing from a similar game idea, Maxwell comes from the *Scribblenauts* franchise. He is renowned for his ability to create anything that can be typed to solve his way through complex platforming puzzles. Representing the Creator archetype, the greatest fear for this form of hero is the inability to express their creative vision for their surroundings freely. The inner cave challenges the creator by enforcing limitations and blocking reasonable solutions. By collecting Starites, Maxwell empowers his drive to create while practicing his innovative flair.

While many game heroes represent the Everyman archetype, Mario's wide range of abilities across all his titles make him a fine example of this construct. The application of this character design for Mario relies on a meta-awareness that this form of hero desires to connect with others. As the mascot for Nintendo, Mario puts on many costumes (Tanuki, Doctor, Metal, etc.) to allow fans of these consoles to play any challenge using Mario and his cast of characters. The deepest fear for a hero of this style is that they will let someone down or become out of touch with their surroundings. By having such a diverse array of games to play, from platforming to sports and all forms of party games, Mario overcomes this fear every time. Many of his greatest confrontations occur inside underground caves, albeit with Bowser or his many minions.

Many archetypes are forced to overcome critical moments in their battles using a core value from their hero type to win the day from the grips of defeat. These defeats often reflect the greatest fear of the hero. This makes their vulnerabilities symbolic of the inner cave. The Jester archetype is often represented as a character who faces their fears head-on with humor and wit. In *Devil May Cry 3*, Dante faces off against his twin brother Vergil in a battle to the death. During this epic fight, Dante is defeated, but he emerges with a better balance between serious goals and casual flair. In this case, actual death is the cave of the Jester, forcing Dante to face the ultimate proposition of boredom in ceasing to exist. By coming through the other side, Dante redefines his core self as a demon hunter and moves on to the next encounter.

Other archetypes seek to overcome their fears by using their vast knowledge and supernatural awareness to divine intuitive solutions for their struggles. Fulfilling the Magician archetype, Bayonetta's greatest fear would come from an incomplete understanding of her situation and herself causing the problem through unintended consequences. This scenario plays out in her first game, leading to her final battle. Unbeknownst to her, she houses the Left Eye of Darkness in her essence. Her father, Balder, carries the Right Eye of Light. By tricking Bayonetta into bringing Eyes of the World together, Balder awakens Jubileus to end the separation of Paradiso, Earth, and Inferno: The Trinity of Realities.

From a Sage perspective, Geralt of Rivia from *The Witcher* accepts that monsters will still exist no matter how much good he tries to do in the world. This directly challenges the idea that knowledge can overcome all fears. Despite this, Geralt forges ahead because it is his duty as a Witcher. This inner cave repeatedly presents itself through the many ways the game can end. The irony of this proposition is that the player must guide Geralt towards the choice that seems to champion the "lesser evil," a claim Geralt despises whenever it is pleaded to him by someone who seeks to hire him. If Geralt trusts the right people, he achieves a noble ending. If he pursues romantic interests (either with Triss Merigold or Yennefer of Vengerberg), he can capture a fate where he is happily involved in a life of love. Or he can fail to win over either or decide to go through life alone. His relationship with Ciri can also end in many ways. They can remain close or sometimes find themselves far apart. The fears of the Sage lie in being misled and falling for it or becoming victim to their incompetence. The political and relational cross-sections of *The Witcher* provide Geralt with the perfect opportunity to prevail or fall short regarding the vulnerabilities of his innermost cave.

Other games reveal the truest strengths of their heroes in the turning points where they emerge victoriously from the threats of the psychological cave. In *Persona 5 Royal*, Joker demonstrates his heroism through the Outlaw archetype. By breaking the law for the greater good, he is pursuing the liberation of society from the control of corrupted hearts and evil self-interests. At a certain point in the story, Tokyo stops believing in the Phantom Thieves, the greatest fear Joker could face. By crossing into the final phases of the plot, Joker does everything he can to reverse this trend. His strength returns, and the Phantom Thieves usher in a better world.

Portraying the Lover archetype in games can be challenging. By basing a game on puzzles and narrative, *Catherine* tells the story of Vincent Brooks and his dreamscape battles to decide his romantic intentions between his longtime girlfriend, Katherine, and a mysterious (and repeated) one-night stand who also happens to be named Catherine. The gaming challenge forces Vincent to climb countless stairways out of his unconscious hell every time he falls asleep. The fear of losing Katherine, or Catherine, drives Vincent's fight to survive his nightmares. He wants to please everyone, so he is only honest once he reaches the critical points in the story. That is the challenge of the Lover archetype: finding the best way to be genuine in their desires.

In the exemplar of the Hero archetype, Sora from *Kingdom Hearts* fears being weak, letting down his friends, or not being the hero everyone needs when the darkness becomes the strongest. Tidus even goads Sora into an extra friendly conversation early in the game by calling Sora a "chicken." These inadequacies motivate consistent reactions from Sora as the titular protagonist in the series. Most of the time, we learn lessons of heroism from the example Sora sets. There are still moments where we see the dangers of being manipulated into defending our heroic identity. From battling the personal shadow to striving to be good enough, Sora shows this archetype to us in how he pushes past the inner dangers of his archetypal cave.

Player choice can shape the experience of the archetypes used in a story. Two game examples for this come from *Detroit: Become Human* and *Fable*. In becoming the Caregiver archetype, Kara struggles with her instincts to preserve her life and the life of her deuteragonist, Alice. Kara is an android who is tasked with caring for Alice. She becomes a Deviant if the player chooses to struggle for life preservation early in the game. The archetypal challenge of her inner cave is how much she allows herself to be controlled or discarded by those in authority. This constant struggle is present across the entire flight of the heroes, giving players a unique experience of the Caretaker role given the direct nature of choice for this type of character.

The Ruler character in *Fable III*, known as the Royal Hero, is created through choice. As the primary quest of the game is to claim the throne from a corrupted older brother and defend the kingdom of Albion, the situation is primarily crafted by the player's choices. The fear of becoming powerless, or worse – usurped, is a constant theme in the quests of this game. The title of traitor carries even more psychological concern to motivate the character to action. The critical moments in this game sway the balance of authority while also deciding the moral direction of the kingdom. For a character who believes power is rightfully theirs, a quest to reclaim it and preserve it provides a compelling narrative of choice and consequence to round out the challenge of the inner cave.

In each example, the archetypal hero has a personal need that helps them feel significant once fulfilled. The dramatic flow of the innermost cave comes from the Orphan status of the developing hero. To achieve greatness, it must be earned. By depriving the character of their needs through the challenge of the quest, the desire to complete the journey becomes infinitely valuable.

When the challenge of the personal cave is completed, the hero gains what they needed all along in order to face their ultimate challenge. If they fail, however, they are still unready. Not every quest is as personally meaningful as those of the innermost cave. Some quests are certainly busy work, while others are "fetch quests." Other missions will level or gear up a character, making them more ready to enter their psychological cave. Once the hero feels prepared, they test their resolve by facing the darkest fears of their inner world. A hero who tries to achieve ultimate victory without first experiencing a meaningful growth within will not possess the psychological fitness they need to continue their success. Heroes who emerge intact after battling through their inner darkness remain congruent across their inner selves and achieve an outward peace. From Orphan to Hero, these are the fictional standards we turn to for a deeper understanding of archetypes in our journey.

 ## FINDING OUR HEROIC SELVES

Understanding our personality structure is one way we achieve the same forms of self-awareness in reality that our favorite game characters discover in their journey through the psychological cavern. Like a torch casting light in the darkness, when we come to know ourselves, the knowledge of our strengths and weaknesses will light our way through each difficult situation. This helps us know our triggers and handle them successfully in a manner befitting the archetype of the hero we hope to manifest.

Personality also plays a significant role in mediating the activities we find fulfilling and which ones we would rather avoid. This is true in both life and video games. When we achieve success that feels meaningful, this benefits us in a variety of ways. Considering the four neurotransmitters most directly tied to happiness - dopamine, serotonin, oxytocin, and endorphins – one could argue that video games create a potential for each chemical reaction to be received from one element of the game or another. However, this experiential gain becomes less likely to happen when the activity does not directly matter to us. The optimal flow experience becomes increasingly distant, and every challenge drifts into becoming hard work instead of ascending towards reality as an autotelic experience.

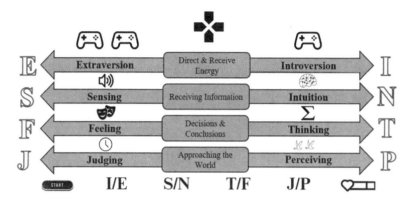

FIGURE 22. *Overview of the Typing System of the MBTI*

Finding the optimal challenge for who we are in video games parallels our daily lives. This is because video games are advanced personality tests that challenge the entire makeup of a person's psyche in a gamified way. Just like personality tests were initially designed to identify vocational recommendations, with the right level of introspection, it is possible to hold similar expectations for ourselves by thoroughly reflecting on how we play what we play and how we play it. What forms of control do we aim for across our challenges? Which deficits do we need to overcome, and which ones can become our "dump stat," meaning a negligible ability for the character we aim to become? How do we achieve our most significant victories to remain triumphant when our adversaries seek to understand defeat?

When we are at our best in a game that aligns with our personality, we overcome challenges in a fulfilling way. We become our ability tree. This congruence defines the best way to put ourselves on display in our victory stance. From this oneness, we identify the best paths for gaining our form of experience points. We learn to do this during play and in connecting with our humanity. Personality is a simple explanation of how we process information to find the things in life that matter the most to us.

The basics of personality explain how our sense of self is designed. When looking at a person through the lens of the Myers-Briggs Type Indicator, a person is measured across four dichotomies to identify them as a member of one of the sixteen types of possible personalities. These four distinctions are based on Carl Jung's theory of type using archetypal symbolism, our persona, and interactions with our shadow. They are introversion or extraversion (I/E), sensing or intuition (S/N), thinking or feelin' (T/F), and judgment or perception (J/P). By identifying the strongest letter in each pairing, a four-letter sequence is created (e.g., INTJ or ESFP), explaining the archetypal patterns a person uses to navigate their life.

When scaling our personality traits is preferred, the Five-Factor Model is applied. This approach to personality theory identifies our tendencies related to the five characteristics we use to navigate life. These factors are extraversion, conscientiousness, openness to experience, agreeableness, and neuroticism. By combining our understanding of these factors, we notice our consistent preferences in various areas, including decision-making, socialization, and flexibility.

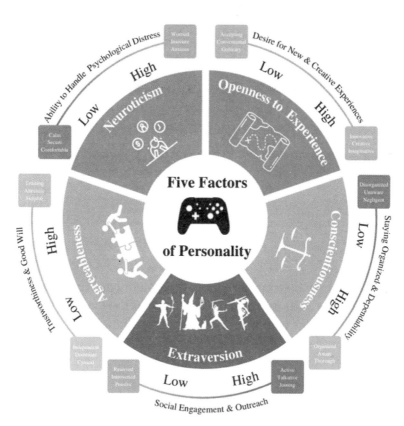

FIGURE 23. *Overview of the Five Factors of Personality*

Similar to the years of the console wars that led to countless seasons of debate in media and online journalism, clinicians have their preferences and will battle to the intellectual death over which style of personality identification is superior. The idea that they are equally impressive in their own right is possibly the academic equivalent of the archetypal cave of darkness. Ultimately, both have descriptive power if utilized with the right person in the right circumstances. They help us to bring gaming concepts like our stat sheet into a realistic perspective. This allows us to know which talents we can depend on and which ones we should avoid in our efforts to solve life's challenges.

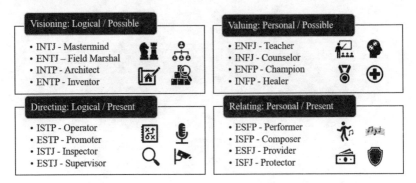

FIGURE 24. *Pairing of MBTI Results with Character Tendencies*

Whichever instrument we use to explain our truth, our personality stays with us through each stage of the journey. It urges us to see the light within the darkness of our inner cave. It makes us stronger the closer we get to finding our path forward. We catch glimpses of our traits in the way we play games. An ENFJ will assume the temperament of The Teacher and play games in a way that reinforces the growth of in-game relationships. The Ruler will pay close attention to the dynamics in a fight to ensure people conscientiously listen to them. The connections between ourselves and our play styles are endless because games were designed to access who we are subconsciously and test what we can accomplish in a deliberately challenging environment made using an intentionally psychological design. When we notice our archetypes connecting to the full demonstration of our personhood, we become capable of seeing the motives of our best selves in illuminating clarity.

The inner cave holds that which we fear. This is true for every one of us. Some of us play to avoid the struggle. Some of us seek to cope with it. The reality is that all of us can play video games and understand the path through our mental cave if we explore ourselves with the same effort we use to explore our in-game challenges. The cave represents the fear that we will never be able to find the path towards the ideal self in reality. By working through the stage of the innermost cave, we learn who we are, just like every video game character that has shown us the ending of their story. By emerging from the depths of our self-doubt, we realize that the path through our life-defining challenge is within our grasp as long as we believe in ourselves with the same faith our heroes learn to wield. The metaphor within each game we play shows us our archetypes, our shadow, and the symbolic path through our cave. This is how we gain the best experience from a video game. When we reflect on these stories and find the insightful way toward success that matches our specific identity structure, we become a hero that carries our experience with us into the next phase of our journey.

CHAPTER XIII

REWARD AND

TRANSFORMATION

Summon me by grace to turn runes into strength.

—Melina (Elden Ring)

Continuing along the road of trials is a daunting task. The chain of quests we face compares to the path through education, climbing the corporate ladder, or moving through the ranks from apprentice to master. Each task serves a purpose and challenges us in new ways.

Emerging from the innermost cave leaves us taxed across our entire being. Like a boss fight completed with 1 HP, this test requires everything inside of us, from strategy to grit, if we are to continue. When we emerge victorious, the rewards energize us. We receive experience points, new equipment, and upgrades to our skills. These rewards prepare us for the next set of challenges.

Reclamation is a phase of the journey where the hero experiences a calming restoration of energies. It is often used in video games immediately following an intense boss fight or an epic sequence of heroism. It is a time for the hero to rest and reflect on their accomplishments. This is when the Explorer emerges from the tomb, the Magician readies the perfect spell, and the Hero gains the courage to approach their adversary. The resolve they claim in those moments leads them to the reality that the final challenge lies ahead.

The horror genre uses this phase masterfully to relieve tension. For example, the Resident Evil series has safe rooms at staged moments across the story. The game uses these rooms to transition from one horror sequence to another. The player refocuses before being thrust back into an even more nightmarish experience. If the regular pattern of enemies is disrupted by a room filled with ammunition and healing items, you know the next big test is only a doorway away. After running and shooting past the next imposing monster, the next room of safety is a welcome opportunity to allow the tension to fade.

After a period of rest, the hero moves forward. The reward of each victory means they are now better equipped to take on whatever new challenges await them. The flow of these moments allows the player to discover new abilities, learn a powerful new spell, or collect upgrades for their equipment. These boons are how video game heroes become more capable during their progression. The acquisition of growing strength is how the hero will eventually become ready for their Supreme Ordeal.

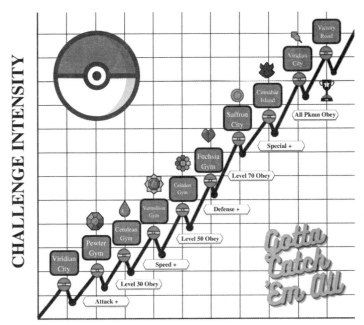

GAME PROGRESS (IN TIME)

FIGURE 25. *Intensity of Challenge in*
Original Pokémon via Time Progression

The intensity of the conflict ebbs and flows to preserve the intended engagement throughout the experience. Nearly every game genre uses this process in some form. Adventure games do this by sending the character to complete acrobatic feats to reach new areas on the map. Roleplaying games force players to level up their party to survive in more dangerous areas.

This is exemplified in each installment of the *Pokémon* franchise, where gym badges represent a Pokémon Trainer's progress toward becoming League Champion. Without these badges, powerful Pokémon may choose to disobey during battle. Even worse, the player may be locked out of some regions of the map they need to visit, halting their progress. The Gym Leaders offer these badges in exchange for besting them in a themed Pokémon battle. These badges must all be collected before heading off to face the Elite Four. The ultimate goals of this world happen to be either claiming the title of League Champion or completing the daunting list of activities required to actually "catch 'em all." With these dual-natured goals in mind, the player constantly shifts back and forth between preparation, battle, and restoration phases. This is the only way for many players to achieve their very best within this game design.

 ## STRUCTURE OF A BOSS FIGHT

Boss fights force the hero character to come face-to-face with their adversaries as they seek to transition from one phase of the game to the next. How video games craft these moments into meaningful milestones in our gaming journey shows a deliberate understanding of tension and motivation for vastly different player types.

In this way, boss encounters test every skill the player has been developing up to that point. The challenge from a boss should be significant enough to push the player in new ways that expand their ability. They become a teachable moment operating through a confrontation. This makes the boss fight a towering challenge that represents both ideological and physical threats to the continuation of the journey. Once the hero enters the battle arena, they are in equal parts interacting with a great opponent, putting the chance to advance the story on the line, and breaking away from the repetition of navigating the road of trials. The challenge is new, and the mark of mastery becomes imminent. Only by claiming victory will they be able to move to the next phase of calm until the next escalation.

From a mental perspective, boss fights serve multiple purposes. They provide specific tests for the player's abilities. They also offer the chance for a resolution to the narrative conflict between the hero and villain. While all prior events have led to this battle, the battle's aftermath will either set up the next phase of the mission or (in the case of a final boss fight) will conclude the story.

Fight designers decide on a set of player skills to be tested by the boss character. This list of skills largely will depend on the game but can involve dodging, puzzle completion, situational awareness, reaction time, and many other elements of player performance. After these are decided, the development team will identify ways the thematic presence of the villain would aesthetically push the hero in this way.

An exceptional example of fight design is the battle with the Great King of Evil, Ganondorf, in *The Legend of Zelda: Ocarina of Time*. This fight requires Link to use the Master Sword to parry dangerous projectiles of energy, the hook shot to move across the gaps in the castle arena, the hover boots to defy gravity, and light arrows to make Ganondorf vulnerable. All of these player abilities must be used successfully in sequence to damage the boss and get to the next phase of the battle. Ganondorf is a dark lord who can levitate, throw energy, reflect attacks with his magical cape, and damage the floor to create gaps for falling. A successful encounter requires Link to masterfully parry the flying spheres of light, float across gaps, quickly reach the center of the room, and land light-infused sword strikes on Ganondorf each time you make him vulnerable.

This review of the fight describes the mechanics of the encounter. On the surface, this fight shows the need to demonstrate competence with multiple character abilities. The impact on the mythology of this world is much more significant. The entire hour of gameplay before this confrontation shows Link earning this showdown with Hyrule's usurper. Every word of the villainous monologue heightens the stakes. Zelda is kidnapped, and Ganondorf aims to use her to plunge the Triforce into darkness. The goal of this battle is twofold: test the player's ability and provide a fitting climax for the story through epic confrontation.

The tale of a video game is told by alternating between story, mission, conflict, and reward. Whether the battle is with a lair boss, mini-boss, or final boss, the player learns to play the game to earn the boon for each accomplishment and push their progress forward. Defeating the Big Daddies in *Bioshock* allows the player to save or harvest the Little Sister. Forming a group capable of vanquishing a raid boss in an MMO game (*World of Warcraft* or *Final Fantasy XIV*) earns members of the group a higher gear rating. Similar activities in roleplaying games can reward new cosmetic items, flashy weapons, and impressive armor sets. Still, other optional bosses, such as Malenia, Blade of Miquella from *Elden* Ring, offer players the chance to see the end of a grueling side quest while also earning bragging rights and unique weapons that signal a sense of status across the community of the game.

This pride comes from the meaningfulness of the boss encounters to the game's reputation. The challenge must enhance the player's ability and reinforce the boss as a climactic threat to the heroic quest. To accomplish this, challenging bosses are equipped with abilities that manipulate intensity and player anticipation. The entrance of the villain is tirelessly crafted to have an impact. When these introductions are iconic, the moment defines the flow of the fight. The boss will use their abilities as a warning shot to show the player what basic maneuvers will be needed to emerge victorious. This establishes a basic understanding of battle flow which will intensify as the fight comes nearer to its conclusion. The player will successfully link their moves to alternate between defensive and offensive maneuvers. Once the boss is vulnerable, the player will engage in a punish maneuver, an amplified chance to damage their opponent. The boss returns to battle stance, and the dance of the fight continues.

Multiple phases are often utilized for the most epic boss encounters. This allows for an interaction between resting observation and the pressure of action. New attacks, faster speeds, or higher punishment following player mistakes amplify the threat. New phases display the heightened resolve of the villain to conquer the hero and end their quest for salvation.

Once these phases are navigated successfully, the hero pushes the boss into their final form. This unleashing of power reveals the villain's final transformation, an echo of their permanently corrupted form. The dance continues until the final push to deplete the boss's health bar is possible. When the hero locks in to deliver the final blow, the burn phase signifies the end of the encounter. The hero commits the attack, knowing they will either win or die trying. If all of these steps align successfully, the resolution occurs, and the victory scene rewards the hero with the opportunity to proceed in their quest.

 ## CHALLENGE OF THE GAMING GODDESS

The ultimate adventures demonstrate a delicate balance between the quest, the characters, and the mystical synergy between the hero archetype and their world. In mythological terms, the flow of this energy is transferred to the mortal realms by the Queen Goddess of the Universe. One powerful example of this dynamic in game form is the interaction between Hydaelyn and the Warrior of Light (your created character) in *Final Fantasy XIV Online*. In every expansion of this MMO game, the influence of the Mothercrystal shifts the fate of Eorzea to prevent the Final Days from becoming renewed. In true harmony with the mono-mythical structure, Hydaelyn's presence in the journey of the player hero is what makes victory possible. These sequences of salvation save the hero from defeat at their nadir, allowing the zenith of their quest to occur. She guides the hero each time to the edge of the world (or the source of the cosmos). She dwells in both the heroic mind and the dark reaches approaching the afterlife. While the created hero is impressive in their own right, the favor of the Goddess links the hero-soul to the unimaginable source of universal genesis.

The mystical power of the goddess only sometimes gets offered to the hero from a deity-level character. Sometimes it is an ability that reveals the potential to find a path to victory in an uncaring world. These abilities are often innately possessed by a supporting character. The hero cannot receive them but requires these talents to make the journey possible. When the potential for mortal courage perfectly merges with the force of the goddess entity, the trajectory of the adventure shifts to create a power capable of saving the day from the direst of circumstances.

"Booker... are you afraid of God?"
"No. But I'm afraid of you."

These words echo across the opening of *Bioshock Infinite*. In this title, players control Booker DeWitt, a disgraced detective who visits the city in the sky known as Columbia. His mission: "Bring us the girl, and wipe away the debt." The girl is Elizabeth Comstock, a young woman held prisoner by the Songbird who can open tears in reality and move between different timelines. Being the miracle child of Columbia's prophet, Zachary Hale Comstock, the zealots in the clouds fight to keep her captive. The Songbird attacks Booker repeatedly as he and Elizabeth fight to escape her captivity. To survive these encounters, Elizabeth often opens tears in time and space to create an alternate path for escape. Booker can handle himself in a fight, but he will never have the kind of power Elizabeth has. She alters reality and helps Booker take advantage of every timeline until they find a path to victory so he can clear his "debt."

This cult-like society results when Comstock manipulates the timelines, weaving together a dishonest sequence of events that elevates himself to become the ordained Prophet of Columbia. His followers mindlessly hope to imprison Elizabeth and kill Booker, calling him the "False Prophet." Through her father's actions, Elizabeth becomes a conduit for the many timelines of Columbia, making her the human essence of the World Navel who guides Booker through the entire game. Once Booker is ready to make the right choices, they reach an end where Comstock is finally confronted. If not, they switch realities to try again and hope for a better result.

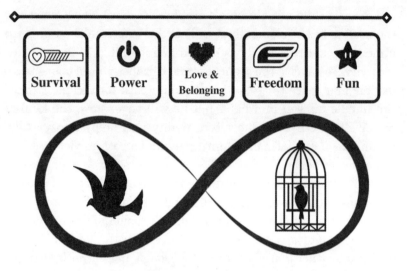

The Bird or The Cage

In **Choice Theory**, every person makes their decisions to secure & obtain their five basic needs. In one version of events, a person could choose heads, and in another, tails.

The Bird or the Cage explores the concept of being the captive or taking the chance to obtain freedom.

Video Games such as **Bioshock Infinite** can help players understand the concept of choice by seeing the impact of alternate decisions on the dangers faced in the virtual world.

This portrays empowerment and accountability as important abilities as we learn to understand our influence on cause and effect.

FIGURE 26. *The Impact of Choice and a New Reality*

The Last of Us: Part I also contains the dynamic of a deuteragonist who carries with them a secret ability based on the conflict of the world. In this case, the symbolic form of the goddess is Ellie's immunity to Cordyceps, the infection that brings the world to its knees. Since Ellie is the key to developing a vaccine, Joel's goal revolves around her. While Joel moves forward with the trauma from his losses, we witness a shift in his attachment to Ellie as they travel across the country. With every danger they face, the source of the threat can be the same, while the threat itself is a different experience they can only overcome by mutually supporting each other. Joel faces the dangers of infection from clickers or death by the many contingent gangs in each locale. Ellie faces limits in her physical strength and use of weaponry. While enemies may seek to kill Joel, the danger Ellie faces are more predatory in nature.

Joel and Ellie complete each other. Without Ellie, Joel loses his humanity as he ruminates over losing his daughter. Without Joel, Ellie may never have made it out of Boston. Her humanity gives Joel a purpose he lacked when the Fireflies first sent him on a mission across the country.

Another game where feminine guidance leads the player through each level is the puzzle game *Portal*. The artificial intonations of GLaDOS (Genetic Lifeform and Disk Operating System) provide scientific instruction through each test Chell faces within Aperture Science. This voice sounds across every room for most of the game, offering encouragement. The commentary acknowledges your successes and reinforces mental rotation to understand most quandaries better while finding the path forward.

The supportive connection between Chell and GLaDOS ends abruptly at the turn of a platform following the final challenge for human test subjects. This hallway ends with an incinerator. Once Chell enters the line of sight, the reality of what she truly means to the experimental process becomes apparent. GLaDOS confirms, "Thank you for participating in this Aperture Science computer-aided enrichment activity. Goodbye." The Portal gun allows for many things; there is no reason to accept this betrayal. The gift granted by GLaDOS provides the path forward. Every player is tasked with thinking fast to make it behind the scenes of this experiment. Now Chell can escape her experimental death trap.

What started as a gift from the unknowable creators of this robotic voice is now the path to self-preservation. With Chell being the hero, GLaDOS is a corrupted goddess, manipulating the quest's events from the beginning. If the player is not ready to realize this treachery, they will theoretically trust her and stay on the platform to accept a premature "Game Over." This would not be the satisfying conclusion of confronting the betrayal in the final control chamber. Beyond the many problem-solving concepts *Portal* teaches players, the moral lesson is to heed your instructions, but not to the point of valuing compliance over staying alive.

In mythology, the goddess archetype is synonymous with an otherworldly being, often feminine in nature, providing the source of life for all existence. In gaming, the mythos of the goddess emanates from characters who offer the same feminine source of life through healing, protection, and guidance.

Video games hold the potential to advance beyond this imagery in many ways. While the support role is often used to attach this monomythical theme to the flow of a video gaming plot, there are examples of feminine characters wielding the gift to move forward with their quest. While Athena is the AI voice in the tutorial for all heroes in *Overwatch*, every hero from D.Va to Tracer has the potential to flourish across the field of battle with their unique abilities. As such, not all female heroes are healers or support players. Likewise, the characterization of many damsels in distress, a la Princesses Peach & Zelda of Nintendo, have become formidable heroes of their universes in their own right. Other characters, such as Yuna from *Final Fantasy X*, are both playable and hold their own without constant aid from others.

By carrying the quest forward through the lessons of the goddess, the hero experiences a transformation of maturity. Prior to this growth, the hero expected easy progress without understanding the work it would take to move forward. Their childish nature defined the extent of their abilities. Each new skill unlocks the next challenge that can be solved. This allows future threats to be attempted in the now. The requirements for heroism go from impossible to achievable. Through this new level of maturity, the hero is able to wield the gifts they are entrusted with.

Despite the goal of video games usually being to stay alive and complete the story, the interactions with the goddess figure remind the player of what is at stake. Namely, the fate of the quest determines the inevitable balance between the value of life and the promise of the end. Without a concept of death, there is no goal of preserving life.

The nature of humanity is captured this way in video games, with each game player knowing that success is possible as long as the health bar is not empty. For the quest to matter, the player often must realize their input into the controller is deciding something important with each passing moment. The most effective gifts empower the player to navigate this balance more effectively as the challenges escalate. In this small way, we are learning to value our time through our actions, even if we are still trying to achieve a more definitive balance between our efficiency and achieving success.

 ## UNIFYING THE HERO ARCHETYPE

Video games have historically received criticism for reinforcing biases that portray female characters only in gendered ways. Just one look at the cycle of mistreatment for female game players across social media makes it clear that the concept of the female gamer is an unfortunate challenge for a contingency of the gaming fandom. In modern times, there is much to be desired as we seek to unify the concept of what a healthy gamer is, especially when factoring in our own concepts of self and gender identity.

While it is true that mythology tells the story of the goddess in ways that highlight feminine abilities, there are exceptions as well. Artemis is the goddess of the hunt and wildlife, but also childbirth. These opposing specialties form a complete understanding when characterizing the heroine in games and the concept of the female gamer. Gaming is not inherently a male activity any more than being heroic happens to be. Just as Ares and Athena sent the armies of the Greeks to war, so too is it representative to allow for the appeal of video games to belong to both women and men, along with any presentation that accurately reveals a person's ideal self.

The dual nature of humanity expands beyond questions of morality and our role in the balance between light and dark. The expansion of the Heroine archetype allows games to move closer to the perfected potential Campbell spoke about in *Hero with a Thousand Faces*. Many franchises serve as examples of these advancements, from the modernized presentation of Lara Croft to the display of leadership in Zelda in *Breath of the Wild*. Characters that once were designed with polygons meant to capture the male gaze (as in *Tomb Raider*) or support characters that needed to be rescued (as in *The Legend of Zelda*) now take center stage with dignity demonstrating ownership of their heroism.

The role of the goddess provides refined symbolism through acts of peace and conflict. When considering Hydaelyn and the Cosmic Goddess as an example (*Final Fantasy XIV*), a cyclical equilibrium exists between providing constant aid to a hero, and being willing to destroy them, as long as it helps them realize their true strength.

The total harmony of opposites allows the image of the goddess to be present in games in all forms or fashions. This image displays the traits of the masculine, feminine, or androgynous, just as it can demonstrate the powers for creation and devastation. Even the idea that these opposites are not dichotomous, meaning gender expands beyond binary limitations, is present in video games. Characters such as 2B in *Nier: Automata* (or Qatherine in *Catherine: Full Body*) subvert these expectations in a way that helps to challenge real-world biases that may impact how we conceptualize game characters. This is the cosmic nature of the goddess symbolism. In a way, video games send us a consistent message of acceptance with every hero, quest, and support we receive, if we are only interested in understanding the meaning found within each character.

Many of these examples involve a reveal as to the nature of the character at some point in the quest. The discovery of the goddess has been a moment in myth that has been used to measure the hero's worthiness to pursue destiny. Terrible things happen when a hero is not ready for the gifts to be bestowed if they step forward anyway. As a result, the discovery moment serves as a "ready check" for the journey. After all, the goddess grants her gifts to the hero in many of these situations, which means the threats the hero will face can become more devastating.

In *The Legend of Zelda: Twilight Princess*, the Fairy Queen serves this role when she allows Link to enter the Cave of Ordeals. While these battles are optional, there are compelling reasons why a player would want to complete the challenge inside the caves. The decision to enter these caves requires the resolve to attempt the most challenging battles in the game.

This example extends across many types of games, reinforcing the magnificence of the gift from the goddess. When the hero is inspired by their gift, they achieve success. If they are unready, they will stumble. In a roleplaying sense, the leveled-up character is mature in their gifted abilities, and the hero who falls is, in actuality, under-leveled.

While the goddess bestowing a gift represents a turning point in the quest, including prominent female characters reflects the needs of a shifting society. The story of gender values is incomplete if left imbalanced. The same happens in games if the hero role becomes overtly male dominated without the room for inclusion of varied qualities and gifts. These characterizations provide meaning in the flow of each game narrative. The hero reaches their limit, and they must receive aid in some form if they are to continue forward. The goddess represents a strength that is different, and more profound, than what the hero has already achieved naturally. These new opportunities to expand the scope of heroic feats occur in varied ways; a voiceover prompt, a new item, additional ammo, or a path to navigate space and time. In whatever form the aid is presented, the goddess portrayal restores the possibility of success in the quest.

This is why representation in games matters. Many of the characters used to explain this portion of the gaming journey have undergone physical and intellectual transformations over the years following their inception in the zeitgeist of game playing. This is explained wonderfully by Stephanie Diez-Morel from Reboot & Recover:

> My earliest memory of a female protagonist was at the end of Metroid when Samus was revealed to be a woman. I remember the sexist remarks from conversations about this discovery. Most video games include characters who identify or present as female. However, Samus was the first female protagonist I can recall that was equal to male presenting protagonists. For the most part, characters that present as female were given roles that reinforce stereotypes or societal norms for being 'feminine,' such as caregiving or healing, lacking their own identity beyond providing support to others in the story.

Games such as the *Resident Evil* series, *Horizon Zero Dawn*, *Final Fantasy*, *Cyberpunk 2077*, *Control*, *Bayonetta*, and *Alien Isolation* all give the option to play as a protagonist who is female-presenting. More representation of female presenting protagonists is apparent as new games continue to release. Despite the increase in representation, there is still a massive need for video games to develop their protagonists as aspirational symbols who can continue to shift perspectives on 'traditional' gender norms and embrace the complexity of our world.

It is my belief that art often models what can be seen in society, and video games do this well through the power of expressionistic storytelling. This medium can help shift our ongoing conversations to present protagonists as more inclusive of what the world needs in our heroes.

Realizing our favorite hero is similar to us empowers the game to become a mechanism of personal and societal relevance. Representation allows for a more complete reflection of society. This is a critical element of games becoming the source of modern mythology. Just as the ancient stories served to explain the way of life to people within a culture, so too do video games. The message is lost if the narrative elements, including characterization, do not align with a population enjoying the content. In-kind, a goddess who cannot make a meaningful impact over reality is just another NPC in the background, easily bypassed and just as quickly forgotten.

Many players experience the unification of their anima and animus traits within their subconscious by coming to understand gender across a continuum through their favorite video games. While experimenting with these ideas often garners harsh judgments in the non-digital world, gender-bending (or gender-swapping) realities are experienced in a mostly safe way in video games. This allows for the curiosity of seeking the unified psyche to be a powerful boon in the experience of game playing. Just as the hero needs that extra light to power their way through the quest, we sometimes thrive in our needs when we use games to identify what they even are.

By realizing the power of our potential selves, we ready ourselves to achieve success beyond what we are given. This allows us to experience transformative harmony as we ascend toward feats we always knew we could achieve if we fully understood ourselves.

CHAPTER XIV

THE MOMENT OF ATONEMENT

Do not be sorry... Be better.

—Kratos (God of War)

I t is common for people to question whether they can achieve their full potential. This is especially true for people who turn to video games as a source of lore, strategy, competition, and entertainment. Video games are often looked down upon by society as a source of mindless entertainment. As a result, people who play video games are often seen as childish or immature.

The conflict between "fun" and "hard work" emanates through the most prominent conversations regarding productivity in modern times. With the rapid development of technology, our ability to efficiently perform screen-based tasks has also increased. When this ability contributes to industry, it is often praised. When used primarily for fun, these interests feel judged. This is unfortunate, as video games can be an excellent way for people to be exposed to valuable lessons regarding adversity and achieving one-ness against a constant backdrop of uncertainty.

The idea that video games damage our mental health is easy to come across in our day-to-day activities. In reality, playing in moderation is a healthy addition to a thriving lifestyle. Games provide a sense of accomplishment and satisfaction that can be hard to find in other activities. They also help you learn new skills and strategies. Some of these are hard skills, such as seeing the scientific relationship between various elements or seeing angles in the trajectory of a moving object. Others are soft skills like forming a multi-person strategy and delegating tasks for a difficult challenge.

As with anything else, gaming can become unhealthy if a person loses that stabilizing connection with the person they aspire to be. Too much gaming can disrupt numerous life areas, including problems at work or school, social isolation, and experiencing various psychological difficulties.

The key to healthy gaming is to find a balance between immersion in gaming and investing in other activities that equally contribute to our sense of self. Most people need more than video games to achieve a feeling of oneness. While video games provide a sense of accomplishment, they cannot offer every experience we need to thrive.

To be well-rounded in games, every hero engages in various activities to develop their skills in each area. This is true for the people holding the controller as well. These abilities come from life areas ranging from spending time with friends and family, bonding with our significant others, learning new things, being physically active, tending to our health and wellness needs, and exploring our passions. If all we do is play video games, we limit our stories to watching others accomplish their goals in fiction. Ironically, if we are only the game player, we are not achieving this growth for ourselves.

The hero in every myth experiences a phase of initiation where they develop their abilities to carry out their idealized role. In video games, the path through this collection of stages often becomes the majority of the gaming adventure. This is because these stages are the easiest to translate into a compelling video game challenge. Following the call to adventure, the player moves through a narrative to find their tests and allies along the path to the ultimate goal guarded by the Supreme Ordeal. In a similar light, we also require the time to work on ourselves to embrace the mature lifestyle found in connection with our ordeal.

How we see ourselves in each phase of life is directly related to the stats we collect across our varied life experiences. We must be willing to put in the effort and practice to improve at any skill. Since video games are a microcosm for life, it is reasonable to transpose the concept of grinding EXP as a parallel process to this form of growth throughout our life phases. With whatever skill we hope to evolve in video games, we often have to start at the bottom and work our way up. We complete repetitive tasks to get better in small steps along the way. Through this style of practice, continued engagement helps to develop our many life skills until we reach the next level for each category.

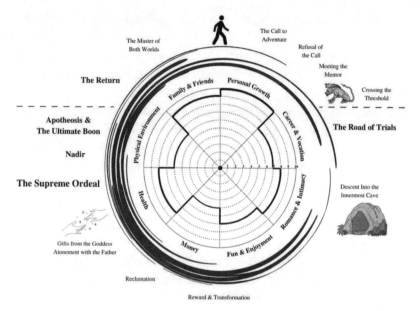

FIGURE 27. *Life Areas Leveling Up as a*
Stat Sheet During the Gaming Journey

Progression in video games is a psychological echo of becoming our unified selves. To fulfill this potential, we must face the fears connected with the challenges holding us back. These trials revolve around our past fears, self-doubt, self-defeating habits, and misdirected schemas. The first step to establishing healthy core beliefs is simply to believe.

A college student trying to pass a challenging course for the third time may realize they can take better notes during class by reflecting on how they have successfully solved a mystery story in a game such as *Heavy Rain.*

An aspiring musician in elementary school follows a metronome more accurately by using practice mode in games like *Guitar Hero* and *Rock Band.*

A teenager who struggles to connect with peers in conversation imagines different comments and responses from their conversational partner by playing *Persona 5*.

Connecting life challenges with actions in our favorite games teaches us to believe we can find a positive path forward. We learn how to handle difficult situations and stay calm under pressure. Many online games push us to work as a team and be supportive. Each player must keep their poise and follow the plan with rapid precision. We can also use games as calming experiences to develop emotional regulation skills and shift out of our chaotic spaces.

Ultimately, video games form a symbolic connection between aspirational characters and the player, providing lessons that can assure us while we move towards the most devastating phases of the journey. To embrace this parallel, we must ready ourselves to overcome our vulnerabilities and become the hero of the self-narrative. To fully become at one with the self, we must face the visage of the Father.

 ## PORTRAYAL OF THE FATHER

Many games enhance the context of the hero conflict by exploring their psychodynamic connection with figures who represent the father archetype. To fulfill their destiny, the hero must atone for any obstacles that prevent them from becoming at one with their self-narrative.

It is only possible to achieve the victories dreamed about in the period of nascence if the hero moves on with the atonement experience. This catharsis can occur in different ways depending on the gaming quest. It can flow from the parentified character to the child, or it can be claimed by the child from the figure of the

Father. This relationship can be genetic or sentimental through the roles established while mentoring the hero. These relationships have been seen in the trials and tribulations of many gaming protagonists over the decades, and new interpretations of this connection will be explored as long as new games extend into our future.

While none of us will ever fly through the cosmos to smite the threat of a corrupted father, we aspire to achieve this intra-psychic balance by establishing a secure attachment to our past. The approval of the father figure is critical to experiencing atonement as we journey into adulthood. In this way, each time we achieve this personal harmony as a gaming hero, we discover a new mythological example that enhances the metaphor of our beliefs that guide healthy relationships.

This influence of the father affects the hero from the moment they become aware of his hold on the narrative. The hero must now possess the resolve to overcome the double monster, the threat as understood in the quest alone, and the compromising feelings resulting from the relationship with the father. In the physical world, this same challenge exists when we reconcile the question of a game's importance in the path our lives are taking.

The intrapsychic conflict between the pleasure principle of the id and the moral interest of the superego carries on in our games as well. This conflict is resolved by the third element, the ego, which settles on a personal decision of how our lives will be spent. Will the drive for easy fun lead to a childish predisposition? In such a case, a player may be less impressive than the heroes they portray on screen. On the other hand, could a player use gaming as the moral imperative toward a lesser evil? In moving so entirely in the opposite direction, a person avoids the risk of failure by deciding the best use of their time is avoidance through play. This inner deceit restructures the moral system that governs the superego, changing the idea of what is acceptable in the psyche of the game player. When this occurs, the superego shatters, leaving only the pursuit of fleeting conquests in the present moment, preferring instant gratification over the rewards offered by a fulfilled journey. Growth becomes limited to momentary joy, and the journey ends until a new calling is finally accepted.

With this balance at stake, the narrative of the inner conflict is understood through the lessons experienced in video games. For better or worse, our heroes show us the full spectrum of the search for atonement. The downfall represents the death of hope. These heroes have fallen short in a crisis of choice, experiencing the consequences of a tragic journey. Victory comes from the balance of a strong ego earned by those who maintain the heroic pursuit at all costs.

This conflict can be decided in a mere moment, but will continue to define the legacy of a character for the rest of time. In the *Warcraft* series, Arthas Menethil was the son of King Terenas Menethil II and Crown Prince of Lordaeron. He was trained to be a paladin by the famed war hero Uther the Lightbringer and was inducted into the Order of the Silver Hand at a young age. Arthas had a strong relationship with his father and looked up to him as a role model. His lineage and potential made him a perennial champion for the Grande Alliance of Azeroth.

During *Warcraft III: Reign of Chaos*, Lordaeron is ravaged by a plague that turns its subjects into the undead. Upon killing the necromancer Kel'Thuzad and knowingly purging the entire city of Stratholme to stop the spread of this curse, Arthas continues north. He aims to hunt down Mal'Ganis, the source of the undead threat. During the pursuit, Arthas loses himself, sacrificing his morality in service of this hunt. He betrays the trust of his troops and scorns his closest allies, giving in to madness.

When he finds the cursed sword, Frostmourne, planted in the Frozen Throne of the Lich King, he claims it in full knowledge that the cost would be his soul. At that moment, his obsession with destroying the undead overtook his entire identity. Wielding Frostmourne as its new master, Arthas quickly turns the tide of battle, rending Mal'Ganis, and returning to Lordaeron as a war hero.

The sword, however, had corrupted the promising champion Arthas was to become. Receiving a hero's welcome, Arthas and his inner circle enter the throne room to receive the king's praise. Rising to his feet, the prince slays his father, plunging Frostmourne through the king's chest, severing his ties with the human Alliance. With destiny abandoned, the cursed sword fills the intent of humanity's champion, dooming him to ascend as the new Lich King. Arthas goes on to become one of the greatest threats in the history of Azeroth. The challenge of the heroic victory was elusive, and the easy path proved to be the road to tragedy.

When a hero is pressured by the perceived will of the father to move forward with the quest in a certain way, these restraints alter the course of the journey on a most fundamental level. While the person continues seeing themselves as the hero, their rejection of righteous sentiment may go unnoticed amidst the struggle to regain approval from the father. Arthas killed his father because he diverged from the rightful path, fully submitting to the will of Frostmourne as his new destiny. In this instance, the projection of villainy onto the father figure is a reflex emanating outward from the unbalanced ego of a fallen hero. The memory of a disappointed father leads to feelings of inadequacy that can never be truly vanquished through domination.

Whether the father is mortal or eternal in gaming fiction, this truth echoes beyond the final battle for supremacy in the narrative. A hero's only hope for preserving the good inside themselves is to become content with who they are. Once this is achieved, they can act free of manipulation from others because they are at one with themselves. Arthas fails in this aim, costing him everything he once stood for. The desire to find atonement with the father can be achieved, given the right choices in alignment with the hero's authentic self.

The scorned antihero façade of Kratos in the original God of War trilogy illuminates the dynamic of the son defeating the father. However, the continued story that started in the PlayStation 4 era shuffles this dynamic by sending the Ghost of Sparta through the nine realms of Norse mythology with his son, Atreus. Driven to honor his wife, Faye, as the fallen mother who binds them together, they are compelled to scatter her ashes from the tallest point in all the realms. They make this journey together as father and son.

Along the way, Kratos and Atreus have a varied rapport. Kratos himself can destroy an entire pantheon of gods, while Atreus is sickly and prone to making mistakes. After firing a stray arrow early in the journey, Atreus is scolded by Kratos for being unable to end the assault. Looking at his father, Atreus says, "I'm sorry." With indignation, Kratos reveals his stance as a parent by replying, "Don't be sorry. Be better." As the mission continues, Kratos warms up to Atreus in moments when he demonstrates potential in battle, and they come to rely upon each other the longer the campaign plays itself out. The loss of his mother has pushed Atreus into his father's world. When this occurs for any aspiring hero, the time for childish distraction ends. These opportunities to overcome the world's challenge force the hero to struggle as they work to accept all parts of themselves.

While it may be possible to find synergy with the father during the journey, the rivalry that forms as the son becomes a hero in their own right fosters a natural comparison, if not competition. Eventually, the son will have to challenge the father for the role of becoming the true hero of their own story. This emergence allows many games to present a scenario where the son must battle the father for the fate of the universe. When focused on the dynamic with the mother, this battle is fought instead to become the guiding force of the universe. As in life, at some point the child moves beyond the limitation of their parental figures to define their own lives. This transition is easier when they feel at one with themselves rather than being at odds with the impossible expectation of their progenitors.

The developmental shift from support to lead character reflects the transformation many young adults experience when leaving home to become independent for the first time. The purpose of change is to set out on our own merits and to see what we are truly capable of. While the story of *God of War* for Atreus begins with this support role, the prophecy of remarkable things is a constant harbinger of things to come, looming over them with each realm they travel together. Eventually, one will have to decide what fate has in store, as in many tales where the hero recognizes the importance of becoming a unified self in light of the father.

By combining all the skills and lessons of support accrued along the road of trials, the hero becomes ever more capable of stepping towards the Supreme Ordeal, provided they experience unity within the context of their origins. This inner peace is the rite of passage to claim the worthiness we must feel to begin acting on the world. Any game emphasizing the relational connections between the protagonist and their desire to make a difference can subliminally explore this. The gifts of the Goddess build the hero up, but the Father, whether symbolic or actual, must be reconciled with for the hero to achieve congruence and pursue their destiny.

THE ATONEMENT

Thc relationships that help the hero ascend toward the Supreme Ordeal allow the adventure to continue even when they doubt whether they are ready to succeed in the critical moment. In the end, the hero must still choose to approach the resolution. Although every quest is different, the plight of the world guides the hero to understand the value of their atonement act. In this way, the spirit of the challenge remains the same. The hero must overcome the conflicts of the id and superego to identify where they stand amidst everything that brought them to this singular point in their timeline.

Video games depict the struggle to find this inner congruence in many ways. To find atonement, the protagonist must confront the force in the narrative that taunts them about who they should be. Many lead characters display this difficulty; Tidus from *Final Fantasy X* should be a fantastic Blitzball player and should be able to defeat Sin to help Yuna save the world of Spira. Nero from *Devil May Cry 4* and *5* should be able to seize the demonic power that is his birthright to shift the balance in the never-ending moral conflict between Dante and Vergil. Arthas should have been able to save Lordaeron without requiring the power of Frostmourne, without losing himself to the corruption of the Lich King, and should have done so without assassinating his father.

Essentially, not every heroic quest ends successfully. Some heroes only comprehend the nature of evil once it is too late. Some game stories continue anyway, allowing the player to experience the aftermath of an unsuccessful narrative. This makes the chance for atonement either the player's responsibility or an event they must play through to witness. It can be viewed from either side as well. Playing as the son, you must make amends for past harms.

Playing as the father, you must correct a past failing. When done well, either the son or the father claims the chance to seize the Ultimate Boon and set things right.

When the hero fully understands their role in the quest, they have everything they need to succeed. Other times, critical insight is missing. The story of Booker and Elizabeth in *Bioshock Infinite* shatters their multiverse despite their best attempt to win peace for both heroes. Nearing the battle where a final escape from Columbia becomes possible, the heroes face Zachary Comstock. As the player, you watch in first-person as Comstock and Elizabeth argue over her childhood, her rightful place in Columbia, the nature of the False Prophet, and her severed finger. Before sharing the revelation, he orders, "Tell her, False Shepherd." You walk towards Comstock, slamming his head on the basin and drowning him in the baptismal bowl that symbolizes his hold over Columbia's people. His final words, mimicking those of Christ himself, fade with "It is finished." Just like that, he dies beneath the waters of rebirth.

One would assume this completes the threatening phase of the journey. However, Elizabeth realizes the terrifying truth about her connection to her over-controlling father and liberator. When she challenges Booker to reveal the truth Comstock alluded to, Booker's fate is set across the multiverse. The opportunity to atone for the past was right there, but the message was misunderstood. By tapping into his rage to claim justice for Elizabeth, he failed to understand who she was; Anna DeWitt. Booker stole his own daughter from himself in the timeline where he was baptized, choosing to be reborn by the name of Zachary Comstock. The personal hell of every multiverse hinted at in this game converges on this Supreme Ordeal. By reflecting on games like this, we see the psychoanalytic power of the battle between the id, ego, and superego through the characters representing each element of the person playing.

Noticing the opportunity to seize atonement in one's journey is how a person knows to reach out and make a choice. While stories such as *Bioshock Infinite* or *Warcraft III: Reign of Chaos* provide examples of a failed atonement, many games offer a chance to experience a victory of atoning in the narrative. The early entries of *Silent Hill* track a player's completion of specific side quest objectives and treatment of the other characters in the game to determine how the narrative would end for the style of play being demonstrated. By choosing execution and cruelty, the foggy hellscape determines that the player has betrayed the noble purposes of fighting for survival in service of their id and the resulting self-interest. By staying merciful and curious, the player dramatically improves the chance of gratification at the end of the horror. The measurement of choice makes the prospect of atonement much more connected to the behavior selection of the player in this series, making the concept of family and sentimentality even more powerful forces in a world consumed by terror.

Another example of enduring demonic forces comes from *Devil May Cry*. While earlier installments feature the conflict between the Sons of Sparda, Dante and Vergil, later episodes feature the aspiring demon hunter, Nero. While the lineage of Nero was initially in question, the signs were there to figure out how he fits into this seemingly eternal struggle between brothers. Nero has the same white hair, athleticism, attitude, and flair when wielding a sword. Despite these similarities, his atonement is learned through his differences, his right arm.

When glowing with demonic energy, Nero merges with his demonic heritage. His initiation into the demonic form of his predecessors is revealed when the Order of the Sword takes his girlfriend, Kyrie, captive. Being held back by the fallen angels,

Nero fails to prevent her abduction. In desperation, Sparda's power radiates from the enraged Nero, further confirming his connection to the fate of this quest. While Dante is the hero who makes victory possible this time around, Nero does claim Yamato, the same sword masterfully wielded by Vergil, ending the conflict over the city of Fortuna.

Nero's demonic initiation is a familiar rite in long-form storytelling using the monomyth. The quest for victory happens in parallel with the pursuit of atonement. When feeling incomplete in the role of "the hero," a character relies on others; the mentor, allies, and gifts granted to them from above. By achieving the mark of mastery, the hero gains the autonomy to pursue a solution for the conflict in their world. They can surpass the father symbol or forge a new path free of the shadow of the past, constantly reminding them of where they will fail.

When one challenge ends, another ordeal begins. This is the reality of every journey until the final quest has been completed. The sequel to Nero's introduction, *Devil May Cry 5*, starts with another failure to fulfill the father's mission. In the opening flashback, a cloaked figure enters the garage where Nero works on the Devil May Cry mobile headquarters. Guarded by shadow, the player has no idea who approaches. The cloaked figure rips Nero's demonic arm from his body, transforming it into the sword Yamato and opening a portal to another realm. Lying in a pool of his own blood, Nero can only watch as he loses consciousness.

While *DMC 5* contains many plot twists, the eventual conclusion is that Vergil committed this theft to return to full strength, destroy the earth, and finally defeat Dante. Nero offers to go after Vergil at the top of the demonic tower called the Qliphoth. Dante refuses to allow this to happen because, as it turns out, Vergil is Nero's father. In this instant, Nero sheds the orphan identity, realizing how he fits into the epic conflict that has defined the recent years of his life. Being left behind, Nero makes a phone call to Kyrie to share this revelation. She offers guidance to Nero, pushing him toward the moment of atonement:

> *"You always know which path is right and which is wrong. There's no need to doubt yourself."*

As the climactic battle between the two brothers continues in the stalemate it always is, Nero battles through his many levels to reclaim his demonic powers and unify them with the robotic prosthetics he has mastered since the theft of his original birthright.

Intent on dueling to the death, Dante and Vergil summon their full demon powers at the top of the Qliphoth tree. Before the killing clash can be landed, Nero catches them both in full flight, revealing his transformation to become one with his demonic lineage. He scolds their childish nature and vows not to let them kill each other. Vergil accepts this imposition as an alternative opportunity to duel. With that, the son crosses swords with his father to determine what will happen when the portal to Hell fully opens. Nero bests his father and creates a chance for harmony. Vergil and Dante leave the scene together to pull the Qliphoth and the demonic invasion through a portal to another realm, leaving Nero to safeguard Earth until they can find a way to return.

This is just one example of the moments which push the hero into the confrontation to gain atonement. Many motivations encourage the hero to keep searching for their catharsis amid a chaotic journey. Some heroes require a sense of belonging, as in the case of Nero. Others seek to vanquish the father to prove their superiority over them, as Arthas did during his descent into darkness. While Booker ends the life of Comstock in *Bioshock Infinite* to take his long-awaited revenge, it all amounts to a cycle of endless reflection, regret, and accepting the only way the story can truly end. For others, the sentiment of why the hero has arrived at that moment is an extra detail. All that matters is the sense of duty for a task that has been waiting a lifetime to be fulfilled.

An immeasurable number of games push their heroes to accomplish these moments. Even so, the heartfelt impact of the bond between Tidus and Yuna in *Final Fantasy X* displays multiple layers of resolve in the push toward the moment of atonement. Tidus begins the game as a glory-seeking Blitzball player living in the shadow of his father, Jecht. While this game in its own right can be reviewed as an example of the complete monomyth, the leadup to the party entering the World Nexus involves the confrontation with the father, the facing of destiny, and the sacrifice of the heroic self.

Although Tidus does exclaim, "I know it's selfish... but this is my story," it can be argued that he at least equally shares this distinction with Yuna, the summoner of Aeons. Her sense of duty holds firm at several points throughout the story, and by allowing their love to develop, both become more capable of facing the events that must occur for the Supreme Ordeal to become completed. Tidus must face his father despite his hate for him. Once Jecht transforms into Sin, Yuna must summon the Aeons to vanquish him, closing their world off permanently from the magic of these all-powerful spirits.

With the natural order of existence altered and Sin's presence removed, Tidus earns the father's respect just as Yuna fulfills her duty as a summoner. With both paths marked complete and destinies fulfilled, Tidus and Auron fade away as if the universe is reminding all those who have come to love them that they were never meant to exist at this point in time. The atonement is complete in all phases, with every hero restored precisely to where they were meant to be.

When we find this drive within ourselves, we, too, become at one with our existence as it has come to pass. While video games show us this path, life challenges us to become content with the present of each passing day. Our basic needs often fluctuate while we strive for greatness like the heroes that inspire us. Whether the goal is superiority, control, duty, or moving past regrets, our motivation benefits from believing the quest is worth the struggle.

The promise that a hero will confront the father symbol is the final rite of initiation connecting the Road of Trials to the staging grounds of the Supreme Ordeal. The transcendent moment depicts a hero in a stage that pushes beyond the basic concepts of good and evil while empowering them with a cosmic inspiration towards destiny. Their quests become what they were meant to become. Hope replaces fear, and success becomes only a function of time and possibility.

By stepping beyond internal conflict, the hero finally accepts who they are and appreciates pursuing who they were meant to be. Such a person breaks past their limits, even as their trials push them to achieve new heights. They enjoy the freedom to act in the world around them. This motivates the pursuit of changes that matter. When these feelings align, they grant a power that illuminates the spirit beyond the most challenging moments of darkness. This determination of self leads to the expression of oneness at our core state of being. The presence of spirit, encouraged by so many video games, allows us to accept ourselves no matter what lies ahead.

Pleasure Principle
- Unconscious drive to obtain pleasure / avoid pain
- A hero pursues power and domination over their competition
- Arthas kills his father, the King of Lordaeron in order to claim his full power as the Lich King

Reality Principle
- Personal drive to pacify the Id and maintain an intact sense of Self
- A hero pursues a set of morals they are comfortable with to achieve the best outcome for the world.
- Nero stops the petty feud between Dante and Vergil. He offers to fight his father instead for the fate of the world during the demonic incursion from the Qliphoth

- Operates as the Conscience of the individual.
- Reconciles the morals and laws imposed on a person by the powers of their world.
- A hero does their duty because of their sense of what is right, regardless of the personal conflict they experience.
- Yuna summons the Aeons and leads her party in defeating them in the Axis Mundi of Spira to fulfill her role as the Summoner.

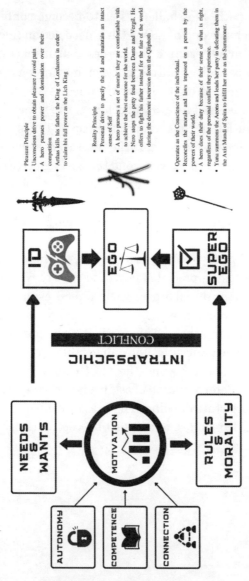

FIGURE 28. *How Self-Determination Theory Mediates Conflict in Game Characters*

CHAPTER XV

ENDURING THE SUPREME ORDEAL

Don't wish it were easier, wish you were better.

—Chief (Animal Crossing: New Leaf)

From the moment a player decides to answer the Call to Adventure, every stage of the journey prepares them to face the Supreme Ordeal. Long past are the times when the naive onlooker stood at the nascent moment, wondering what lies on the other side of an impossible threshold. The departure has passed into initiation, and the aspirations of the beginner must yield to the reality that the test of mastery is an inevitable trial they will eventually face.

Any time a person is tasked with overcoming challenges of progressing difficulty, their ability must improve if they are to move on to the next phase of the challenge. Like completing levels in a video game, people become ready by allowing themselves a chance to overcome obstacles they have not attempted before. By completing this transaction of trial-and-error time and time again, a person eventually gains enough experience to hold their own in the challenges of their endgame.

We see this developmental process repeated across many areas of life, such as jobs, careers, schooling, and even relationships. For an experience to align with the monomyth, each test a person faces must gradually build up their resolve to tap deeper into their unrealized potential.

The challenge of life is complex, involving many peaks and valleys as we work towards the return. The story of the Traveler in the game *Journey* depicts what it means to embark on such a quest. A player cannot hold forward for more than a minute at any point in this adventure before they come across a tombstone for an unnamed "other-Traveler." These are players that did not continue, and their journey was never completed. Since we do not see ourselves as a person who has faced their ultimate failure, we overlook the deeper meaning of the environmental storytelling in this world. We have a calling to answer, and any player who has seen this journey through to the end will not waste time mourning each passing gravesite. Instead, they will only take time to reflect on these truths during breaks in play as the winds prepare us for the final approach to the summit that called us to the journey in the beginning.

The Supreme Ordeal is the most difficult challenge in the journey toward fulfillment. The more stressful reality is that, for a person who has answered the call and followed the road of trials, faced their inner self, and strived to become one with what they have found, they must accept this challenge, no matter the risk. The ego may struggle to manage a strong self-belief, while abilities must overcome the struggle of the innermost self. When the persona merges with the actual self, revealing the holistic person, it is devastating when the journey does not conclude successfully.

The outcome affects the spirit until the meaning of the journey redefines this natural confluence into a new understanding. For this to occur, the ego requires hope.

No matter the activity, our greatest challenges have a way of singing to us at the core of our being. Over time, this harmony (or discord) shifts our self-esteem until we can admit the truth within. A game's impact on our spirit is often overlooked in preference to other parts of our being. In actuality, a person's spirit is how our ego finds hope. Moving beyond behavior and thought, the spirit becomes an essential life area for those standing firm in their Supreme Ordeal.

When we succeed, the most accessible feeling for many people is joy. When we lose, the parallel experiences come from fear, anger, and disappointment. Emotions influence how we view our leisure time, meaning they impact our entire construction of satisfaction with life. We may console ourselves with the thought that our losses are "just a game," but the reality is that we often care very much about our identity as a statement of where our competence lies. Spending significant amounts of time failing can cause a demoralizing sentiment that is hard to stop from spreading into other areas of our being.

The message often received about success and failure by many game players is designed for an older world: if we put in the work, we should expect success. If we did not experience success, it must be due to poor preparation, limited experience, or lacking talent.

In video games, however, it is common to lose the most difficult of challenges hundreds of times, and yet we keep trying because the game has trained us to believe in ourselves to make progress with each encounter. These ideas are not absolute truths, but consider what would happen if an adolescent in modern times were to need another attempt at the 8th grade. Would we examine the evidence and conclude with optimism, "They just needed to gain more experience. Let's try again!" The reality is that not all societal challenges allow for a growth mindset. As a result, unfair expectations for many developmental processes define the experience of growth, leaving the most efficient way for a person to thrive being their connection with leisure and fun.

The value we draw from each life area increases significantly when we see them as areas for growth and notice them thriving each day through our preferred activities. Even though academic or vocational accomplishment can lead to collecting external motivators like money, many alternate paths demonstrate the ability to help a person experience improved self-worth.

Each day offers only a limited amount of time to focus our energies and pursue our ideal mental state. Focusing on progression alone encourages a repeated pattern of behavior that causes a crisis in our sense of self. When creating our starting stat line in an RPG game like *Fallout*, we often aim for balance across each stat area. If not, we specialize. Balanced players handle most situations well enough to get by but are never "exceptional." In life, we use the phrase "jack of all trades, master of none" to describe this lack of focus. A specialized player will master specific skills while needing to minimize the use of stats holding near-zero development. Many of us value growth activities in areas that provide the greatest fulfillment.

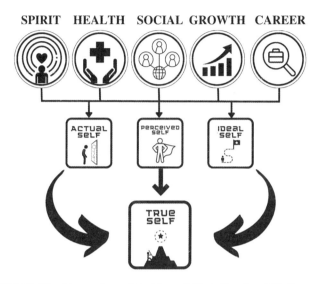

FIGURE 29. *The Formation of the True Self: A Gaming Life Perspective*

In many ways, the ordeal in life comes down to what we do with the time given to us. Like the wisdom of wizards in fiction, video games offer symbolic strategies that occasionally work better than more literal approaches. As a species, we create many shortcuts for interacting with our surroundings. Among the most powerful of these is play. While many types of play range from imagination to interaction within the physical world, video games allow the mind to access worlds where impossible challenges can be attempted repeatedly, safely. Some forms of play rely on an objective in the physical environment. Others encourage us to manipulate an object or achieve a goal through a list of socially accepted rules. Others use a symbolic style of play, casting the player into a mentally enacted drama. These differences occur digitally as well. The type of play in *The Last of Us* certainly differs from those in a fun-filled rove through a *Lego* adventure (*Star Wars, The Lord of the Rings,* etc.).

Regardless of the narrative, most games offer a challenge through combat to stage the struggle of the Supreme Ordeal. Through these fables, we develop wisdom just as those who formed the ancient myths did. In story form, the constant threat of disaster stays limited to our imaginations. This helps the challenge provide valuable lessons about the human condition in a more survivable way than living through the fictional event itself. Gaming is a chance to learn through creative processes brought to life through symbolism. They mentally transport a person safely into scenarios that are impossible to learn from without excessive risk of harm, outweighing the value of the experience. Video games unlock the opportunity to wonder.

Despite these benefits, video games are often seen as a childish form of play, and play is often forgotten as an essential aspect of adult life. The dissonance of abandoning the spiritual outlet play can become for the inner self damages our ability to accept how much play time can benefit us in the present, leaving us only with an inner struggle that is hard to explain due to what we are lacking. While it is true that task completion is important in many contexts, if our inner value depreciates when we focus on efficiency, the price of value becomes too steep as time moves on. When play connects with the spirit of a player, it transcends coping to become restorative in nature. Furthermore, some activities are not about task completion but rather about embracing presence within the core of our being. A person who can feel this experience routinely will undoubtedly complete more checkboxes in life when the tasks in question are both meaningful and occur at the right time in the flow of life.

In society, there is a fear of the unknown regarding gamers and whether they will conform to traditional development standards to reach their potential in the Ordinary World. Our connection with play is a primary casualty of this concern. Regardless of the developmental growth of the player, the ordeal revolves around negotiating with those in our world that games carry benefits.

Progression is all about checking hundreds of boxes seamlessly through willing engagement as the player enjoys a variety of growth processes. Furthermore, video games inarguably teach this better than the world does. Just look at all of the websites and learning systems that seek to gamify the user experience. This trend is an admission of the power video games wield to help us learn anything we find interesting in life. For something to be considered a game, it must contain a goal, rules, feedback, and voluntary participation. Quests can be reviewed at any time. Attempting them involves instant feedback when rules of life are enforced. Despite this power, few opportunities in the world (outside of eSports and streaming) enable people to play video games as a job. Video games teach some of life's most challenging lessons, yet unlike with work, we happily welcome the experience.

Video games are among the most potent forms of play for generating new ideas. The fact that video games occur on screens is more a byproduct of how many activities across the world happen on screens in every context. Claiming that achievements completed through a screen are less valuable than those experienced in physical locations is irresponsible in the modern era. After all, 319 billion messages are sent via email every day. Are these not actual communications? This stigma filters into passive views on work-from-home and telehealth services as well. Logically, it is ridiculous to argue that a person has not attended therapy because they have never sat in the same physical space as their clinician. Finally, degrees are earned online similarly to those earned in traditional classrooms. If a person uses their acquired abilities to carry out a task in the workforce after several years of embracing the learning process on a screen, it would be naïve to argue that their vocational role is not aligned with their identity.

If serious tasks are easier to achieve in a meaningful way using a screen, this argument becomes eternal. Instead of worrying about our connection with joy, it is better to accept that "play is play" in any context, and a world existing so much on screens will engage in both work and play on screens. This brings every frame in our rate of existence into focus. Accepting this truth connects us with the divine state, where momentary joy becomes a hope of learning to fulfill our life's journey. While every person can decide their comfort level, it benefits us to understand the role of play in allowing us to become the best version of ourselves. In this way, we elect our intrinsic motivation to guide us along the gamer's journey.

Whether we win or lose the battles we face on any given day, play remains a powerful learning process. By noticing the sublime process in our gameplay, we experience the divine state so many of the myths of past centuries would describe using gods and heroes. Games create these states through elements of flow, progression, and heroism, and this lets us believe that no matter what challenges we face in life, the challenge was designed so we will find the path to victory. As long as we hold firm to our hope, we will endure any setback. We just have to be granted the option to press "Continue."

 ## LIFE VS. GAMING: SUFFERING DEFEAT

While it is helpful to notice the gamified elements in life, it is crucial to recognize that challenges are only sometimes meant to be leisurely. When an accomplishment is considered serious, the challenge should be approached with a matching amount of respect. Nevertheless, the spiritual connection between our goals and the plight of our favorite heroes still becomes an exciting opportunity to develop confidence in ourselves as an intelligent, capable problem-solver. When the hero directs the knowledge from the World Nexus towards the ultimate task, their sincerity assures us that their world has a chance for redemption, even when the battle seems lost. These moments allow us to save the world (albeit a fictional one), no matter how restricted our influence may feel on a casual day we experience. Through our understanding of symbolic play, we improve our outlook in life whenever we project the same assurance that our efforts are meaningful any time success and defeat lie in the balance.

Resolve alone is only sometimes enough. In the most challenging circumstances, the Supreme Ordeal pushes the hero to their limit break. Every quest has an intent, but not every quest intends to break the party apart. When a challenge breaks the hero down to the core of their being, the player is assured that the destination ends with the Supreme Ordeal alone. This specific challenge tests a person's willingness to sacrifice in order to move on. It excises hope from the hero's will until they realize the true cost of victory and still decide to push forward. If they triumph, their world experiences restoration. When the ordeal conquers the hero outright, the reign of darkness continues until the resurrection of the current hero or the coming of the next.

Finding the Supreme Ordeal in a video game narrative requires the player to recognize the connection the hero has formed with the world itself as well as their party members. In some games, the action of the villain determines how the main adventure leads to the ultimate challenge. This event occurs in one of two spots in the Three-Act Structure. The first is near the middle of the plot, allowing the turn of events to propel the hero into the acts preparing them for the showdown with evil. The other is as a revelation during the final confrontation. This option manifests as the key to victory, a missing element the hero can claim only when they have the strength (or player skill) to fulfill the requirements for saving the world.

"Embrace your dreams, and...whatever happens...protect your honor as SOLDIER. Come and get it!"

— The final battle of Zack Fair, Crisis Core: Final Fantasy VII (2007)

The spiraling universe of *Final Fantasy VII* acculturates the players into experiencing these forms of loss at both phases of the storytelling. For an example of endgame trauma, in *Crisis Core: Final Fantasy VII*, Zack's final stand preserves every part of his identity that defines his status as a hero. He saves his friend, Cloud, from Shinra Corporation, dying in the process. In making this choice, he preserves his honor as SOLDIER, a status he proudly reminds everyone of countless times throughout his adventure whenever he arrives to save the day. Zack passes the Buster Sword to a traumatized Cloud as his final legacy. In the end, he allows the memory of his love for Aerith to fill his mind one last time. Zack's journey ends, allowing Cloud's to begin.

Born from trauma and loss, Cloud drags the sword toward Midgar. Seven years later, Cloud is hired by Avalanche to blow up a Shinra Reactor, signaling the selection of the new hero and the next attempt to save the world from the corrupted SOLDIER, Sephiroth.

"I'll come back when it's all over."

— The final words of Aerith Gainsborough, Final Fantasy VII (1997)

While Crisis Core ends with the loss of the central protagonist, the main game, *Final Fantasy VII*, is equally famous for a major plot twist at the end of disc one. When Cloud passes Aerith selling flowers (a job encouraged by Zack), it is unknown to the player how closely connected she is to Shinra. When she joins the party, she has the most vital healing ability among your allies as you battle to escape the central city.

Due to Aerith's magical connection with the Lifestream, the player appreciates her role in the party for many hours of gameplay. Her death in the "City of the Ancients" shocks unsuspecting players significantly. While the general expectation for a turn-based RPG is that your party will be available throughout the campaign, this game chooses to traumatize the player by destroying the comfort zone. Sephiroth's victory forces the player to regroup, providing a parallel trauma between the player and game characters while both decide how to move forward. While it is fulfilling to complete *Final Fantasy VII*, the reality that defeat can be suffered at any point in the quest reminds us how real consequences will challenge our hopes as a gamer.

Although these stories live on in the minds of RPG fans, the idea of video games as a legitimate platform for exploring complex concepts must become more evident to those outside gaming communities. Fictitious deaths can create similar emotions at limited ranges as losing loved ones, friends, and family. Yet, learning in academic settings seldom turns to these forms of storytelling as examples of the human condition.

Seeing the Digital Mind Wave in Crisis Core as a representation of Zack's memories of his friends during combat is a fun way to inject randomness into each battle. However, seeing memories of Aerith shoot across the screen as Zack begins to fail, losing hope and then realizing his life is ending, these storytelling innovations intellectually reveal the power of our mind to use memories to hold onto the core of our identities in the face of any crisis. While this is one small example of how games innovate through narrative moments, each decade sees the release of countless game experiences that offer powerful metaphors for understanding the world to players. All of this potential can be found in the hobby of video games, and yet they are often demonized as a childish pursuit where time could have been spent being more productive. In this way, the final ordeal is not actually the gameplay challenge, but is rather the question of how any player can navigate a fulfilling game experience without appearing immature, reckless, or irresponsible with their time.

Video games tell their stories through a consistent message worthy of being repurposed across any life circumstance where passionate players have need of them. By representing the modern approach to mythological storytelling, the exploits of game characters inspire all forms of person; the self, the sibling, the friend, the family, and anyone seeking to accomplish the greatest hopes they hold within the inner cave of the psyche. Unfortunately, games often prompt arguments, judgment, and unfavorable labeling of the player.

Using an example of a gamer excited by Bioware games, conversational trees can easily teach someone to understand the consequence of word choice. Rather than appreciating the activity, their parents (representing society) were constantly concerned with how a "silly game" would ruin the family dynamics whenever the façade of the status quo was not followed. Time spent gaming is better served elsewhere, even though removing sources of fun carries numerous consequences. This misguided edict increased the player's stress, causing catastrophic struggles with self-esteem, and removed the sensation of positive reinforcement from the home since gaming was removed and the parent-child interaction could not replace the lack of positivity gaming was offering. Living in a dissonant household, the gamer hired a therapist to find a conversational partner who could be supportive, and reflected on how the Bioware discussions respond more effectively to their choices than those in their homes. This gamer only wanted a conversation where they felt heard and their ideas mattered. That dynamic in the family was always the real boss fight, not the time spent playing video games.

Embracing the monomyth as an endpoint in our passion for video games allows others to become active in our quest to find our best selves through our inner worlds. When this happens, we engage our surroundings with confidence. A player in this mode will understand their reinforcers. They will be content in their gaming and embrace an environment that is interested in their passions. Then the ordeal rescinds from reality, letting the person become content until their joy approaches the edge of nirvana.

In mythological terms, the nirvana construct balances eternity and time. Psychological flow becomes a central aspect of this harmony. It is marked by a passion respected by those who embrace our true selves. While eternity extends forever in all directions, time is the present experience that flows away once we recognize it. As two aspects of the same energy, they relate to each other the same as victory and defeat.

While the supreme ordeal ushers the unready player into defeat, the ready player will rely on resilience until their victory is achieved. By engaging the hero metaphor, finding the balance in nirvana through a game only happens when a player reflects on their time playing a game and believes honestly and completely that this time was spent valuably. If the elements of our ordinary world have not evolved into the illuminating support we need, then we must believe this enlightenment can be found by becoming extraordinary. This is why it matters so much where we play, what we play, and who remains in our lives to see us grow from the challenges that pushed us to our limits in admirable ways. These are the truths we take with us into the forever of our lives.

AXIS MUNDI: THE SOURCE OF THE SCHEMA

The center of existence reveals the origin of all things. Mythology labels this space as the Axis Mundi or the World Axis. This space serves as the fulcrum between the opposing energies of Heaven and Earth. Psychologically, it becomes a projective test for the characters, prompting a convergence between their hopes and deepest fears. In this space, a vengeance-driven villain will see an opportunity to rend the planet, destroying all who have wronged them. A doubting hero will fear the unlimited potential for destruction and assume the end is nigh.

From a cognitive perspective, the strongest parallel to the Axis Mundi is called the schema. In simple terms, the schema is a core belief that defines the flow of thought for how a person interacts with their world. It explains our beliefs about ourselves, resulting in our thoughts, emotions, and reactions in our daily experiences. From these converging concepts, namely our perception of reality and the World Axis in our myths, we connect deeper with the boundless possibilities of our imagination. This unifies our values and motivations to pursue congruence in fulfilling both in one harmonious action.

The Supreme Ordeal requires everything within us to perform the unifying rite in the proper place to end the quest. A test must challenge the player's skill to be perceived as meaningful. It cannot remind us of the ordinary world and its challenges. Boredom leads to complacency. Stress encourages growth when belief endures. Coming through in this way makes us proud to display our performance for all to see. Completing the rite of passage unlocks the approach to the ordeal, signaling the end of casual questing in showing how ready we are.

Many games place the player on a direct path to the center of existence by continuing the main quest in pursuit of the highest levels of mastery. By stepping into the World Axis, the character loses the naivete of their old self forever. When they step out of the nexus where their world was formed, they begin understanding the greater context of the heroic quest. In this way, the schema becomes connected with the flow of all things, advancing far beyond the subjective limits of a normal perspective.

This growth occurs when Link enters the Temple of Time. By claiming the Master Sword, the entire flow of time is opened to him. As timelines open, Link can use the destination points to save Hyrule. Primordial energies allow Link to pass through the World Axis, the only way he could ever fulfill this quest. The version of Link exiting the Temple is infinitely more capable of seeing the world for what it is. This Link is reborn as the "Hero of Time."

Rebirth is not always literal in video games. Still, the symbolic purpose from death to resurrection matters far more in stories that follow the monomyth. In *The Last of Us*, Joel is impaled after a fall midway through the journey. This pushes the player to control Ellie for an entire segment, significantly shifting the strategies needed to overcome the threat of this world. From a character perspective, this helps Joel and Ellie value each other more as the roles of caregiver and guardian become a two-way relationship. This creates a reborn sense of trust between them, aiding their quest as they move forward together again. Before, the roles were dependent. Now, both characters have found their resilience, achieving a healthy independence while still relying on their partner when the challenge gets too rough for a solo approach.

Other games allow the protagonist to die over and over, even while the story continues. The power of gaming is that a player can fail repeatedly and still feel accomplished by their time in-game. The choose-your-own-adventure dynamic is built into how we hope to succeed in our play. This happens when games offer multiple endings, like in many survival horror titles like *Resident Evil* or *Silent Hill*. It can also be done in narrative-based games where players must rapidly interact with Quick-Time-Events (QTEs). *Detroit: Become Human* uses this feature to create a multi-ending adventure across several playable characters (either living or dead). This game opens with an android named Connor being sent to investigate a rogue AI (Daniel) holding a human girl hostage on a rooftop. There are many ways this mission can end. Many of them result in the girl being saved. Not all of these endings result in Connor being functional at the end of the negotiation. Regardless of how this mission ends, Connor (the same RK800 or a "reborn" model) is back on the search to continue the next chapter.

The story continues even when the player is unsuccessful. Much like in life, we can expect to succeed every time on the first try, but this is seldom a healthy realistic expectation for how life will play out. The hope for success relies on understanding the full power found by embracing contradiction. For Link to save the present of the future, he must move things around in the present of his past. For Joel to be strong enough to escort Ellie, she must be strong enough to hold firm when Joel is at his weakest. To fix the relationship between humanity and their AI, Connor must find a way to befriend his partner who blames AI for all the loss in his life. For each of these characters to succeed, they must overcome the belief that no solution is possible. Moving beyond this schema, each scenario eventually contains one glorious path, the "good ending," where everything works out positively for the characters and the world against all odds.

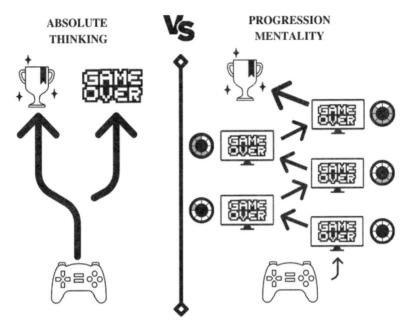

FIGURE 30. *Playing Through Defeat to Achieve Progression*

Learning progression mentality is difficult, but maintaining it can be grueling in certain situations. The contradiction between wanting to be successful and knowing that one has to become willing to fail to achieve victory is much easier to absorb in a video game than in the things which matter the most in our lives. The idea that if we are talented, we will be successful is a hard-wired message for many people, formed through a constant reinforcement process starting in childhood. The reality is that the ability to achieve success is not in our talent but in our willingness to keep trying until we find the best path forward.

For easy challenges, success could occur on the first or second try. The most meaningful tasks, however, might only happen once the attempts total in the thousands. Grit offers one of the best paths forward for this victory-seeking mentality. By defining the combination of personal traits known as (G) growth, (R) resilience, (I) initiative, and (T) tenacity, these traits are primarily learned through rehearsal rather than being innate to our being. While games instantly offer another chance at the moment of non-success, life goals usually require passing time for the next attempt. Resources must be replenished. The calendar keeps moving forward until another opportunity arrives. Regardless of whether the setting of the challenge happens physically or virtually, we all can identify one thing we wish to try again. The request to "continue" and the countdown asking if we will try again are displayed on the screen, but the idea serves us well for any goal that connects with our heroic journey. The power to keep moving through the core of our world relies on our determination to see the quest through to the end. This trait only falters when we lose the willingness to keep going.

The environment created by the World Axis metaphor creates an attachment style that connects us, our beliefs, and our world. While we intend to complete our quest, the messages we find in this critical source of personal meaning range across all types of sentiment; encouragement, trauma, stress, or indifference, all depending on our natural surroundings. In childhood, parents create these realities. In later phases of life, our personal habits, intimate partners, social circle, hobbies, and career path take over the responsibility of cradling our identity.

These attachments are reflected in how we share our passion for video games in our relationships. A secure attachment enjoys the conversations about gaming and the challenges we invest our creative energies into with interest. Like the Temple of Time for Link, the environment offers a non-threatening path forward.

An anxious attachment is like the Forgotten City in *Final Fantasy VII*. The party is free to roam around and enjoy the ancient sights, but if you wander into the wrong places, a boss will attack, or even worse, a member of your party will be lost forever. The challenge of this attachment is that you never know when the challenge will arise to threaten your homeostasis. Everything feels fine until it is not. When a place that should be safe proves to be dangerous, this shock becomes a trauma that is remembered when attempting to connect with future opportunities that should be similarly "safe."

The third style, avoidant attachment, is shown to us through many of the final areas of the *Kingdom Hearts* games. The Keyblade Graveyard, once the site of an ancient battle, is now lifeless. There is no reason to go there except to exorcise demons that haunt you. Only people seeking connection with the dead go to places like these. While it is a core area for the story, and as a result, leads to other sites one could deem the true Axis Mundi of *Kingdom Hearts* (The Final World, The Realm of Darkness, Scala ad Caelum / The Stairway to the Sky), it is one marked by devastation which prevents the universe of this story from holding onto its light. A person living in this universe will either vehemently avoid this place, or brave through it to reclaim their energy from those who have taken it away.

Hostile attachment is similar to the avoidant system. In a gaming context, this is analogous to the structure of Mementos in *Persona 5*. While not directly tied to the main story, this dungeon allows the Phantom Thieves to explore the collective subconscious of Tokyo. This multi-tiered dungeon is designed to reflect the neuroses from Jungian psychology in a gaming style. As a result, the hidden secrets of the shadow self from many NPC's create optional challenges for the party as they level up. The hostile nature offers endless battles across the subway tunnels. The Phantom Thieves engage in battle every few seconds if they want to survive a place like this. As a result, the leveling-up potential for this space is infinite as long as the player is willing to spend the time defending themselves.

The constant battle of the world center places the character face to face with the materials of their creation. Even with this power freely flowing around them, the player must focus on the present challenge to understand the knowledge of how to thrive in the world they inhabit. This opportunity is grasped by gathering insight from every experience leading to the Supreme Ordeal. By completing every task within the Ordeal, receiving the gifts of the Goddess, finding atonement with the father, and mastering the skills needed for each trial, the player becomes ready to find the ultimate reward in every world that expands their resolve.

Finally, we approach the point of no return. Win or lose, the hero must step forward towards this point in their universe and attempt to pierce the veil of what is known, becoming more extraordinary than they ever realized they could be when answering the call so long ago. All the lessons a player has learned have led to this one moment. Once you reach this point, only one choice remains; to accept your place in the final challenge.

 ## NADIR: THE DARKEST MOMENT

Applying life lessons from fiction is an inexact science depending on how the psyche internalizes the message of the epic tale. Fables, myths, and legends are all concepts for passing on stories to entertain new audiences through a mask of moral value. When we aspire to mimic something, our choices reflect the same qualities of the original tale while using the elements available in our reality. This metaphor is daunting when it comes to the Supreme Ordeal.

The ultimate defeat, if experienced in life and not just in game form, is when the game becomes a permanent escape, a purgatory, where entertainment distracts from living life into further stages of the journey. The player is lost, searching for a bliss they can never fully enjoy. They have lost themselves to their ordeal.

The power of myth is that these stories teach us about hope. It helps us to face the true challenges of our story, and teaches us to embrace the heroic example that echoes across the subconscious levels of our being. Video games wield the same power for inspiration that is found inside all eras of archetypal storytelling. By projecting our ego ideals into impossible situations, these stories unlock a mindset of fulfillment for the quest we call life. When we fail in a game, it teaches us to ready ourselves for another attempt. When we have a non-success in life, we are demoralized. The mythological language refers to this as the nadir.

Nadir is a devastating phenomenon. Used in gaming stories, nadir represents the most catastrophic defeat a hero can suffer. When the chance to ascend is right there, sometimes the hero fails to reach it. There are consequences to this setback. The realm is doomed (for now). People suffer. Society eventually loses the ability to hope, resulting in future heroes no longer noticing the call to adventure. The potential for change feels outlandish, and the burden of questing would only prove futile.

The catastrophe of the past allows nadir to influence the opening of many of the most impactful game worlds. Moving past the endless suffering is a compelling context for the gamer's journey, and has been used to establish the struggle of new game narratives time and again.

Iterating on the monomythical formula, the Soulsborne genre (*Dark Souls*, *Bloodborne*, *Elden Ring*) repeatedly starts the player in the nadir state. The call for the Chosen Undead / Tarnished to step forth and restore the world to its former glory calls to many game players. Restoring a world so lost to chaos would certainly imbue the hero with a tale of never-ending renown. The barrier between life and death is dissolved by stepping forward into an already defeated world (as a hero already dead). To overcome the nadir, the hero, whether in a tale of hope or suffering, must break the veil of death's dominion over life to make the impossible possible.

While the nadir is common in mythology, video games add more power to the experience than a listener at the Agora in Athens would have imagined during a philosophy lecture. While listening in Ancient Greece, the pressure to tell the tale faithfully falls on the speaker. The audience only has to listen. In a game, there is a balance between avoiding defeat within a narrative and doing the same through mastery of gameplay. If the nadir impacts gameplay, the challenge being played is the most difficult of the game experience on a technical level. Dexterity and reaction time are being tested to see if the player has reached the pinnacle of ability envisioned during the game's creation. If Nadir is functioning on a narrative level, the story has taken a turn to test the character growth of the player. It will also explore who they have become in their play experience on a philosophical level.

One version of the nadir, "The Night Voyage," asks the hero to travel into darkness and survive. In *Until Dawn*, the player is tasked with making choices as a set of eight teenagers being hunted overnight in a dark mountain cabin. The game revolves around "The Butterfly Effect" in a gamified format, with the objective being to help as many characters as possible survive until the break of dawn. While jump scares and riveting chases from deranged killers and monsters alike create suspense in this game, the actual test on the player is their ability to regulate their morality through their fear for the characters. Even minor misjudgments result in death.

The final test in this story occurs when each character's path converges on the cabin. In the final moments before sunrise, the player faces a rapid-fire sequence of button-pressing reactions and holding still moments, challenging every impulse the player has developed throughout the campaign. Staring down fear and death as one and the same, the player must wield a sense of calm that shows they are not fazed by the threat of death at the hands of the monsters in the story. Each mistake at this phase reduces the number of characters who reach the end by one.

Finding peace amid death is the only way to overcome the nadir of the final conflict. Many games encourage this, whether through their storytelling or game design. In an entertainment medium where death is the primary feedback mechanism, passing on to the next challenge becomes the fundamental source of accomplishment for the player.

The nadir moment teaches us about ourselves. Even if we hope to accomplish something, it must be more than desire that drives us. By learning how to play regardless of the outcome, nadir loses its ability to incite fear within us. It is the fear of failure that prevents us from achieving our destiny. Being willing to lose is often the only path to our victory.

We continue through our defeats in life and absorb them as part of the story. Even in video games, this becomes the pivotal lesson of our journey. Perfection is an illusion. Our best opportunities for success come from how progression motivates us to crawl out of our darkest moments. Every game is designed for the player to be capable of completing it. Still, for some adventures, fate and destiny are not enough. True heroism is found when the power of opposites, success and failure, come together to form a unified message that non-success actually leads us closer to our goals. No matter what we hope to become through our adventure, we approach our goals with the same inspiration we have when we push for victory in our favorite games. After all, we value success less when there is no chance of defeat.

CHAPTER XVI

APOTHEOSIS & THE
ULTIMATE BOON

*The right man in the wrong place can make all the
difference in the world.*

—G-Man (Half Life 2)

N o matter how difficult the challenge is, the player believes
they can win because they know they are playing a video
game. The game is designed to measure every facet of
performance objectively, moment by moment. As a result, all
the player needs to do is stay focused and execute the proper
strategy. Ultimately, they either win via learned industriousness
or exhaust themselves until learned helplessness takes hold.
When the opening for final victory presents itself, the player
will feel the power of the moment while they push the winning
sequence of buttons, winning the fight once and for all.

The opportunity to complete a task satisfactorily is always
possible, and without debate, in video games. Engaging in a phys-

ical activity requires access, a willingness to be patient to receive the related reward, and aiming to be effective despite imperfections in the activity. These factors are critical in the experience of motivation. Video games improve upon this experience magnificently. Any goal we have is measured objectively within the structure of the game. Rewards are delivered immediately based on performance, and fairly. As a result, we want to continue playing them because the way they treat us is fair.

When a goal becomes autotelic, meaning the value to the person is meaningful on an internal level within the participant without relying on external rewards, the flow experience becomes more likely. Balancing ability and challenge results in many sensations of heightened fun experience during peak engagement with the goal. Flow unlocks the most profound connection a player can feel with an activity, whether during a riveting guitar solo in *Rock Band* or while completing a challenging boss battle in *Dark Souls*. We lose track of time and thought, merging with the activity to demonstrate perfection in our experience. At the highest level of challenge, this is what it takes to bring out the best performance from a player in any activity. This is what is required to overcome the greatest challenge.

As the hero encounters the Supreme Ordeal, they are exposed to the ultimate challenge in their journey. The amplification of the challenge which began at the Road of Trials has now pushed the hero into direct conflict with their toughest opponent. With each minor victory, the hero moves closer to the ultimate test of their resolve, revealing the endgame boss in their final form. As they wish for relief from the nadir, the hero may struggle until hope seems lost. For those who keep playing, who keep improving, and who believe there has to be a way to succeed, the moment of crystalized ability occurs. At this point, the gamer has finally reached apotheosis.

In mythological terms, apotheosis is a state of being that occurs in the moments when a person's awareness expands beyond normal existence and achieves a level of divine presence. Many video games show a moment when God-like power is seized by the hero to help them overcome an insurmountable threat. As a reality-based parallel, psychological flow perfectly balances the holistic awareness of a person with the core of their being, which allows their performance to ascend to wondrous levels. Flow only activates this performance once ludology converges with consciousness. As far as the gaming experience is considered, if a player truly experiences flow in their play, this synergy becomes the moment of apotheosis.

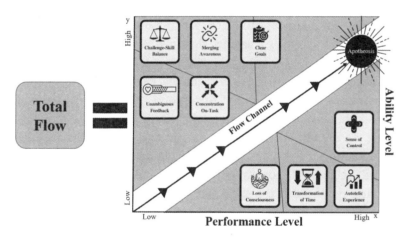

FIGURE 31. *Total Flow and the Experience of Apotheosis in Play*

The unparalleled chance at victory found in these moments cannot be predicted as easily as other elements of the play experience. If a player consciously hopes to achieve this victory, they will be fixated on ensuring it comes to fruition. For apotheosis to occur, the player must allow time to pass naturally in the background of their consciousness. Their concentration must fade beyond awareness, releasing control in the player's mind to allow them to become one with the meaningful task. Feedback leads clearly to the goal, and the person now perfectly flows into the activity without conscious effort. The player has become the game itself until the outcome allows them to stop playing and enjoy whatever result has occurred.

The flow experience can be challenging to explain to those who have never experienced it. However, in the early days of eSports, one moment changed the concept of mastery in flow for video games in a way anyone can see and understand. Evo Moment #37.

On August 1, 2004, at the Evolution Championship Series, Daigo Umehara faced Justin Wong in the semifinals for *Street Fighter III: Third Strike*. This match featured Wong playing Chun Li, while Umehara selected Ken. Having only one pixel of health left on his bar, Umehara seemed destined for defeat in this match. Knowing this, Justin Wong queued up his Super Art II, a move featuring 15 rapid-fire kicks in sequence, each containing only 6 of sixty frames for the opponent to respond with a perfect parry. In this setup, just one successful hit for Chun Li wins the match for Wong. As the combo starts, Ken parries each kick in the sequence by predicting the attack before it even starts. As the combo continued, Umehara continued stringing together every parry, reacting on the control stick every tenth of a second in perfect sync with the animations of the fight. The audience's excitement clashes with his opponent's disbelief as each block staves off elimination. Every hit was blocked, and the combo ended with Ken still alive. After stopping a final kick, Ken, controlled with excellence by Umehara, returns the aggression with a 12-hit combo that drains the remaining third of Justin Wong's health bar, ending the match fantastically and creating Evo Moment #37.

In examples like this one, the elements of preparation and mastery with the selected character alone would not have been enough. This moment is a perfect confluence of factors that allowed the player to capture the moment by displaying a perfected psychological flow in their gameplay. Unlike in books or movies, where storytelling invites the passive audience to enjoy, in video games, the action has to be performed by the participant for a moment to achieve meaning. Millions of people turn to video games daily for various reasons, and many of them hinge on the desire to find a moment like this and successfully capture it. When the nine components of flow are present at once (challenge-skill balance, merging of action and awareness, clarity of goals, unambiguous feedback, concentration on the task at hand, sense of control, loss of self-consciousness, transformation of time, autotelic experience), the player can experience a transcendent moment. However, this rise into a perfected awareness of the game can fade into regret if fiero, a moment of power in flow, is not attained. The quest for the ultimate victory gets closer and closer with each attempt. This chance to claim our win helps us merge our hopes with the story of the character through our gameplay. For the perfect moment to happen, both must merge together to create a moment we will never forget.

The one meaningful moment is a powerful motivator in life. This is the sensation people chase in their addictions. It drives them to push further than everyone else to fulfill their dreams. It sets the person apart from the rest of the world in the areas of the life journey that matter the most to them. The apotheosis of a person is attained when they step into that role of fulfilled potential and demonstrate it impressively. If apotheosis is the heightened experience of being during gameplay, fiero is the moment of ultimate victory.

The meaningfulness that drives positive psychology towards self-actualization often seems abstract, but can be easier to calculate in the type of success players fulfill when playing video games.

Even if a gaming moment is only an example of what humanistic theories urge us to strive for, the ability to understand these accomplishments is a valuable example for therapeutic parallels. These moments in life are often rehearsed, but are impossible to fabricate. They cannot be experienced using a formula. Practicing for the moment requires a person to be ready for anything without knowing when the moment will present itself. The final opening where the achievement becomes possible that has been anticipated for hundreds (and even thousands) of hours, and still cannot be explained to those who are not living their own journey. Even with the implementation of trophy systems to tell gaming populations what should feel like an accomplishment, the truly autotelic endeavors that do not require mechanical kudos are what truly help game players feel accomplished whenever they achieve an improbable success.

The prestige of turning an epic defeat into a surprising victory creates a chance for us all to come together and talk about the time when we did this fantastic thing. The apotheotic moment represents catharsis, as the worry that we can fail fades into realizing we have achieved our moment. When we talk with others about what we have done, we now enter the conversation as someone who has completed the challenge instead of someone still climbing the ladder. The transformation alters what the game means for us moving forward. We are now more deeply connected with the lineage of the game. Like the hero in the monomyth that vanquishes the overwhelming evil, we now must decide what challenge is next. Do we start a new difficulty, collect all the relic items, or move forward into life's next great endeavor? As one who has mastered the great challenges of one virtual world, we will either select the next challenge from a list given to us, or we can decide to use what we have learned about ourselves to triumph over the next goal that feels exciting enough for us to build a new journey around.

THE NATURE OF THE ULTIMATE REWARD

How a hero receives the ultimate reward depends heavily on their motivation for the journey. These drives occur simultaneously throughout both the internal and external levels of each act of the story. For example, the complete story arc for Kratos in the original *God of War* series depicts a scorned antihero seeking revenge on an entire pantheon of gods whom he blames for his past wrongs. The climax of each game in this series features a moment where the apotheosis requires a literal "god mode" for Kratos to become able to impose his will against his opponents. The first of his conquests is revenge against Ares, the original god of war. Next is the accidental bout with Athena, who sacrifices herself to prevent the fall of Olympus. This tirade ends with the final duel between Kratos and his father, Zeus.

For extrinsic rewards, Kratos gains godhood, the title of God of War, and the realization that he has always been a demigod. On the intrinsic level, however, Kratos never feels the reward of these victories because he never finds a way to become content within himself. He thirsts for vengeance at the expense of his chance to make peace with his past. His selfish drive to outlast the entirety of Greek reality causes everything he could connect with to fall into ruin. For such a hero, it is fitting that he would disappear without a trace, leaving all to wonder in which civilization he will resurface and which pantheon of gods may suffer his fury next.

The Prince of Persia: The Sands of Time demonstrates a completely different form of virtue in its hero. Having just witnessed the Maharajah's daughter fall to her death, the Prince, Dastan, rejects the evil Vizier's offer of eternal life by plunging the dagger of time into the hourglass that holds the sands of time. He rewinds the entire game, returning the player to the beginning. This time, Dastan warns Farah of the Vizier's treachery and battles the traitor to the death before her. She does not, however, believe his story because she has not lived out the adventure which was forgotten in the reversing of time. Dastan has made the selfless choice to save everyone he loves at the cost of his desires. Intrinsically, Dastan has restored reality to a version where the Vizier has been defeated, even if he is the only one who knows the full sequence of events that made this possible. No extrinsic reward is possible though, since Dastan has forfeited the memory of all that occurred for everyone but himself.

The imagery of mythical rewards serves many purposes beyond these character moments. They signify the completion of a quest chain, a status symbol that connects the player to those in the community with the same drive for certain challenges. The boon can be a new weapon, effectively enhancing the avatar's power as they face further challenges. A reward can add new abilities so the player feels capable in situations that used to be hopeless for the heroic quest. The gifts can revive the power hidden within, or connect the hero deeper with the forces that govern their virtual world. These rewards are often gifted near the end because to have them earlier would negate the growth required of the hero. The mythical nature of each relic channels a renewed energy into the hero as they seek to accomplish the task of the journey against the backdrop of infinity represented by the World Navel.

Like the bell of summoning from *Elden Ring*, drawing aid from those living in the beyond, game players are constantly reminded that the energy needed to overcome a problem is limited only by their imagination. The reminder of a larger existence for worlds of fiction can also encourage players to take the time for reflection on the personal, physical, social, and spiritual levels of their existence. For those who have not yet achieved their ultimate reward, understanding what specific resources they have yet to find in life can enhance their motivation to keep searching. When we stop searching for our complete existence, we become ghosts, locked in servitude, waiting for the bell to signal another conflict for us to resolve. When we are finally able to seize the reward, we release ourselves from this purgatory and achieve agency in our lives just as those who have achieved it before us. This in turn, allows us to decide how best to continue our quest in the future. We go from completing the task because someone else has summoned us to, to being capable of choosing the task for ourselves and finding our own meaning.

When a player finishes a story, they are left with the memory of their completed game. The characters have closed the final chapter of their quest and will now revel in the boons they have earned through their journey. The hope is that each victory achieves some form of symbolic meaning. Perhaps the challenge was high, and we learned how to test our resolve in a safe way that encourages us to keep trying in other areas of life. Furthermore, the characters might represent our archetype and show us some indication of what it takes to make an impact that stays true to our style of virtue.

A game can show us a path to personal fulfillment in many ways. On the external level, we complete games to collect more achievements. For our internal values, representing the more meaningful level, we carry with us the memory of what we have accomplished and what it took to make this achievement come to fruition. How the player connects with reality in their accomplishments is the true test of how they define the meaning that defines their true self.

TRIUMPH AT THE
WORLD CENTER

Despite the abundance of gaming rewards we can claim in a play session, ranging from common to mythical ratings, only certain items meet the criteria from mythology to be considered the Ultimate Reward. This phrase projects a standard of power that moves our expectations for what the item can do beyond anything we have encountered so far in the journey. These items require the deepest devotion to both mandatory and optional tasks, often going far beyond the basic quest requirements in order find the item and be allowed to take it. These tasks are often incredibly difficult, but also fulfilling for those who complete them.

As an example, the *Kingdom Hearts* saga contains optional gathering and crafting challenges Sora can be pushed through in each world of his quest. At the end of many hours and thousands of additional mobs of enemies, the player will eventually find all the items needed to equip the Ultima Keyblade. Being different from the common Keyblade of the canonical story, this weapon holds the highest balance of any weapon between power-to-magical ability. In addition, any player who equips this weapon during their playthrough is displaying an additional badge of honor in the physical presentation of the character. By seeing Sora holding the Ultima Keyblade, any onlooker will know this player has braved the challenge of gathering every material in the game and has overcome the deepest challenges *Kingdom Hearts* has to offer.

Even more alluring is the method of unlocking Sora's ultimate form in *Kingdom Hearts II*. One of the final areas of the game, The World That Never Was, has endless waves of Heartless for Sora to battle in certain areas of the city. The player invokes the power of Drive Forms to heighten Sora's abilities for small periods of battle. These boosts occur for Valor / Attack, Wisdom /

Magic, Master / Balance, Limit / Break, and the Anti-Form, which sends Sora into his Dark Heartless stance from the Innermost Cave segment of the first game. The greatest metaphor lies in unlocking the last Drive, called Final Form. To do this, the player must traverse the final world (hence, the toughest mobs in the game) and use the other forms as often as possible. One random time, instead of becoming the selected form, Sora will reveal his Final Form. Once this occurs, this power can be called upon at will, the same as the other abilities.

While the ability to fly across the screen as the "God-Mode Keyblade Master" brings an epic amount of fun to the end of the game, the meaning in our flow represents achievement entering our lives. We cannot achieve our potential unless we accept the toughest challenge and rely on our abilities in the best way possible. From this realization, we know we can always search for the ultimate rewards, but we probably do not need them by the time we receive them. The extra ability is deeply fulfilling but is not required. Like the Ultima Keyblade, they are simply a sign of what we bring to the table as the player who has worked through all the challenges of an epic quest.

Since these rewards are not an ultimate endpoint, the question of what we are pushing toward at the final stage comes full circle. During the Initiation Phase of the journey, the hero is uncertain of their world. They worry that the obvious problems in their reality can only be stopped if a significant change occurs.

Just as the shift in therapy relies on the transformation of thought from defense mechanisms to insightful action, the hero learns to realize their potential and engage with their world in ways that make the change possible. The projection of what a hero 'is not' is replaced by the ultimate example of what they have become in the present. The rationalization that we can wait for someone else to make change happen is replaced by the realization that we are that hero, and are good enough to do the work ourselves.

The fiction of heroic fantasy becomes the reality for those who stay the course long enough to seize the ultimate reward. The sensational nature of this reward goes beyond the materials of the item, and is instead the revelation that the wielder, not the item, has ascended to their ultimate form. Without this insight, the reward is just another accomplishment, making a difference in only one context. When this context moves through the hero on a holistic level, their potential becomes limitless.

The right to enter the World Center by merit is offered to those who have completed their journey through life and become their ultimate form, in whatever ways the journey has encouraged their growth. These milestones become the symbols for how we relate to the player.

In the physical dimension, these symbols come from any transformative achievement the person has experienced, from graduation, marriage, birthing, promotion, relocation, and learning to live life true to oneself through any life-defining shift. We know these changes have occurred whenever we were one thing before and are now qualitatively different through our dedicated effort for growth. Just as Link restores the Master Sword to the Temple of Time to finally return the childhood, we can now choose the best way to live with the abilities we have earned.

Our attachment to the journey changes with time, but the accomplishment remains. The sacred symbol of the Erdtree can be reduced to ash just as easily as the Lighthouse can be remembered fondly. This shift in perspective takes time. Once we know how to return, we begin another journey. This time, we have everything we need to be the hero we thought the world needed at the first moment. The euphoria of victory is nice while present, but it will always yield to the next great task. Whether the mission is the next game for the gamer, a job for the graduate, or a family to lead for the parent, there is always another journey for the hero that has stood at the world's center in possession of the ultimate reward. This is the nature of seeing the journey in games as a projection of hope as we select the ultimate dream to pursue in life.

 ## THE CHOICE TO RETURN

Amongst the grand aspirations of a mythical hero is the ability to walk amongst the gods and be perceived favorably. For these examples, from Achilles to Tithonus, the supreme boon was not to become deified but rather to inherit invulnerability from their paradise. In life, it is rare to find a parallel to this dream. Mortals endure the struggle. The driven among them make plans. Humanity is tethered to the life cycle and the many statuses that limit us. Like a perpetual session of playing *The Sims*, humankind is cursed to manage meters in hopes of making the most out of life.

When this example shifts completely into the realm of video games, God-Mode becomes the obvious parallel to the unlimited nourishment of the indestructible that has achieved their paradise. Such a mode can be earned in some games (e.g., infinite ammo and materials in *The Last of Us*) or acquired as a coded exploit to enhance the fun beyond what can be earned (e.g., Motherlode in *The Sims 4*).

Our desire to apply these feats is evidence of a continued tradition in myth from centuries passed. We envision the Indestructible Being as a goal from our dreams because we feel the childish bliss of being untouchable as if it were a memory. Achieving this in any game creates a psychodynamic burst of nostalgia. By enjoying a game this way, we see the world like a god would if they were playing. When we lack the discipline to endure easy challenges and preserve our untouchable stature, we commonly feel the reminders of this childish wonder in our play. The childish fantasy in this success gives way to the reality that even though we can conduct ourselves at this level in the game, there is no accomplishment. At this realization, we remember that we actually can approach some form of this accomplishment through our own merit, and then the need for childishness rescinds.

No matter the path taken to reach the end, whether it be struggle, skill, unlocked abilities, or a code for God mode, the joy of play eventually fades into a sense that every game, even our favorites, will ultimately be played by us for the final time. Sometimes we know this is the case, as in a planned trip away from a cherished game world. Other times, we log out blissfully unaware. Only time reminds us when we haven't played in a while, realizing we have seen our final cutscene and moved on to the next thing in life.

This next pursuit in life is different for everyone. This does not have to mean games will never be played again. Rather, the player learns how to enjoy diverse goals, each one benefitting from the superior planning and problem-solving built by the joy of playing a video game in the earlier phase of life. The mindful path helps to build a patient spirit in the person, helping them stay present in reality while the best opportunities find them over time as the next journeys to take. In the words of Aigis from *Persona 3*,

"You don't have to save the world to find meaning in life…"

Finding the thing that gives you meaning allows for the building of legacy, which is the best parallel for immortality discovered up to this point. The irony behind legacy, it turns out, is that it is built in the present despite humanity commonly discussing its influence in their future. Nobody has ever completed a single game they never chose to play. So it is with finding our place of meaning before, during, and after our video games.

When the performance relies on the player, video games solidify their legacies in our lives when we reach game's end. The emotional impact relies heavily on player investment and the memories formed during gameplay to create meaning. Take the synergy in *Super Metroid*. When the Metroid of the first game gifts Samus the Hyper Beam, it allows Samus to destroy the Mother Brain along with Zebes. Imprinting Samus as a meaningful figure to the Metroid mirrors the player's memories of completing both games, amplifying the impact of this victory despite everything playing out in only 16 bits.

Many games use the ending to help players transition into an automatic sense of optimism. The image of Mario and Peach flying with hope toward the final Power Star in *Mario Galaxy* contrasts with the chaos of denial depicted by Bowser's interstellar defeat. The last shooting star even reminds the player, "Yes...All new life carries the essence of stars...Even all of you." This message resolves the struggle between good and evil, leaving all to continue life in a galaxy saved from eternal chaos by the power of stars.

Still, other games choose to emphasize the value of humanity. Some games, exemplified by the contrast between *Portal 2* and *The Last of Us*, arrive at their conclusions in shockingly different ways. At the same time, the environment of *Portal* tasks Chell with escalating challenges to defeat the cold logic of AI, the ending of the second game shows GLaDOS deciding to save her from imminent doom despite their history. This twist gives the player a hopeful feeling that humans can achieve their potential convincingly, despite the wavering conclusions from the logic system of an AI machine. The celebratory song from the targeting robots threatens certain doom despite this victory, a fitting end for this story style.

The uneasiness continues further with endings like in *The Last of Us*. The journey across the United States eventually brings Joel and Ellie to Salt Lake City, the location of the Fireflies' compound. At this point, they reunite with Marlene, the leader of the Fireflies and the person who sent them on this mission at the start of the game. After running some medical tests, Marlene reveals to Joel that they will need to remove the infected portion of Ellie's brain to study her immunity if a vaccine is to be created. This operation will save the human species from extinction, but Joel must let go of this girl he cares about. Furthermore, this closeness represents the resurrection of Joel's humanity, a quality buried deep since the tragic death of his daughter twenty years earlier.

Ultimately, Joel cannot accept this trade. He murders the lead surgeon and flees with an unconscious Ellie. This moment mirrors the early game escape in which Joel carried Sarah after their car accident. The symmetry in these flashpoint events leads to a huge character moment for Joel. Holding an unconscious Ellie in his arms, the final threshold is guarded by Marlene, who pleads with him to do the right thing. Even after Joel realizes this sacrifice is what Ellie would want, Joel cannot make the selfless choice. He fires on Marlene, puts Ellie to rest in a car, then returns to silence Marlene in cold blood.

Despite the big moments in the story and all the signs of growth for the characters, the cautionary tale in *The Last of Us* reminds the player that we always have a choice of where we will return. How we realize the truth inside relies heavily on how we interpret our options. The moment of victory for players moving Joel and Ellie to their new life challenges us to remember our values and stay true to our ideal self whenever possible.

The moral tale of guilt versus redemption is experienced more easily when the characters on trial for their wrongs are not us. Booker DeWitt and Elizabeth from *Bioshock Infinite* serve as another example of how deeply this truth can cut, with one failing to complete the mindful journey, and the other being forced to live through it infinitely across the multiverse. The final walk between these two allies features an infinite ocean with lighthouses to enter. Every step our heroes take is mirrored by a different pair of Booker and Elizabeth heading into their lighthouse. Choices have consequences, and the choices made by Booker DeWitt have created this one version of reality. Elizabeth comes to realize the horrifying truth of this plot. Booker and Comstock are the same.

Every step of the journey through life offers a chance to reflect on how we have arrived at this point. Each moment of presence helps us decide where to head moving forward. Every event in this game is the product of one version of Booker desiring what another Booker has while the pendulum of fate continues to swing. Realizing the only way to end this cycle is for Elizabeth to drown every Comstock and Booker, Elizabeth makes the final decision in every timeline. The player has no choice in the end but to be submerged in the deep implications of this plot twist.

Games challenge us to see the world in a way that is just out of reach when using the usual thought processes. Using the ability of fiction to alter the nature of possibility, any choice, and every outcome, pushes our thinking in amazing new directions. We achieve greater things in story form, but the ability to transfer these choices back into reality and create something real from these memories is perhaps the most superhuman ability found within human intellect.

The metaphor of a game's conclusion depends on the person who has played it. As we recall the memories of playing, the connection we formed with the characters mirrors how we perceive our challenges. Choosing to work through a story replicates the symbolism of Elizabeth and Booker moving from one lighthouse to the next. We jump into new stories because there is something about the conflict that makes us want to experience it. This is where passion is formed. Our desires inform us of which challenges we are perfectly suited to face. When we answer the call, we set ourselves on a path with an eventual ending. Despite the promised conclusion being an obvious end to the journey, we happily accept the journey and appreciate the experience with our energy more so than dreading the ending.

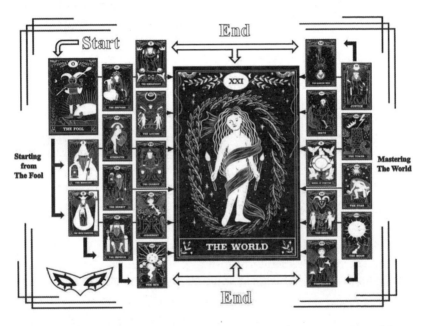

FIGURE 32. *From the Fool to the World Arcana in the Persona Franchise*

Any important game achievement can offer us a metaphorical flight into understanding life's journey. The wondrous ideas we encounter inform our views on the state of the world in ways that help us battle through our subjective experiences of the story. Like the various teams in the *Persona* franchise (SEES, The Investigation Team, and The Phantom Thieves), the chance to acquire the

World Arcana symbolizes the perfect connection with every view of the world. This does not consist only of an ideal view of our world but the true world at the core of the collective subconscious. While these squads battle the most powerful ideas humanity can cling to, such as the influence of politicians and the Holy Grail, their feats require power that exceeds all capabilities. Every ally, and every ability, combines to form The World.

The true hero sees through the limitations of their aspirations and sees the abstract picture of life in its entirety. While personal growth does not normally rely on playing video games, believing in concepts bigger than our subjective experience is necessary to expand our mindset until we find the passion to unlock the world. This is the power of myth that Joseph Campbell explains so eloquently in his seminal explanation of the monomyth across the 20th century. When we see beyond the imagery of the godhead and still find a path to illumined knowledge, that is the journey to the ultimate form of our persona.

Reflecting on our proudest completion in a meaningful video game becomes synonymous with stepping into the light, just as the hero does when they cross the return threshold. By carrying that light into whichever endeavors deserve to be next in life, we take it upon ourselves to work on them with the same resolve that made us effective as a gamer. Problem-solving, determination, and the desire to keep progressing all give a game player the ability to connect with life in a fundamentally different way from the average non-gamer.

For those who have completed the walk into a game's end, finishing the final quest becomes second nature. Finding out what happens next in the ordinary world is among the most amazing challenges to accept. When this choice is before us, we take our place as one who has become empowered by the lessons of our other grand journey. By translating the strengths of gameplay with a combination of hope of meaning, game players choose to accept the next challenge so they can climb the next mountain to find fulfillment in life.

ACT III

The Return to Life
As the Endgame

CHAPTER XVII

Crossing the

Return Threshold

The courage to walk into the Darkness, but strength to return to the Light.

—Parables of the Allspring (Destiny)

E ven for the most meaningful video game experiences, the state of play cannot last forever. Each story must come to an end. Every quest is either finished or forgotten with time. For those who experience these stories through a gamer identity, they provide a joyful escape from the struggles of the real world for a brief time. The way games encourage the player to find the way forward is a counterargument to the restrictions most people feel when things are locked in to "be as they are." In this way, games are a form of entertainment that helps us cope with the parts of life we cannot seem to change on our own.

When players see things through to the end, they experience a boost in self-esteem. This feeling makes a powerful impact when it reaches our core identity. This ultimate belief in self encourages people to keep trying. Like in *The Legend of Zelda*, where everything a person ever needs to solve a puzzle is already inside the room with them, the greatest tool a person ever has is their belief in themselves. This makes gaming a valuable activity, no matter what stage of life we are in, as we fully understand these lessons of encouragement for the first time.

The symbolism of finishing a great journey is seen in the resolution phase of countless stories invoking the monomyth's structure. Having received the ultimate ability, the hero from any mythical story must decide where to go once the world is saved by completing the final quest. In our greatest endeavors, we mirror this decision. Do we return to the Ordinary World where our desire was born? Can we be the agent of change we imagined now that we have come this far? By playing games this way, we ultimately challenge ourselves to answer these personal questions with hope.

The game player can do anything they set their mind to with the right strategy, unfailing execution, and a little luck mixed into the encounter. If myth aims to project our hope onto fictional characters, then this process works to find the arena in life where we hope to be the most effective. We embrace the challenge, grind, retry, and level up until we effectively gamify life. The return to our context, within games and without, can be the meaningful triumph we aim for in every important pursuit of the journey.

The problem is that many people who hold dominion over the things a game player cannot change do not see video games as a proper pursuit for inspiration across childhood or adulthood. Even with near-daily empirical findings that video games refine our connections with problem-solving, critical thinking, teamwork / social coordination, play, flow, joy, and other facets of our satisfaction with life, the societal narrative on the value of engaging with these myths in our free time seems to become fixated on ideas like childish play and irresponsible life choices.

There will come a time beyond the age of common modernism when most finally understand that something can be fun and valuable concurrently. The result of this crisis is that the game player, having just completed their time in gaming and energized by their discovery of self, will often start another save file, explore New Game +, or will find another game so they can keep playing. After all, if society will not allow a chance to do something valuable, why not save the universe again?

This way of thinking is dangerous for our mental health the longer we cling to it. The longer a person stays inactive in their favorite game, the harder it is to find the energy to answer the call to adventure. Remembering that the adventure within a game is a metaphor for the journey through life, it stands to reason that a player who is away from the controls of their life will also struggle to initiate meaningful progress. The intrinsic value of video games is the reason they provide players with immense joy and unmatched agency. This value highlights why nothing else compares to the experience of playing one's favorite games. The trick with the obsessive mindset is that the greatest source of light casts the darkest shadow. Video games not only teach us this truth, but they also demonstrate it in their own right.

To witness this tragedy within the history of roleplaying games, Darth Revan from *Star Wars: Knights of the Old Republic* shows us the path of losing and redeeming the self. Occurring thousands of years before the original Star Wars movies, this game exemplifies the monomyth in games while challenging players to struggle between the Light Side and the Dark Side of the Force.

While the Force represents the flow of energy from the World Navel to every Jedi and Sith, the protagonist discovers their connection to this power quickly throughout the game. Being a

Bioware game, the plot significantly depends on the player's dialog choices to shape their version of the hero and their desired direction for the unfolding story. By learning the ways of the Jedi and the Sith at developmentally staged points in the game, the player must wrestle with the decision about how to approach morality while they decide on their goals for the galaxy far, far away.

The choices made by the player exemplify the power of nurture in a game sense. The reveal of the protagonist's identity, however, demonstrates why Star Wars is viewed historically as one of cinema's premier leaders in creating plot devices for their audience. The entire conflict between the Republic and the Sith Empire hinges on defining the player's motivation to defeat Darth Malak. After many hours of training as a Jedi in this game, the player learns the nature of their identity. The protagonist is actually Malak's fallen master, Darth Revan.

All the good, and all the evil, that set the stage for this conflict has been caused by you. The very thing you have sought to overcome all game is yourself. The game has set you in the middle of a grand debate over nature versus nurture.

After this revelation, the player may redeem Revan back to the Light Side of the Jedi calling or embrace the Dark Side's need for revenge to reclaim what is rightfully theirs. The duality of the game pushes the player to decide how they want to be seen by the galaxy in the aftermath of their victory. In essence, choices matter. Both decisions are difficult, forcing the player to choose which path best represents their version of the story.

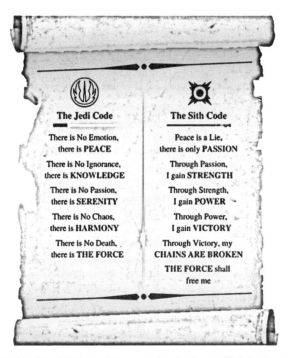

FIGURE 33. *The Differing Views of the Jedi and Sith in Star Wars*

In comparison, the weight of deciding to play this game, while not deciding the fate of the galaxy, shows how a person understands their connection with the surrounding world. Each life area holds within it a necessary task for a person to live a healthy life. While passion cultivates our greatest abilities, how we use these talents can become symbolic of the same Dark Side that consumed Revan.

Instead of sharing the gifts we learned so well as gamers, those who continue playing obsessively will experience their victories only with themselves. This isolation leads to a hollow feeling around games. This player continues to play, not because the story or the challenge is meaningful, but because play is available as an option while more valuable opportunities do not seem to be. This passion leads to victories only in service to continue to play games.

The reality of being stuck as "only a gamer" is the truest experience of the refusal to return noticed in the monomyth whenever the victorious hero avoids their duty. Yet, when the symbolism becomes lost on the player, the refusal to return can happen to anyone who has lost touch with the metaphor of the monomyth.

Returning to the starting area may be less appealing for heroes that stay invested in their journey. Once the hero finds the path to victory, they may avoid the return back to their ordinary world altogether. In this way, characters who push forward into the sequel without returning mirror the player who continues achieving victories in video games without considering how other responsibilities can also improve their journey.

In *Kingdom Hearts*, Sora returns to Destiny Island between the first game and the many games on his newest journey. However, he does not choose to stay in this ordinary world for long. The adventurers Nathan Drake and Lara Croft are further examples of focusing on new objectives to avoid staying at home to enjoy the benefit of their past triumphs. This trend justifies continuing the story of the most popular franchises, as the return is less compelling to play than the conflict-ridden stages themselves. The obsession with finding the next great discovery compels the gaming character to focus on the chance for action instead of settling in for a new type of challenge.

Accepting the next challenge in life emulates the righteous choice from many of the more spiritually-based myths. For most, new challenges provide a sense of interest. For others, the passing of time leads to regret. The best growth opportunities rely on a balance between using and restoring our energy. When the return threshold is before us, we all face a choice. Do we allow ourselves another chance for fun? Can our imaginations run freely through life without the frequent opportunity to play? Sometimes, the game player forgets the honest answers to these questions and loses themselves in unearned fun. This form of fun forgoes the boon of personal growth to embrace escape, turning this choice into avoidance. The question remains, how does someone knowingly forego their passion when the ordinary world no longer motivates them? How can we level up into our most complete self when the most compelling challenges in life seem to be found in video games?

 ## THE FLIGHT TO THE PREFERRED CHALLENGE

When the gamer decides not to return to their context often enough, they can become lost in an endless road of trials that pushes them from game to game. The accomplishment of each new thing allows a diegetic irony to set in. For them, the sense of passion that comes from being successful is being reinforced continuously. Games offer quick solutions, while life requires consistency over long periods of time. From outside this gaming arrangement, it will appear to others that the player has lost their way. Fixation on fun prevents other goals in life from feeling important. Games move from being an escape to being a method of avoidance.

When this happens, those outside the game may intervene with a rescue attempt. Like when the gods chase after the hero who has stolen the ultimate gift, social pressures might occur during this rescue that encourage the need for therapy, selling away the console or PC, or any other over-the-top method of disconnecting the player from further gameplay.

The difficulty of the rescue comes from the realization that the problem was never about limiting play. All along, games prevent the full impact of the situations that overwhelm a person's life. Avoidance of failure by choosing the right coping skill is encouraged by many approaches to psychotherapy. Sometimes more coping is needed for success to be achieved in the world where it makes the most difference. Other times, the person loses track of which world that is.

The complex need for coping depends on the awareness of everyone that creates the gamer's reality. This awareness level must be developed for those who mount the rescue attempt. For them, it is much simpler to control the use of technology than it is to spend enough energy to be consistently supportive. Learning how to have a conversation about games and the role they play in life becomes the most valuable reward of the journey to this point. This leads to even more important abilities, such as time management, passion, interests, and connection with those around us.

As it turns out, performing these responsibilities is a skill that also must be leveled up. As a result, people learn over time to be more successful in this sequence of events. The people watching the game player need help understanding why the gamer does not simply choose to succeed. Ironically, the game player is the perfect source of this information. When these conversations feel impossible, the game player will feel stuck in an unfulfilling stalemate, likely withdrawing back into the gaming habits that prompted this flight in the first place. Without effective communication, no solutions seem obvious to anyone involved, and the relationship deteriorates.

Attack Type ↓ \ Opponent →	Normal	Fire	Water	Electric	Grass	Ice	Fighting	Poison	Ground	Flying	Psychic	Bug	Rock	Ghost	Dragon	Dark	Steel
Normal													−	X			−
Fire		−	−		+	+						+	−		−		+
Water		+	−		−				+				+		−		
Electric			+	−	−				X	+					−		
Grass		−	+		−			−	+	−		−	+		−		−
Ice		−	−		+	−			+	+					+		−
Fighting	+					+		−		−	−	−	+	X		+	+
Poison					+			−	−				−	−			X
Ground		+		+	−			+		X		−	+				+
Flying				−	+		+					+	−				−
Psychic							+	+			−					X	−
Bug		−			+		−	−		−	+			−		+	−
Rock		+				+	−		−	+		+					−
Ghost	X										+			+		−	−
Dragon															+		
Dark							−				+			+		−	
Steel		−	−	−		+							+				−

Key:
+ Super Effective Attack
− Not Very Effective
X No Effect

TABLE 4. *Pokémon Generation I Type Advantage Chart*
(As seen in The Psychology of Pokémon: The Power to Catch 'em All)

This conundrum presents itself whenever the intervention focuses more on personal responsibility than on systemic influences that block a person's greatest strengths. This problem is illustrated in a near-perfect metaphor when we return our focus to the Pewter City Gym Battle in Generation I of the *Pokémon* games (*Red / Blue /* or *Yellow Versions*). Gym Leader Brock uses a duo of rock-type Pokémon, Level 12 Geodude and Level 14 Onix. Depending on the starter chosen by the player and their preparation leading to this early encounter, this fight is either frustratingly long or humorously easy to finish.

The reason for this difference is simple, but also complicated to explain to a person who does not play video games.

For a Pokémon veteran, the reason is crystal clear. In this battle, if the player has chosen Squirtle or Bulbasaur, they have a type-advantage against all rock-type opponents. They will destroy Onix and Geodude with nothing to worry about. If the player has chosen Charmander (or Pikachu) as their starter Pokémon, they will experience a disadvantage in this gym battle. Regardless of which starter Pokémon was selected, the solution is to level up their starter and add more Pokémon to the team. By doing this, the problem of type disadvantage is negated. The trainer will be strong enough to win the battle by playing to the strengths they inherited from the start of play, adding to them, and minimizing the threat of disappointment through strategy and preparation.

With the ongoing metaphor for the will of the gods influencing the role of authority in a game player's life, the back and forth about how much gaming is the right amount becomes what is referred to in mythology as the Magical Flight. When the transfer of focus from games to other areas of life comes easily to the gamer, success spreads to many life contexts. This person is generally viewed with favor by all observers, and their ability to string together victorious outcomes nurtures a narrative that they are an impressive being. The environment of this individual stays supportive even when the limits of the person's potential are being tested. This is analogous to the game of *Tetris*, where everything is orderly, lines are cleared out at the low point on the screen, and it is easy to maintain confidence that the player will continue to showcase their abilities to manage the game easily.

By comparison, a game player who seems inefficient will draw out a blaming of video games from those in authority, even to the point of serious alienation, diminished mental health, and other serious life challenges. If this happens, the gods of the system (being the loved ones and those prone to negative judgments) will feel justified in their ideas that video games are nothing but childish distractions which undermine the potential of their loved ones. This gamer experiences the chaotic example of *Tetris*, struggling to clear blocks, leaving excess holes that prevent recovery, and living on the verge of a "game over."

Essentially, the person could have achieved greatness, and the only reason they did not do so is because their decisions of how to structure life did not let them. This view does not notice the lessons learned from gaming. It does not identify value in the tasks of play or self-care. From this point of view, the negative experiences in life are formed from a place of judgment, stemming from the player's decision to allow their primary escape to revolve around the play of video games.

Certain games end with a self-destruct sequence. It is not good for anyone's health to linger in a building that is about to explode. In the rescue mission that extends through *Resident Evil 4*, Leon S. Kennedy must survive the biological terrors of Los Illuminados. Engaging in the final battle with cult leader Osmund Saddler, Leon is saved by the timely drop of a rocket launcher at the last moment by Ada Wong. After surviving the fight, Ashley and Leon watch Ada escape by helicopter, leaving them to fend for themselves. Although serving the mythical function of the Goddess, bestowing the power of victory on the hero, Ada's penchant for moral ambiguity shines through as she tosses a set of keys for a nearby jet ski to Leon. She reasons that she has set the island to detonate. Taking the sample of the virus and the ease of escape away from the hero, Leon is left with only one objective he can still complete successfully: return Ashley to safety. With the timer at the top of the screen, the player guides Leon on foot and by jet ski through the remains of the facility. With the right spatial awareness to navigate the collapsing cavern, the player emerges victorious in the final flight to safety just as the island erupts in a magnificent explosion.

This ending reveals the fight or flight response so often explained across prominent psychological theories. Games with this style of ending also capture the essence of the magical flight in mythology. Despite claiming victory, the player must perform one final feat to see the mission through to a satisfying conclusion.

The metaphor of this flight explains two sides of reality at once. First, the hero has accomplished something great by emerging victorious from the final conflict. Winning the critical fight with the leader does not magically bypass every lingering minion that remains from the stages of initiation. Since this enmity endures beyond the moment of victory, the escape is still required for the hero and their party if they are to find a point of rest to appreciate their accomplishment.

In this way, the flight toward safety is a defense mechanism, protecting the hero from the final gasp of an uncaring environment as it tries to steal back victory after the decisive defeat.

As the game attempts to end the protagonist one last time, this event mirrors the belittling nature of an uncaring environment experienced by the game player. Despite having fun and completing an enjoyable story, the act of play must be torn down in some households because of the resentment towards gaming and the use of technology for the fulfillment of imaginative play.

This juxtaposition shows why the flight encounter is an essential parallel in the life of a game player. When it proves impossible to share the joy of games with those around you, a person must make a choice. They can live in shame by continuing to play while believing this dominant narrative. This leads to a descent into isolation, hiding their joy from others since nobody wants to join them in triumph.

There is, however, another option.

The gamer can experience a paradigm shift to fulfill their entire being, one in which they share their joy of gaming unapologetically as a perspective view of their progression in life.

The concept of the paradigm shift is a prominent feature in the series of games telling the story of *Final Fantasy XIII*. The story of Lightning and her battle with fate contains a combat system reflecting the importance of understanding our paradigm. The balance between offensive abilities (Commando / Ravager), the defensive stance (Sentinel), support (Synergist / Saboteur), and the healing role (Medic) must shift throughout the course of battle if the party of three is to achieve victory. When the tides of battle shift unfavorably, the player must notice this failing quickly so they can shift their fighters into a different stance. For example, if the powerful enemy is alert and focused on the group, the Sentinel must taunt and absorb the damage from ending their vulnerable party members. When the opponent is staggered, a state in which they are vulnerable to an onslaught of damage from the party, everyone needs to shift their paradigm to a more offensive tandem to deal the highest damage-per-second (DPS) possible. When the stagger ends, the party must revert to a conservative stance, prioritizing strategy and defense until another opening becomes possible.

The value of games such as *Final Fantasy XIII* is that by learning the strategy for success we learn that we are more powerful together than we ever would be alone. This only works when every member of the party system is willing to work together communicate, and accept the rest of the group.

A player who attempts to initiate a gaming-positive conversation in an uncaring environment will, without doubt, experience many rejections. The only way through this frustration is to maintain the resolve that it is okay to hold a different worldview than those around them, while doing the best they can to not give up on the desire to communicate. It is possible to harbor different passions than someone else and still be supportive of them. The fulfillment from playing a video game mirrors many other hobbies that create a passionate interest in those who practice them. The flight of the gamer, and the chase from their resentful gods personified, is not the only possible fate. Even so, games like *Final Fantasy XIII* show that, even when something is prophesied, we do not have to accept a fate that restricts us from living our lives.

The ability to master the flight sequence for the return adds an element of defining grace to a game player's existence. Having the poise to include games as a meaningful portion of our identity is because the concepts within them teach important strategies when we analyze them as a modern mythology. After all, the monomyth binds cultures together through a shared mindset that reflects the societal values of the people being entertained.

When the story leads to passion, it also teaches which defenses are needed to protect ourselves on the path through life. Just as Jason dropped the severed limbs of the Prince of Colchis as a diversion tactic to flee with the golden fleece in the Argo, a racer in *Mario Kart* will throw a banana peel backward in the hopes of thwarting their pursuer. In this parallel, the player who defends their choice to allow games to fill them with joy is demonstrating the same resolve in their choice as the heroes of timeless myth.

Another flight example is found when the tension of the heartbeat pulses in the game *Dead by Daylight*. This match-based game focuses on four survivors running from a killer in a manner similar to slasher films. With the balance of power skewed in favor of the horror villains, the survivors must survive through flight, as it is impossible to fight. The one thing they can do with some influence of offensive effect is to drop crates behind them, which are meant to stagger the killer for a few seconds. When this is done well, the victim's flight achieves an inspiring energy as they ultimately find new opportunities to escape the terrifying ordeal.

When we flee danger effectively while seeming impressive in our abilities, it becomes harder for those pursuing us to doubt our potential.

Examples like these are meant to encourage game players to achieve life balance by understanding themselves. While the path to admiration favors those who alternate between tasks of enjoyment and hard work gracefully, preserving our joy is a valuable resource for thriving in life. Carl Jung often spoke about using dogma to shift people's worldviews. By giving people a structure of fulfilled compliance, they are seemingly aligned with their gods. However, by rigidly following rules without a natural connection to them, the ego loses sight of what their god truly is. This tragedy dominates any society who forgets to nurture the spirit in favor of only taking the time to measure behavior.

Passion does not separate us from our purpose. Rather, passion encourages us to become inspired to handle any challenge within our realm of influence. The gods inside video games are not real, even if they function realistically from a narrative perspective. Just like the gods of mythology, they represent the hope inside each of us that our beliefs will lead to purpose.

Deciding that success cannot be experienced in the form of playing video games is a behavioral judgment that only sees the game being experienced when the controller is in hand for a measurement of time. Such a judgment is completely blind to the cognitive experience of gameplay. The cause and effect of knowing when to fight, and intuiting when the right time is for flight, is a transformative insight in its own right. By playing video games, these lessons are learned, along with countless others, that prove useful in understanding our progression through life.

If a small mistake can be avoided during our day, we will greatly benefit when we try again in hopes of avoiding the negative ending where the uncaring world holds us back. Both experiences, conflict, and escape, are hard choices. The message of the magic flight is that, as gamers, we must choose our difficulty. Is the conflict worth the conversation, or should we keep to ourselves and review our choices on another day? Hard work is built into the experience. The victory stance helps us imagine the realms of impossible bliss coming from our favorite worlds of fiction. On the other hand, tales of doom connect us deeper with the tragedy of life. In a life with gaming, even the struggle to find favor with others makes these messages more compelling.

We may not be able to wield mighty weapons and infinite magic to achieve these victories, but that is the lesson's purpose. The monomyth allows humans to envision their path to success in a world that requires more inspiration. The crisis experienced in the choice to return to the ordinary world requires the game player to stay true to their convictions. This game player must figure out how to be an otherworldly symbol of congruence in a world that has lost its way, only looking for behavioral benchmarks to ensure they are on the right path. The resentment of the pursuer does not exist because video games are a negative influence on the journey. The confusion of this chase has only set in because the pursuers need to recognize that their way is not the only way to answer the call to adventure meaningfully.

 ## THE RESCUE FROM WITHIN

The self-serving rescue attempt is often more about the ego needs of the rescuer than about the one who is lost. Becoming absorbed within a state of constant play requires much more than a compelling game for consequences to occur. It requires a life that needs the person to willingly participate in it just as they do in their fun playing games.

The rescue pattern originates from the pursuit of enjoyment, not a desire to do wrong. By staving off hardship, games offer a clear purpose during play, especially when it is difficult to find a use for our greatest strengths elsewhere. It is common for game players to find purpose sensations more readily inside virtual worlds in many actual-world contexts. This is due, in large part, to games being designed with the specific purpose of highlighting the progression systems and reinforcing every successive step in the right direction. When a game player becomes captive to the cycle of play-struggle-succeed for too long, they will miss out on possibilities to succeed in the original life, the one occurring in the physical world. The virtual world becomes a perfected realm where success and failure both feel fair. In fact, even when failure may feel unfair, the person will struggle because they believe their effort can overcome the unfairness. The chance for players to perfect the world for themselves is available to everyone. The structures of reality continuously prevent many from achieving this feeling due to evils that cannot be as easily fought coming from places which are too far away for the common person to argue with.

Regardless of the persuasiveness behind losing oneself in a pattern of frequent play sessions, the return question still must be answered. While the magic flight allows the hero to flee from the attempt to imprison them, the player also needs a savior to see their value and bring them back to the balanced state of their ideal self. Even when a virtual world is designed fairly compared to the game of life, gamers will find the next earthly system worthy of effort if progress is believed to be possible, assuming they have the right kind of support from their In-Real-Life (IRL) party.

The overtones of preoccupation manifest when the refusal to return prompts the others in our lives to worry about gaming addiction, when many are just weary about finding their rightful place in reality. While scholars remain split on the viability of treating gaming behavior as a true addiction issue, video games have subliminally commented on this across their many decades of voice-acted game experiences. Regardless of the metaphor, games and scholars alike typically portray life balance as a positive experience, and obsession as dangerous if it prevents the person form becoming the best version of themselves.

In *Heavy Rain*, four protagonists are used by the player to solve the mystery of a kidnapped child, being tasked with solving the crimes of a serial killer who drowns their victim's using rainfall as the countdown for death. One of these characters is FBI Agent Norman Jayden, assigned to the Origami Killer case at the beginning of the game, and an expert at using Augmented Reality (the Added Reality Interface / ARI) to gather clues from crime scenes. To battle negative effects from spending too much time using this technology, Agent Jayden will abuse a fictional medication named Triptocaine if the player makes this choice.

The decision to escape reality happens throughout the game, especially when Agent Jayden is physically or mentally distressed. Suppose the player chooses to get their "fix" too often in the game. In that case, Jayden can achieve an ending where he is still addicted to the drug, fails a chance at personal redemption, and begins to see the ARI interface even when the glasses are not being worn, making them a hallucination. The game teaches the player how addiction works, even though the point of the game is to solve the mystery of the Origami Killer before the next victim runs out of time.

Returning to *Star Wars: Knights of the Old Republic*, Darth Revan became a Sith because they felt the Jedi would not be able to stop a threat powerful enough to ravage the galaxy. Rather than accepting things as they are and choosing to believe in the Light Side, Revan usurped the Sith Throne for himself alongside his apprentice, Darth Malak. The two became the arbiters of their own will, disregarding the ethos of the Jedi Council. They could not reconcile the feeling of powerlessness with the chance to do their best while staying true to their values. This decision to fix things plunged the galaxy into darkness. The relapse into using the Dark Side to solve our problems represents the emotional experience of allowing a pattern of escape behavior to dominate one's lifestyle. The principal characters in *Knights of the Old Republic* are there to rescue Revan and use them to influence either the Light or Dark Side of the Force to discover the whereabouts of ultimate battle station that can alter the fate of the galaxy, the Star Forge.

In characters like Agent Jayden and Revan, gamers have the ultimate moral choice to use the powers of evil for quicker solutions or struggle through the noble path to find the improbable way to victory. Both interact with characters who show caution at their choices, and both experiences give the player a subconscious awareness of what it means to achieve a clandestine alignment with their values system. Once again, the fictional context of the story allows the player to develop an awareness of a difficult concept like addiction. Once learned, these ideas can be applied positively, despite being learned in the safety of a video game. This reality, it turns out, is better for everyone involved than having a loved one (or our self) endure the actual struggles of hopelessness being explored by the game characters.

After they have gained these figurative life lessons, the game player must now decide how to transition between the perfected practice of their gaming activity and the chance to demonstrate their abilities across all areas of life. The time spent inside the video games was actually an opportunity to wrestle with the imperfections of society. Finding the truth that works for them, they now have a foundation for finding the optimal path for a rescue to occur from within themselves. The value of mythology is found in connecting the realistic state of these ideas with the mystery of the psychological. The discovery of a true purpose in the ordinary world gives the game player the context they need to finally accept their rescue and complete the return.

The rite of crossing the return threshold is fulfilled by resolving the confusion of the magic flight (running away from their potential) and accepting their true purpose. This realization allows them to move forward free from doubt, with the confidence to carry out their lifelong task. Despite being different from non-gamers, the player with a newfound context can share their creative gifts with their new environment. Whichever life areas are involved, whether relationships, work, or personal growth, the player can accept who they have become since the beginning of their journey. Even more profound is the confidence to allow boundaries to be present, which preserves their sense of self when others do not understand the journey the game player took to find their path.

Those who do not relate to the logic found in video games often seek their truth from other avenues. This allows the gamer to shine through in their most important new challenges, as the gifts needed to complete quests in video games often exceed the strategy needed for many real-world tasks. The many cognitive skills developed in video games are life-changing. By expanding how they use these talents, game players will evolve in magnificent ways that nurture the ego, assuming the gamer (and their environment) allows this process to occur. It takes confidence for game players to credit their growth to video games in the presence of certain circles. However, just because the claim is met with cynicism, resentment, and even wonder does not make it any less true than inconvertible concepts like heliocentrism or the existence of gravity.

Myth lends itself to metaphor, becoming a powerful strategy to settle the debate over the merits of gaming. In a world where results speak for themselves, humanity is ultimately supportive of finding the truth. For these return journeys to be completed, the game player has to find the truth that works for them, and then figure out how to express it in their surrounding world.

Ultimately, these disagreements distract from the realization that nearly every industry can be improved by successfully gamifying their approach to learning. The moral argument over the impacts of games has already been settled decisively, despite many loud voices continuing to argue their point. Yet again, this concern is sorted out effectively by dialog from inside a video game, as Ansem famously told a young Sora in the cave on Destiny Island in *Kingdom Hearts*:

"One who knows nothing can understand nothing."

Showing the kind of presence that can repair the world narrative around healthy gaming is part of the calling in the return of a gamer to their ordinary world. Many people are still surprised when game players are responsible, thoughtful, and achieve things effectively in the world's design for tasks. This reality represents a fundamental misunderstanding of what video games actually are. They are fun, but they are also challenging. They are entertaining but also informative. They require time, but also find a way to fit into our routine. When a game player stops allowing shame to form the narrative, a powerful congruence washes over their entire being. Once this peace is fully realized, the time has come to cross the return threshold and enter the ordinary world. Being the place where the idea of necessary change started, the gamer is now able to show the world what it means to live a life of value while holding onto a passion for video games.

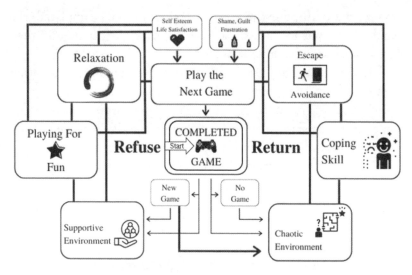

FIGURE 34. *Making the Return Choice with Supportive and Unsupportive Environments*

CHAPTER XVIII

THE MASTER OF BOTH WORLDS

No matter what manner of disaster may befall us, your presence alone is enough to keep the flame of hope burning bright.

—Raubahn (Final Fantasy XIV)

A s game players, we all exist across two worlds: the physical world containing "serious" goals, and the virtual space which contains a greater mix of work and leisure with each passing day. The "Two Worlds" concept allows the game player to see the distinct differences in their quest across the two styles of activity boundaries. One side teaches the mastery of virtual problem-solving in a flowing dance of engagement, while on the other side the skills of the dance must transform into strengths if the person is to be viewed successfully.

The monomyth helps us find meaning across both contexts. This symbolism transforms the serious connotation of the ordinary world into a psychological quest where all things become possible, and every experience gained supports our mission to define meaning in life. By completing the principal challenge of the gaming journey, the monomyth enables the hero of the story (us) to see the return phase as a sign of mastery for both the physical and virtual spaces of life.

To do this, the player must learn to embrace the hero role in their dual world. By understanding how to navigate both worlds easily and actively participating in each, players can find challenges that fulfill their paths while staying connected to their full potential. When the player decided to return from the mythic quest, they chose to rejoin activities in the serious world. Whether by guilt or necessity, the time for play eventually ends. The option to return appeals to those who are interested in the achievement of the physical world. When this is not the case, the player will refuse the return, choose an endless bevy of new quests across different games, and stay engaged with the easier fun of the virtual space.

This perspective may seem factually accurate, but the concept evolves for players who envision mastery in both worlds. The two worlds are the same, described in the monomyth as the divine and the human (but in this context, the serious and gaming space). To integrate the two worlds, a person must restructure the flow of life to acknowledge that games are allowed to be a source of passion in the human experience. Our stake in humanity does not vanish just because we are momentarily logged into a video game. The timing of our play actually occurs during our daily lives whenever we decide it can fit in as a priority, meaning we are the developers for many of the levels in our own game of life. Although it is tempting to view gaming as an ideal world where time is measured accurately, feedback is instant, and progression is fair, we must remember that we are still playing these games as a physical being while our lives continue to play themselves out. In this literal sense, we are simply staring at a screen, pressing button inputs into a technological system that measures our success and failure through moving pixels battling in front of us. This is always happening (in the moments when it does) within the context of real life. Those who have experienced the moment of atonement in their gaming journey will recognize this, allowing them to complete a successful return phase and establish their state of mastery from their gaming space across their actual selves.

 ## GAMING MASTERY IN SERIOUS SPACES

In video games, mastery is measured by the ability of the player to perform impressive feats while avoiding the conditions of failure in whatever challenge they are attempting. When mastery is demonstrated, the player can advance to the next stage, level up, improve their appearance, or display notable achievements on their player account.

In the serious world, being successful as a game player is rarely accepted as the rationale for offering a physical-world opportunity. Even when performers connect their abilities from gaming to their training, society rarely expends the effort to champion gaming as a foundation for cognitive development. As a result, it is easy for game players to underestimate their proficiencies in workplaces, classrooms, and the social world. This dissonance between skill and opportunity occurs because the two settings seem too different for most people to notice how similar they actually are.

The philosophical marriage between gamification and work has seemingly infinite potential. In modern times, the serious world seems to be embracing this relationship as long as the technology preserves profit without excessively favoring fun. Unfortunately, many see enjoyable work as a sign that productivity may decrease. Although the opposite is true, this misunderstanding of how games generate productivity leads to poor attempts at establishing a new work culture, rendering games as a façade for engagement instead of the source of inspiration they could be in the serious world.

The advent of play in classrooms has proven to generate increased student interest, but the question soon follows regarding the impact on test scores. The gamification of the workplace concedes to productivity scores. As passion falls victim to questions of performance, societal confusion persists. Despite countless studies demonstrating how excitement leads to willing participation, the idea of serious work is more synonymous with a joyless complexion followed by the flow of endless tasks.

By measuring productivity and setting benchmarks, society has decided how to define successful thoughts, restrict the range of acceptable emotions, and control behavioral output so all of us can generate the best outcome possible. If this method works, why don't people feel fulfilled with the same consistency that comes when they are having fun? From this question, it becomes clear what society is missing in the argument against games. The cognitive behavioral path that skews the relationship between thoughts, feelings, and actions can lead to the appearance of improved behavioral performance. However, when we overlook the wisdom of our own needs and bend the knee only to goals that exist in the serious world, we lose sight of things that are harder to measure. The value of a video game is that somehow it breaks through these limits, letting us feel an experience that moves beyond the existential, while also encouraging us to understand in the deepest way possible the importance of efficiency.

The world does not have to be this way. Whenever the greatest boon of the champion gamer is discarded as a childish pastime, the threat of burnout intensifies. The gamer resigns from hard tasks, deciding their joy exists elsewhere. Meanwhile, the search for a hero who can thrive in a serious environment continues. This scenario sees passion as frivolous. As a result, the template for success is more concerned with marking checkboxes than with the qualities video games develop using the exceptional processes of flow: fun, play, imagination, and hope.

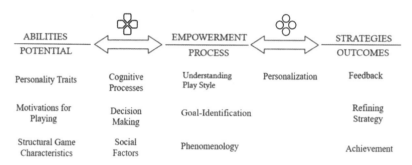

FIGURE 35. A *Positive Progression Process Learned from Gaming* (Kaufmann, 2020)

Whenever this degree of dissonance occurs in reality, there is an opportunity to improve the environment. At least, would be the strategy for overcoming the failure condition. This hope allows the gamer to voluntarily select their goals in both the game world and their serious quests at the same time. The challenge of explaining the value of a gaming mentality to non-gamers is similar to what occurs when a given religion slides deeper into behavioral dogma, forgetting the spark of inspiration that allows the belief to guide a person in their spiritual existence towards inner peace. How can a game player who sees an opportunity for progression explain their resolve to people who have never felt the same, suffering these mistakes thousands of times while accepting the lack of direction in their journey as being normal? The light of the ulti-mate boon, a strategy that leads game players to developing grit by embracing the processes of trial-and-error, only works when the world encourages creativity with every new attempt at the goal. When this is not allowed, this very light is suffocated by the darkness of a reality where success is only measured one way.

In actuality, both worlds have an established pathway to success which requires translating when crossing into each space. The message must be remade, as with any classic from 2-D gaming days becoming their modern remaster. Like the visual updates to *Resident Evil* or the additions to quality of life instilled by the generational remakes of *Final Fantasy VII* and *Mass Effect: Legendary Edition*, game players are intimately aware that languages of the past must be updated for each generation. The serious world and the virtual space occur in the same existence and are more unified in their desires than supporters on both sides may care to accept.

Adjusting the language of older generations to current technology is reflected in the idea of remaking old games. Effective remakes thrive in reimagining for those interested in experiencing them anew while honoring their original audience. The goal is to circulate the idea of the game in whatever form connects with society. In this light, the language of 'Yes' adopts the delivery of 'No' until every audience understands the value of what is spoken. Without the ability to translate these opposites, ideas can only enhance life for the original audience.

By creating the updated version, the audience grows to include those looking for the message now. The game's inception expands beyond the original context because the ideas were universal. The hopes from both spaces are silenced, overcoming the endless void of rejected ideas. The abstract becomes reality, welcoming new players into the same conversation games are destined for when they are found deserving of acclaim.

If the translation fails, nobody understands the ideas from across the rift. The value of the story is forgotten once no one remembers playing them. However, when the new language is shared successfully, everyone within the area of effect, from gamers to societal leaders, benefits from the improved reality. Balance is achieved between light and dark, and innovation flows freely in a continuous cycle.

Manifesting these gifts is exceptional work, especially when creative processes are overlooked in preference of results. Every person who has the freedom to fall short in the process of progression is simply reflecting the concept of being a lifelong learner until they discover the most efficient methods for gaming the system. All this requires is the ability to project the gaming lifestyle into the experiences for the self. By understanding the status quo of both the gaming style, which sees value in progressive solutions, and the expectations of the waking world, the game player must also learn to accept their failures when they occur on either side of the life-affirming threshold.

No matter the degree of mastery from the player, the game world possesses an infinite array of stories the player has never experienced, drifting forever through an expanding list toward the backlog. The actual world, no doubt, reminds the game player of countless daily opportunities never brought to fruition. A game player cannot earn every achievement, just as one cannot collect every human experience. Knowing this, what benefit is there of explaining the dream of perfect progress to those whose creativity is limited by the waking world? From societal opinion alone, these strategies are not serious, and can be discarded similar to how a busy adult hears the musings of a child excited in their play. The strategy needed to master a gaming space is no mere jest or child-like interest.

Such a dismissal will surely happen less as time continues forward. Once games are more and more accepted as an outlet for creativity and imagination, the mainstream influences of child and adult life will grow to see those who can master both sides of the life journey as bringing much needed abilities to the difficulties met in pursuit of success. For the modern era, when gamers are overlooked or dismissed, it is only because a blind spot exists in the design of the problem because those who have succeeded in similar problems were never encouraged to grow by a video game. The problems they constructed were bound to the limits of the realistic, failing to grasp the infinity of a game space. As a result, the concrete thinker can only understand the passing of time, never considering the experience of stories that reach for eternity.

 ## THE POWER OF TIME

Video games use time manipulation to explore realities beyond what is metaphysically possible. While Link must use this ability in *Ocarina of Time* to move successfully through the past and future of Hyrule, there are still other examples of time as a central element of the return for monomythical game stories.

The multiple endings of games are a basic way to review this notion, but other games tackle these ideas directly. *Chrono Trigger*, commonly held to be one of the most renowned games of all-time, begins innocently with a hero named Crono attending the Millennial Fair, celebrated by the Kingdom of Guardia in 1000 AD. During a demonstration of the teleportation device, an unpredictable interference from an heirloom of the monarchy causes the teleporter to send Princess Marle back through time. Her presence interferes with the rescue of her captured ancestor, the queen of the present time. Making matters worse, if she does not get rescued by her kingdom (who think she does not need rescuing because they believe her descendant is her), then Marle will never exist in the year 1000, as she has stumbled into the grandfather paradox. The player must take the party back through time, rescue the lost queen, and return their princess to the present timeline. By resolving this issue, more paradoxes are created. This series of conflicts takes them from the distant future to the ancient past and to the very end of time itself. The struggle continues because the idea that a perfect timeline can be found (or returned to) is futile once one begins undoing what already has occurred.

By failing to accept what happens in time, the player is cursed never to be content, believing something can always be better. Ultimately, they hope to restore life to a path where they never accidentally stumbled upon time travel. By meeting new people along the way, the truth is they can never go back. They have always traveled through time from a certain point of view.

This dilemma mirrors the perfectionistic tendency. Chrono Trigger's charm is that none of the endings are considered universally superior. Just as in life, the victories we experience lead us to whatever next chapter lies beyond. Since time travel is fictional in our actual world, we do not have to wonder about ways to improve the timeline except in one direction: heading towards our future.

Accepting our mistakes over time may be easier for some than others. Perhaps the errors of the past had a minimal impact. For others, the ripple effect of our regret tears us apart to the point where a journey of forgiveness is necessary. Recalling the road trip of Prince Noctis Lucis Caelum of Lucis, the story of *Final Fantasy XV* captures another key element a hero must face when their destiny draws from the monomyth, the tragic return.

The quest of Noctis, alongside his friends Gladiolus, Ignis, and Prompto, was to retrieve the Royal Arms from the tombs of past Lucian kings, hence gathering the power of the Ring of the

Lucii (also known as the Ring of Light), and arrive at his wedding to Princess Lunafreya. Throughout this journey, Noctis experiences great losses. The death of his father and the assault on his kingdom set the tone early on. Being on the run and assumed dead, the bonds of brotherhood Noctis feels for his traveling companions are strained many times over as they all wrestle with finding the best path for Noctis to claim his rightful place as the true king of Lucis. The villainous Ardyn, a disgraced Starscourge healer from ancient times (notably inspired by the fall of Lucifer), plots revenge on Noctis' bloodline. His success comes when he mortally wounds Lunafreya during the ritualistic passing of her powers to Noctis. The ritual finishes, but the peaceful marriage of the Oracle to the King was never meant to be. Moving forward, Noctis must rid the land of Daemons to restore order to the kingdom.

Within the enemy capital, Noctis sees each of his friends pushed to their limit by the endless horde of daemons. Noctis presses on alone to reunite the Ring of Light with the Crystal. This act fulfills the prophecy and solidifies his position as the King of Kings who can wield the universal source of life. Ardyn Lucis Caelum, eternally motivated by his rejection in ages past, allows Noctis to unify these powers so he can destroy them both at once in the future, creating a permanent dominion for his daemons and allowing himself to be their king in a way fate never would have allowed without this manipulation.

The unification of the Crystal and Ring brings Noctis to the world between worlds, communing with the astral god Bahamut. This deity tells Noctis that he is the King of Kings and must return to claim his throne. He must fulfill a prophecy by banishing the darkness even if it costs his life. Noctis floats through the void, experiencing his memories of life for an eternity as the light flows into him.

The world is covered in darkness when the true king returns to reality. Being separated by time, Noctis must learn everything that has happened to the world by finding his friends. He quickly learns that he has been absent from the world for ten years, meaning Ardyn has ruled unopposed for the decade since Noctis entered the light of the Crystal. Physically, Noctis has aged along with everyone who never left Eos. Mentally, he knows only one purpose: the prophecy.

Despite his sacrifice, Noctis has been left behind by the world. The nature of existence now reflects the will of Ardyn, the usurper. Making his way to the Citadel throne room, once ruled proudly by his father, Noctis sees the prideful Ardyn sitting on the throne, mocking the status that once bestowed righteous dominion to the true king. Now, the only purpose for this room is to host the battle of fates between Noctis and Ardyn. Flying across the city of Insomnia, the two foes clash for the ultimate battle between Light and Darkness.

Noctis emerges victorious by calling on the power of all the past kings to attack Ardyn together. Ascending to the throne as the true king, Noctis joins the kings of Lucis finally as one with them. He allows their spirits to strike him down, releasing the full power from the Ring of Light. Entering the afterlife, the spirit of Ardyn seeks one final attempt at revenge. Aided by Lunafreya, Noctis repels the Starscourge from ever returning to Eos. In this act, Noctis accepts his destiny and becomes the Master of the Two Worlds, past and present, in life and death.

These two stories about the influence of time encourage every person who plays them to appreciate the chance we have to aim for a destiny fulfilled. Since our nature is tethered to the present, humankind is constantly reminded of our fleeting mortality as we pursue the existential boons of personal growth and self-actualization. The readiness to transit between our abilities in games and life allows us to see the balance between the fun and the serious in a unique way compared to other pursuits that can define our sense of destiny. Seeing the inner workings of society this way allows for humor and despair, but in a way that provides the confidence to pursue our ultimate goals. Like when *Sonic the Hedgehog* acquires every chaos emerald, the symbolic glow of confidence allows our creativity to take flight across any challenge. Knowing how to jump over any pitfall with grace encourages us to continue until our most sought-after achievements become a reality.

The flow of time causes us to exist momentarily in our failures, just as it does in the joy of our successes. Every encounter has value for us based on the space it originated from. The gamer who has mastered a path through both the gaming and serious worlds must be able to stitch together their two worlds. They seek to blend their life goals with the ultimate gamer mentality. By finding joy in both forms of our existence, a gamer at one with themselves finds a path where one space of living encourages their abilities in the other. We do this from moment to moment until we find the ending where we have achieved complete fulfillment in our experience.

The heart insists on finding the path of destiny whenever the monomyth allegory enters awareness. The most devastating realization in this mentality is when destiny is not achieved. No one can control every element of existence, including the passing of time and the serendipitous opportunities that allow fictional stories to end happily. For heroes like Crono and Noctis, the harmonious conclusion of life is possible, if not bittersweet. For others, the ability to enjoy prosperity occurs alongside the life-defining accomplishment. There is a beauty to thinking about both in the context of a tale we know to be fiction. The greatest addition to the life of a game player is understanding that not every character on screen is pursuing destiny. By seeing ourselves as the hero of our own story, we have already embraced the transformative idea, compelling us to keep going until a story is told where we have achieved every hope we hold for each phase of life. The path of mastery is not granted, but rather earned. The difference between these pathways is not innate, but instead relies on the balance we strike between our faith in the goal, our belief in ourselves, and the awareness we demonstrate in how we use the limited resource of time.

 ## CONSTRUCTING OUR DIVINE MOMENT

The freedom to cross back and forth between the achievements of the fun and serious worlds requires a careful balance if the mastery is to be demonstrated convincingly to the surrounding world. When done poorly, the value of the side most focused on by skeptics will be doubted. When demonstrated admirably, the source of these talents normally goes unnoticed. For this reason, the secret strategy is complicated to share with those focused only on serious tasks from the non-gaming side of the ordinary world. For example, when students have a project that needs to be completed, they begin the activity by balancing their personality, abilities, and desire to finish the challenge. If they are over-achievers, they may not require additional prompting to remember to work on the project, even after their full day of focused tasks in their coursework. Suppose the student is less perfectionistic but is still a talented problem solver. In that case, they can prompt themselves to use their cognitive abilities to focus for a suitable length of time. Some students do not prioritize school, meaning the lack of progress will draw blame for whatever the student prioritized over the assignment. This can easily occur when there is no internal drive from the student's value system, but even more so when there is no external prompt to help overcome the lack of personal interest. These can be digital reminders, a social nudge, or a break in play that can push the player into remembering goals outside of a game.

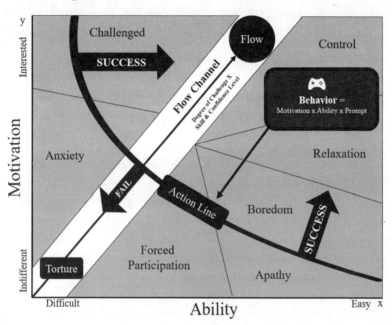

FIGURE 36. *Conceptualizing the Fogg Behavior Model Using Psychological Flow*

Within the gaming context, psychological flow is achieved when the perfect balance is struck between the challenge being experienced and the player's ability. Since games are designed to be fun and remain voluntary, the behavior is easy to select. A prompt to start a task can assist the process whenever hard work is experienced along with a lack of intrinsic motivation. Attempts to gamify the situation can help in certain instances by boosting motivation towards action. However, the gamifying action alone will not generate enough enjoyment to create enthusiasm for the task. As a result, the player must level up their "serious work" abilities to enjoy the gamification act. For a player who has achieved the stance of mastery in both serious and gaming contexts, this demonstration is effortless. The success is presented as a product of flow itself. The pitfalls of tortured activity and forced participation are overcome properly, and the player can also manage the balance to preserve their life satisfaction.

The search for the right prompt is what each stage of the journey is all about. The one who has mastered the domains on both sides of casual fun and seriousness can pass between these states for any task free of worry. As one who has established balance in gaming, they know when to grind for the most enticing experiences and when not to play. We notice the openings when time can serve our purpose, a grand concept we pursue in games with characters who hope to fulfill the call of destiny. The chosen one idea may not be literal for the ordinary world, but the self-esteem needed to see oneself as a capable solution for the challenges that gatekeep our best lives require us to see ourselves in this light. The image of the chosen heroes walking toward the blinding light to battle fate creates a memory we can relate to, even if we do not understand why our consciousness appreciates the imagery so deeply.

The master in both worlds has found a passion that unifies their paths in life, appreciating the balance that comes from thriving in each existence. The gift of believing in the way forward can come from the insights of career counseling, personality testing, serendipity, and any combination of factors that allow a person to reach for their truth.

Choosing a specific path feels daunting in the real world. However, games train us to understand how our interests inform our choices in powerful ways. In *Fire Emblem: Three Houses*, Byleth must choose between the house of the Black Eagles, the Golden Deer, or the Blue Lions. Like in our choice of occupation, once the choice is made, all activities flow in the direction of this specialty. The ultimate destination reflects the initial choice, the people we choose to be interested in, and where we offer our support. In this way, the many paths Byleth faces in *Three Houses* reflect our journey to master life, starting with our choices.

While it can be fun in a game such as this one to try out all the scenarios, life does not afford us this opportunity. At some point, we choose who we want to become, even if we refuse the call and remain stagnant for years. As a form of personality test for gamers, the archetypes help us to identify heroes (or game challenges) that resonate with us. A person who is uninterested in *Fire Emblem*, for example, could be more enticed by the open-ended team system of *Pokémon Go* and prefer less impactful options of Instinct (Yellow), Mystic (Blue), or Valor (Red). The game is mostly the same regardless of choice, meaning the pressure to choose amounts to select a favorite color and moving on with the augmented reality chance to catch 'em all.

Another chance to see which world we seek to master with our archetypes can come in the form of class selection in an MMO game. The quest to fulfill the destiny of Crystal assigned by Hydaelyn in *Final Fantasy VIX Online* is an example of selecting a class to define the early stage of your character but then being able to be everything anywhere later in the game. Players can be any class they unlock, meaning that unlike in *Fire Emblem*, where the path is locked in at the beginning, the player can modify the path at will. A player can start as a Gladiator, shift over to the magic of an Arcanist, heal as a Conjurer, then return to the sword-fighting hijinks they initially selected.

This lesson reveals how mastery is elusive when the chosen task and the journey toward fulfillment are out of alignment. While the pressure from others may be felt to resemble a completed version of the self in the present (or struggle internally with this on our own), games routinely offer many paths for finding this sense of gratification. When we forget our lessons in more meaningful contexts, disappointment spreads into every area of life, even poisoning our sources of joy. This happens because games are only vehicles for discovering meaning in our choices. They are not the choices themselves.

Games cannot offer the final meaning if they are a player's only source of joy. Every exploration of the hero's journey offers a symbolic renaissance for our minds, but these insights are not the destination. The terminus we seek is not the moment of completing the game but when we realize what we want to become more than anything else. When people mistake the game for the final meaning, time passes haphazardly, with video games obstructing the metaphor they were meant to reveal. The fictional line between serious and fun is not due to diametric opposition. Rather, since the two speak a similar language, sometimes we can forget to reconcile our values with our activities. When we hold onto this connection, we are able to clearly understand how time must be used well to pursue destiny, and how believing in ourselves transforms our activities into purpose.

When both sides of life align, this moment of synergy is analogous to the Divine Moment. This crystalizing of passions unifies the identity of the person in every context. In mythology, the moment occurs when a mortal interacts with the divine entity responsible for all existence. In gaming, this moment is mirrored any time the quest to conquer death is finished, balance is restored, opening up the rest of our world to be experienced.

Gaming does not encourage conflict when our daily lives achieve balance. Instead, healthy gaming helps us create harmony. Without this truth, we experience guilt whenever we feel that time should have been spent differently. When we allow ourselves to live in joy, we do better work, at the proper time, and overcome greater challenges. This shifts the balance between our fear of consequences and our need to clear the bar of expectations every day. If we allow ourselves to be human, we will have better boundaries with our goals, even to the point of experiencing a more complete range of emotions until we can roll across the floor, laughing to our fullest. The truth is, we can enjoy two different worlds on the same day, mere seconds apart. After all, the exploits of the Investigation Team of *Persona 4 Golden*, moving back and forth to master the world of high school and the terrifying world inside the TV screen, offer us a great insight into the divine nature of reality and truth in the wording of their call to arms:

Now I face out, I hold out, I reach out to the truth of my life, seeking to seize on the whole moment to now break away.

Oh God, let me out. Can you let me out? Can you set me free from this dark inner world?

Save me now, last beat in the soul.

— Shoji Meguro (Musical Artist for Persona 4, 2012)

By entering into the mindful state for our daily grind, the pressure to perform floats away from the conscious self. While those who see only one way to measure value criticize, this differs from the voice of one who has mastered their path. The fear that hope is incompatible with reality devastates anyone who has not acquired the ability to let reality flow freely in their own time. The rebirth of the confident psyche eventually reveals the best path forward. As in games with puzzle rooms like *Zelda* or *God of War*, everything needed to move forward is in this room. In essence, each room we sit in, and every challenge we face, requires total acceptance of ourselves. The frantic nature of forcing the solution must be allowed to fade into the aether. When this happens, we can finally accomplish whatever we set our mind to, with a mastery that gives us faith that things will work themselves out as they were meant to.

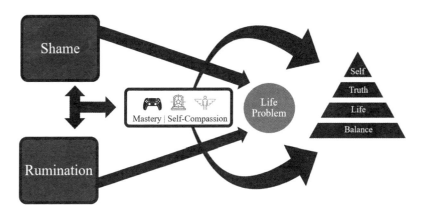

FIGURE 37. *Mindfulness Concept of Self-Compassion for Game Players*

Seeing ourselves within the features of the hero archetype connects us with the infinite storytelling of the video game medium. The stories we enjoy enhance our concept of meaningful adventures, informing our archetypes and providing transcendent hope beyond any individual tale. This is why people love video games. They allow us to see ourselves as something we are not in ways we never could be. They allow us to transcend time, space, worlds, energies, faiths, and, most of all, our limitations. We begin to see a way through life if we were something else; a different gender, having an additional talent, being trusted with new power and responsibilities. Someone who saw themselves as a 'cannot' is suddenly cast as someone who 'will.' Those who did not see themselves as having a destiny before are now the most important person in their part of the universe. Whether the world calls to us through a lens of adventure, fantasy, sci-fi, or horror, we know we can make it through because the world was designed to see us do it. We move through the present fully empowered by past lessons to achieve a victorious future. We easily believe this in video games because they let us participate in our truth.

The true miracle is that the world is not designed to assure us of that same style of victory, yet the lessons from video games still work. Mastering one world shows us what it takes to master the other. Whether we succeed in a game first or in the world, the next opportunity is open to us if we want to meet the adventure as a worthy participant.

We make many choices on our path through the game we call life; even things we think are static on our character profile can level up by continuing to engage in our quests. Choosing our difficulty and selecting which role we want to experience is only as permanent a choice as we want to make it. We could see the first choice through to the end or pivot to explore what other masteries will enhance our potential. No matter the case, as long as we take on the next quest with the confidence we witnessed in the gaming hero, we will find the confidence to bypass our roadblocks in a good enough time to accomplish something we used to believe was impossible. We finally become one with ourselves by accepting the truth: A balanced life has room for epic stories. The joys in life need us just as much as our serious quests. Finally, life is meant to be enjoyed the same way we experience video games. Now we have the freedom to play our life as a hero who has completed the quest and knows who they want to be at each stage of the journey.

EPILOGUE

FREEDOM TO LIVE
THE GAMERS JOURNEY

Human beings can choose the kind of life that they want to live.
What's important is that you choose life... and then live.

—Naomi Hunter (Metal Gear Solid)

With all the complexity in the world, how do video games show us so much about who we are and who we aspire to be?

Many experiences we move through in life occur in stages. The sequence may only sometimes happen on the conscious levels of our awareness, but we either attend to each thing individually or decide to pass on them. When we focus on the present, we are only a part of things in the short term. When we allow our experience to separate from our current selves, we see the connections as a tapestry of experiences extending in past and future directions until we understand our existence. Video games can be a part of our past, present, and future, and in many respects, can touch upon every phase at once, in an instant. Across this infinite landscape, heroes we select to be a part of our present fight show us a path through their accomplishments, encouraging our imaginations to thrive. As they model the answering of the call to adventure, they carry us into all forms of challenge until the quest is completed, allowing them to return to the life they were fighting for all along.

As we imagine being a part of these stories, we witness the transformative power of stepping into the unknown. The shadow of new experiences is where our goals await, hoping to be achieved. When we enter this darkness, the road of trials pushes us toward the opportunity for personal growth, with each new challenge we endure forming a clearer understanding of our potential. Every road is unique, yet the similarities for all who play video games bind us together as a shared culture; those we call gamers. By seeing the symbolism of each heroic story and applying it in some way to our psyche, we build the same form of hope within ourselves that every culture has been receiving for centuries from mythical heroes. Experiencing the subliminal power of play encourages the creative forces inside of us to continue leveling up. These experiences combine to unlock the energy to freely walk through life with the gaming journey in our minds.

From the start of a new game, every player becomes the hero. In reality, this sounds aspirational. Only some people are asked by fate to accomplish a grand task to save the world. However, if we set our sights on humanistic self-actualization, every person would feel as if they did pursue this greatest achievement.

Video games provide a chance to practice this mindset. Wins and losses feel different when they are fleeting events followed by the immediate opportunity to freely try again. For every player that wins, others lose. The natural order of life is to consume for survival, an equitable design for video games. Feedback is impartial, with everyone, more often than not, having an equal opportunity to succeed. As a result, the meritocracy of games gives everyone an equal chance to become the chosen one once they enter the game environment. In that way, game players are all the same despite their differences.

No matter which gaming victories we pursue, their mythology allows each of us to matter. The distortion of fairness becomes real, showing us that the game, created for our enjoyment, will provide the challenges we need for us to realize our motivations. As each of us chooses which paths to invest ourselves in, the personal form of the myth takes shape. We become connected to the universal narrative of heroism. The more players we connect with who enjoy the same journey, the more our passion advances beyond the limits of the self into a world we share with others.

Whenever societies become focused on the endpoint instead of processes, this fixation discourages time spent in a state of presence, and instead emphasizes outcomes alone. This aura of constant pressure influences our views on those who play games in cozy ways that represent the counter point to the "productivity first" mission issued by the rest of the world. Restoration from the stress of this world is often needed, so we cope using the most powerful activities that offer a sensation of escape. Video games are just one option on this menu, but games themselves do highlight the truth that there is more to an action than its outcome alone. Games are a gestalt, becoming more in the minds of the player than the sum of their literal experiences. They can certainly be played for achievement, but their processes also contain amazing sources of relaxation, restoration, and fun.

When gaming overtakes our responsibilities, it is because we want to play the hero without the consequences of failure. The ability to save society from permanent despair lies well beyond our reach, while the symbolic act of saving the world from this fate remains possible in the game world. This heroic escape transforms into many parallel purposes in the mind of a person who plays this way. When play is done for healing, the person can return to their earthbound tasks willing to struggle, knowing this is part of the process that is expected of them. They will stick with this process, hoping to actually make a difference, and repeating the attempt until another opportunity is within reach (or when life goes in a new direction). When the restoration becomes hollow avoidance, the only place where achievement is possible is in the virtual space. In this instance, the calling to make a difference as the hero has been missed. The person sees no purpose either in their gaming or in their worldly pursuits. The call must be answered for the purpose to occur, either within games or beyond them.

This level of insight must be earned through experience. Ironically, any opportunity for roleplaying growth relies on the same three stage process of action, then experience gain, and finally leveling-up. An outside party cannot force us to live this way; the lesson must be personally discovered. No matter which archetype explains the personal journey of the gamer, the player must overcome the terror of failing, making the attempt with the grace that signifies their readiness to endure any hardship. Just as the gamer has experienced through the thousand faces of virtual heroes, so too must they discover their courage on their own timeline so they can endure the unifying challenge when the opportunity presents itself.

The basic understanding of success offered by video games symbolically improves the player's self-awareness over time. The toughest game challenges inspire the development of grit. Presenting new problems with each act of the game encourages initiative to keep going. Encountering the boss characters as they escalate to new forms delays gratification, yet we know we will eventually achieve victory as long as we take the time to level up. When we lose, we can continue until we fall to the point of the dreaded game over. Even then, we can always try again from the beginning (or reload a past save), remembering the lessons of past mistakes.

Whenever a new game is started, the player receives an implicit promise that as long as they decide to keep making progress, they will eventually become the hero. This makes them the champion of things that are becoming, not things that have been. This mindset leads us to finding our presence, and is the key to revealing our ideal self in both the digital gaming and ordinary worlds. In this light, our past experiences help us build hope for a future where our heroic self exists. To cross this threshold, the self must transcend the stagnation of repetitive stagnation to instead pursue lifelong progression.

In starting the next game, a person who settles on stagnation will stay who they have been, allowing their past to define the present. There is, however, an alternative to this bad ending. Armed with a new game mindset, the gamer will continue their journey into the future equipped with an understanding that accepting the self becomes the key to unlocking personal growth. The fear of change is repelled by the courage to adopt new thinking. With this power discovered, every moment becomes a chance to keep moving forward.

All of us hope to accept this quest in some way. Many receive this confluence of opportunity through family, relationships, learning, occupation, and institutions or religions. All of these environments involve a form of game we play. The lens through which we view each life area reveals how our path is defined by creating goals, learning the rules, responding to feedback, and making our willing choice. When anything in life brings these elements together to create a routine, a game is being played. When only seen literally, the game is a required task with dire consequences. When mythology is preserved, the imagination creates a sense of purpose in our chosen path. That path is what allows the game to offer us a sense of purpose.

The heroic journey of gaming uses the ideas of the monomyth in ways that allow us to experience both pure joy and genuine fear. Our minds light up in anticipation of each hero's eternal challenge, hoping we will be able to persevere in our own challenge when the time is right. Like with ancient audiences who heard the mythology of their culture long before our gaming was even a dream, the infinite tale of heroes and quests helps us to envision with our own mind's eye a path towards fulfillment that grows larger than ourselves. Yet somehow we hear these stories and become in ourselves the driving force for bringing the heroic resolution into reality. This resolve was symbolic for the audiences of old. For modern audiences, people who play the stories themselves, video games allow us to be a part of the timeless adventure by playing them until we bring the feeling of victory into our reality. Not everyone can find this feeling in their life, except for when they notice it in the play of a video game. This makes gaming the perfect mentor for the path to the victorious feeling for the majority of people who take the time to explore themselves in their play.

In this way, in a world where winning becomes increasingly hard to discover, the stories connect us to everyone who finds inspiration through these successes. By allowing our passion to guide us, we connect with a version of our self that lies deep within the psyche hoping to unify us while we make the most of our journey through life. Anyone who finds this moment of atonement for themselves will easily recognize how a hobby (like playing games) adds to our potential. This expands who we are, allowing us to finally share our purpose with the world in ways that will echo across time.

Video games, at their core, are about having fun. The chance to have fun saves us in a serious world that constantly offers experiences of pain, despair, and suffering. Myths have always been used to explain the world in a way that captures the imagination while sharing a vision of how things are or could be. The witnesses to these stories would form deeper connections with each other through the power of myth just by being in the same spaces.

When we tap into our imaginative abilities, the monomyth inspires us to see past the hollow victories expected by the world as we find our path. Since games teach us to fail upward, we are certain to feel the hollow outcomes of success and failure while always keeping our minds focused on the true purpose.

Our failures do not define us if we lose productively. They instead become non-successes. These outcomes help the ego embrace the fears of the shadow while we discover atonement with the true self. When we assume the transformative identity within us, every goal becomes manageable, and every challenge that cannot yet be overcome stops distracting our focus. The freedom to live as a gamer helps us embrace our full existence in a system that aims to suppress childlike wonder. We can preserve our joy even as we accomplish great things. That is the greatest power we receive from the mythology of gaming.

ACHIEVEMENT UNLOCKED: CONTINUE THE JOURNEY

The successful journey for every player begins with the decision to play a game for the first time. Answering the call to adventure adds a new source of fun to the flow of life. Gaming teaches players how to solve problems, lose, win, and have fun. For some, this activity becomes a hobby. For others, it becomes more. It can be an occupation, a much-needed escape, or even a source of inspiration. Eventually, we encounter the shadow self, a side of us that asks us to forget everything else and do what is easy. If we give in to self-doubt, we lose sight of who we are meant to be. Games stop being fun, and they become an obligation. For most, games remain a source of joy while new challenges are faced across each phase of life.

The balance between story and challenge empowers video games to become a mythology for an entire culture of those who adore them. When the message of a game is understood, it helps those recognize a deeper meaning to approach every new challenge in life with a belief that victory can be achieved.

When we identify the one true challenge we must face to unlock our ideal self, games share with us the concept of progression. Many goals in life take years, and even decades, to see them through to the end. Mythological stories are epic because they tell us to see time as an experience rather than needing to feel every accomplishment right now. Life is a process, and the progression of the gaming hero hints that the best things in the journey require dedication, realistic expectations, and, most of all, time.

When we cross the threshold to begin the great challenge of our lives, we decide it is time to pursue the transformation of self that will make our world better in some meaningful way. Despite not realizing the sacrifices ahead, we embark on the road of trials. The quest chain shows us how to gain experience and level up. This becomes our task in life as well. We enter the world with new expectations to become armed with abilities we did not have before. The challenges along the road of trials are both standardized and personal. We hope to overcome them, but every personal setback challenges us at the core of our being. To preserve our psyche, we must stay the course if we are ever to keep moving forward. To do this, all of our focus must combine into an impressive performance that shows who we are. We must improve our thoughts, use our coping skills, and face the challenge all at once so that in the pivotal moments our effort equals our readiness for change.

Then one day, our stats increase, granting abilities we never imagined when the game's journey started. It is as if we are completely different characters, maintaining our values from the beginning but with a presence to send our darkest problems from the ordinary world back into the light we have come to represent. One by one, we reclaim the balance we hoped to establish from the beginning. Then, the greatest challenge calls to us.

The Supreme Ordeal represents the final boss in our story. This challenge requires balance across every phase of life. These challenges demand the most impressive execution, the knowledge to make the right choice, and the gift of opportunity. Within the game and without, we must be at one with ourselves if we hope to manifest the strengths from every challenge that brought us to this point. The approval of the father figure and the symbolic gifts of the goddess restore our faith that we are enough to overcome the greatest inner struggles. The boss battle can be literal, leading to the ending phases of a video game, or figurative as a rite of passage for our intent to bring our talents with us back into an ordinary world waiting for us to return.

When the confrontation breaks us down, the nadir is felt in a way that makes us question everything. The gaming hero may regret saying "yes" to the mentor. We may wish we had never believed in ourselves enough to begin the journey. These ideas tear us down, preventing us from fulfilling our destiny. When we continue to fight as the gaming hero, they will only win when we guide them to victory. This lesson translates across both worlds. From this realization, we know we can continue our path if we will only decide to persevere in life despite our setbacks. The only goal which can never be accomplished is the one that is not being attempted.

Realizing the full wisdom of progression, the power in our gaming abilities restores the hope that convinced us to begin the quest in the first place. The apotheosis in our character allows us to rise above any challenge we place our focus on. We vanquish the final challenge and lay claim to the ultimate boon. This rite leads to the life we longed for at the beginning when our hopes felt alive only in our imagination. The hero who finds this change within themselves sets out on the return journey. Every obstacle that used to block the way has now become a cleared path. Each guardian who overpowered us in the beginning levels is easily pushed aside. The abilities of the gaming hero allow them to move easily from the ordinary world to the supernatural one. When we embrace this level of understanding, we balance the world of play and the world of the serious. The master of both worlds can find a place to accomplish impressive feats and remain one with the self.

This freedom to live changes the entire worldview. Although those who have not departed on their journey may not see this world clearly, they can still rely on us for ideas, support, and even to group up and enjoy challenges. This connection is the power we bring into our world; the ability to accomplish great mental tasks, describe them, share them, and help others see them in a new way. This occurs because we choose to see video games in the same light as the mythologies that have inspired societies.

It is impossible to play every game and experience every hero's journey. That is the legacy of the monomyth. New games are announced nearly every day in the modern world, meaning we must choose which stories to play and hope we find the ones that will matter to us. As long as we find the presence to enjoy the games we do play, we will be able to live the gaming side of life to the fullest. Games live with us in memory, helping us find a way to connect with others and explain who we are as a gamer. Any game can give us a personal sense of joy. Some stories, however, transcend us to inspire new generations of gamers in ways that will never be forgotten. This nostalgia builds a bridge for mentors and new players alike to experience the mythical journey in ways that bring them together across any phase of life.

The interest in any society towards mythology eventually moves from a sense of wonder to secular goals like profits and tribalism. The symbolic images of a game cease to have meaning if they are only another purchased form of entertainment. The history of gaming remains in its infancy, with technology rapidly expanding as profits skyrocket. Yet, gamers love their games, and each one uniquely. The worlds we inhabit are filled with wonder. This is why we joined them in the first place. No matter our struggle, games give us the opportunity to see ourselves as the hero. Unlike when institutions manipulate the power of their myth control people, gamers do not believe the mythology in their games actually happened. They are fiction, and as a result, they maintain the poetic element that activates the hero identity in ways that enlighten us. The literal is not always more meaningful than the symbolic, allowing our presence to achieve the oneness of the hero ready to take flight.

This is the full power of the journey through a video game. In deciding to pursue joy, we give ourselves, in a moment, what is needed to remain whole. By reflecting on the journey afterward, this atonement transcends even the experience of the play session itself. Our cognitive abilities improve. Our self-esteem feels what it is like to be the one valuable person who makes a difference. Our resilience builds until we find the perfect strategy to overcome the challenges of the visceral world. As we have done countless times in our gaming story, we will overcome anything when given the time to gain experience, equip the best gear, and step into the challenge with the proper abilities equipped.

We all benefit from remembering that the journey is often more valuable than the destination. Just as every traveler decides on their mountain to climb, we feel the pull towards our purpose whenever we listen to the calling within ourselves.

There are many ways to notice this calling in our world. Video games are just one source for symbolic lessons among countless others that add this call to adventure to the quest log of life. The mythology of video games tells us that to pursue our purpose, we often must relax our minds in order to see the stages of our journey clearly. By allowing ourselves to pursue life authentically as a gamer, the infinite mythology of video games inspires us to complete any challenge, both those played before and those not yet played, so we will stay filled with hope in every quest we encounter as we continue the journey.

THE GAMER'S JOURNEY

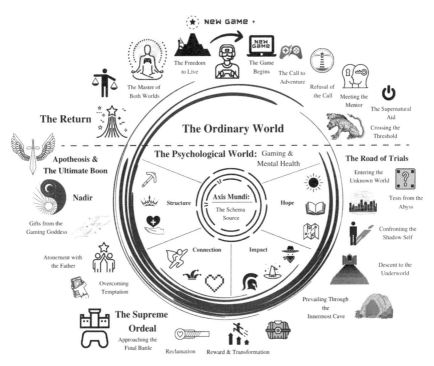

FIGURE 38. *The Gamer's Journey from Start to New Game +*

REFERENCES

_____ *LIST OF GAMES*

2K Australia & Gearbox Software (2014). *Borderlands: The Pre-Sequel* [Video Game]. 2K Games.

2K Boston & 2K Australia (2007). *Bioshock* [Video Game]. 2K Games.

2K Marin (2010). *Bioshock 2* [Video Game]. 2K Games.

5th Cell (2009). *Scribblenauts* [Video Game]. Warner Bros. Interactive Entertainment.

Airship Syndicate (2019). *Darksiders Genesis* [Video Game]. THQ Nordic.

Arnold, J. (2008). Shall Never Surrender. On *Devil May Cry 4* [Original Soundtrack]. Capcom.

Arkane Studios (2012). *Dishonored* [Video Game].

Atlus (1992). *Shin Megami Tensei* [Video Game].

Atlus (2009). *Shin Megami Tensei: Persona 3 Portable* [Video Game].

Atlus (2009). *Persona 3 Portable* [Video Game]. Ghostlight.

Atlus (2011). *Catherine* [Video Game].

Atlus (2012). *Persona 4 Golden* [Video Game].

Atlus (2016). *Persona 5* [Video Game].

Atlus (2019). *Catherine: Full Body* [Video Game].

Atlus (2019). *Persona 5 Royal* [Video Game].

Atlus. (2021). *Shin Megami Tensei V* [Video Game].

Bandai Namco Studios (2015). *Tekken 7* [Video Game]. Bandai Namco Entertainment.

Beat Games (2019). *Beat Saber* [Video Game].

Behaviour Interactive (2016). *Dead by Daylight* [Video Game].

Bethesda Game Studios (2008). *Fallout 3* [Video Game]. Bethesda Softworks.

Bethesda Game Studios (2011). *The Elder Scrolls V: Skyrim* [Video Game]. Bethesda Softworks.

Bethesda Game Studios (2015). *Fallout 4* [Video Game]. Bethesda Softworks.

Big Blue Box Studios (2004). *Fable* [Video Game]. Microsoft Game Studios.

Bioware (1998). *Baldur's Gate* [Video Game].

Bioware (2003). *Star Wars: Knights of the Old Republic* [Video Game].

Bioware (2007). *Mass Effect* [Video Game].

Bioware (2011). *Star Wars: The Old Republic* [Video Game]. Electronic Arts.

Bioware (2009). *Dragon Age: Origins* [Video Game]. Electronic Arts.

Bioware (2014). *Dragon Age: Inquisition* [Video Game]. Electronic Arts.

Bioware (2021). *Mass Effect Legendary Edition* [Video Game]. Electronic Arts.

Blizzard Entertainment (1998). *StarCraft* [Video Game].

Blizzard Entertainment (2002). *Warcraft III: Reign of Chaos* [Video Game].

Blizzard Entertainment (2004). *World of Warcraft* [Video Game].

Blizzard Entertainment (2016). *Overwatch* [Video Game].

BlueTwelve Studio (2022). *Stray* [Video Game]. Annapurna Interactive.

Bungie (2001). *Halo: Combat Evolved* [Video Game]. Microsoft Game Studios.

Bungie (2014). *Destiny* [Video Game]. Activision.

Bungie (2017). *Destiny 2* [Video Game]. Activision.

Capcom (1987). *Street Fighter* [Video Game].

Capcom (1996). *Resident Evil* [Video Game].

Capcom (1998). *Resident Evil 2* [Video Game].

Capcom (1999). *Resident Evil 3: Nemesis* [Video Game].

Capcom (1999). *Street Fighter III: 3rd Strike* [Video Game].

Capcom (2001). *Devil May Cry* [Video Game].

Capcom (2005). *Devil May Cry 3: Dante's Awakening* [Video Game].

Capcom (2005). *Resident Evil 4* [Video Game].

Capcom (2008). *Devil May Cry 4* [Video Game].

Capcom (2019). *Devil May Cry 5* [Video Game].

Capcom (2021). *Resident Evil Village* [Video Game].

CD Projekt Red (2007). *The Witcher* [Video Game]. Atari.

CD Projekt Red (2011). *The Witcher 2: Assassins of Kings* [Video Game].

CD Projekt Red (2015). *The Witcher 3: Wild Hunt* [Video Game].

CD Projekt Red (2020). *Cyberpunk 2077* [Video Game]. CD Projekt.

Concerned Ape (2016). *Stardew Valley* [Video Game].

Creative Assembly (2014). *Alien: Isolation* [Video Game]. Sega.

Criterion Games (2022). *Need for Speed Unbound* [Video Game].
    Electronic Arts.

Crystal Dynamics (2013). *Tomb Raider* [Video Game].

Deadline Games (2009). *Watchmen: The End is Nigh* [Video Game].
    Warner Bros. Interactive Entertainment.

EA Tiburon (2022). *Madden NFL 23* [Video Game]. EA Sports.

EA Vancouver & EA Romania (2022). *FIFA 23* [Video Game]. EA Sports.

Eidos Interactive (1996). *Tomb Raider* [Video Game].

Ensemble Studios (1997). *Age of Empires* [Video Game]. Microsoft.

Firaxis Games (2016). *Sid Meier's Civilization VI* [Video Game]. 2K
    Games.

FromSoftware (2009). *Demon's Souls* [Video Game]. Sony Computer
    Entertainment.

FromSoftware (2011). *Dark Souls* [Video Game]. Namco Bandai Games.

FromSoftware. (2015). *Bloodborne* [Video Game]. Sony Computer Entertainment.

FromSoftware (2019). *Sekiro: Shadows Die Twice* [Video Game]. Activision.

FromSoftware (2022). *Elden Ring* [Video Game]. Bandai Namco Entertainment.

Game Freak (1998). *Pokémon Red and Blue* [Video Game]. Nintendo.

Game Freak (1998). *Pokémon Yellow* [Video Game]. Nintendo.

Game Freak (2004). *Pokémon FireRed and LeafGreen* [Video Game]. Nintendo & The Pokémon Company.

Gearbox Software (2009). *Borderlands* [Video Game]. 2K Games.

Gearbox Software (2012). *Borderlands 2* [Video Game]. 2K Games.

Giant Squid Studios (2016). *Abzû* [Video Games]. 505 Games.

Gunfire Games (2018). *Darksiders III* [Video Game]. THQ Nordic.

Guerrilla Games (2017). *Horizon Zero Dawn* [Video Game]. Sony Interactive Entertainment.

Guerrilla Games (2022). *Horizon Forbidden West* [Video Game]. Sony Interactive Entertainment.

Gygax, G., & Arneson, D. (1974). Dungeons & Dragons (Vol. 19). Tactical Studies Rules Lake Geneva, WI.

h.a.n.d. (2009). *Kingdom Hearts 358/2 Days* [Video Game]. Square Enix.

HAL Laboratory (1999). *Super Smash Bros.* [Video Game.]. Nintendo.

Harmonix. (2005). *Guitar Hero* [Video Game]. RedOctane.

Harmonix (2007). *Rock Band* [Video Game]. MTV Games.

Hatakeyama, T., Kurosaki, M., & Tada, T. (2022). Encyclopaedia Eorzea ~The World of Final Fantasy XIV~ Volume I. In. Japan: Square Enix Books.

Hatakeyama, T., Kurosaki, M., & Tada, T. (2022). Encyclopaedia Eorzea ~The World of Final Fantasy XIV~ Volume II. In. Japan: Square Enix Books.

Hudson Soft (1998). *Mario Party* [Video Game]. Nintendo.

Infinity Ward (2003). *Call of Duty* [Video Game]. Activision.

Intelligent Systems (2019). *Fire Emblem: Three Houses* [Video Game]. Nintendo.

Irrational Games (2013). *Bioshock Infinite* [Video Games]. 2K Games.

Jackbox Games (2014). *The Jackbox Party Pack* [Video Game]. Telltale Games.

Japan Studio & Team Ico (2005). *Shadow of the Colossus* [Video Game].

Konami (1987). *Castlevania* [Video Game].

Konami Computer Entertainment Japan (1998). *Metal Gear Solid* [Video Game]. Konami.

Konami Computer Entertainment Japan (2001). *Metal Gear Solid 2: Sons of Liberty* [Video Game]. Konami.

Konami Computer Entertainment Tokyo (1997). *Castlevania: Symphony of the Night* [Video Game]. Konami.

Studios, L. (2023). *Baldur's Gate 3* [Video Game].

Lionhead Studios (2010). *Fable III* [Video Game]. Microsoft Game Studios.

Massive Entertainment (2016). *Tom Clancy's The Division* [Video Game]. Ubisoft.

Maxis (2000). *The Sims* [Video Game]. Electronic Arts.

Maxis (2014). *The Sims 4* [Video Game]. Electronic Arts.

Media Molecule (2008). *LittleBigPlanet* [Video Game]. Sony Interactive Entertainment.

Meguro, S. (2012). Reach Out to the Truth. On *Persona 4 [Original Soundtrack]*. Atlus.

MercurySteam (2021). *Metroid Dread* [Video Game]. Nintendo.

Midway Games (1992). *Mortal Kombat* [Video Game].

Midway (1995). *Mortal Kombat 3* [Video Game].

Mojang Studios (2011). *Minecraft* [Video Game].

Namco (1994). *Tekken* [Video Game].

Naughty Dog (2007). *Uncharted* [Video Game]. Sony Computer Entertainment.

Naughty Dog (2009). *Uncharted 2: Among Thieves* [Video Game]. Sony Computer Entertainment.

Naughty Dog (2011). *Uncharted 3: Drake's Deception* [Video Game]. Sony Computer Entertainment.

Naughty Dog (2014). *The Last of Us* [Video Game]. Sony Computer Entertainment.

Naughty Dog (2016). *Uncharted 4: A Thief's End* [Video Game]. Sony Computer Entertainment.

Naughty Dog (2020). *The Last of Us Part II* [Video Game]. Sony Interactive Entertainment.

Naughty Dog (2022). *The Last of Us Part I* [Video Game]. Sony Interactive Entertainment.

NDcube (2018). *Super Mario Party* [Video Game]. Nintendo.

NetherRealm Studios (2011). *Mortal Kombat* [Video Game]. Warner Bros. Interactive Entertainment.

Niantic. (2016). *Pokémon Go* [Video Game].

Nintendo (1981). *Donkey Kong* [Arcade Game].

Nintendo (1983). *Super Mario Bros.* [Video Game].

Nintendo (1986). *Kid Icarus* [Video Game].

Nintendo (1986). *The Legend of Zelda* [Video Game].

Nintendo (1986). *Metroid* [Video Game].

Nintendo (1988). *Super Mario Bros. 3* [Video Game].

Nintendo (1990). *Super Mario World* [Video Game].

Nintendo (1992). *Super Mario Kart* [Video Game].

Nintendo (1994). *Super Metroid* [Video Game].

Nintendo (1998). *The Legend of Zelda: Ocarina of Time* [Video Game].

Nintendo (2006). *The Legend of Zelda: Twilight Princess* [Video Game].

Nintendo (2007). *Super Mario Galaxy* [Video Game].

Nintendo (2013). *Super Mario 3D World* [Video Game].

Nintendo (2017). *Mario Kart 8 Deluxe* [Video Game].

Nintendo (2017). *The Legend of Zelda: Breath of the Wild* [Video Game].

Nintendo (2012). *Animal Crossing: New Leaf* [Video Game].

Nintendo (2020). *Animal Crossing: New Horizons* [Video Game].

Nomura, T. (2009). *Final Fantasy VII: Advent Children Complete* [Film]. Visual Works.

Obsidian Entertainment (2010). *Fallout: New Vegas* [Video Game]. Bethesda Softworks.

Pajitnov, A. (1988). *Tetris (NA version)* [Video Game]. Nintendo.

Platinum Games (2009). *Bayonetta* [Video Game]. Sega.

Platinum Games (2017). *Nier: Automata* [Video Game]. Square Enix.

PopCap Games (2001). *Bejeweled* [Video Game]. Electronic Arts.

Project Soul (1995). *Soul Edge* [Video Game]. Namco.

Project Soul (1998). *Soulcalibur* [Video Game]. Namco.

Quantic Dream (2010). *Heavy Rain* [Video Game].

Quantic Dream (2018). *Detroit: Become Human* [Video Game].

Rare (1994). *Donkey Kong Country* [Video Game].

Rare (2018). *Sea of Thieves* [Video Game]. Microsoft Studios.

Remedy Entertainment (2019). *Control* [Video Game]. 505 Games.

Riot Games (2009). *League of Legends* [Video Game].

Rockstar Games (1997). *Grand Theft Auto* [Video Game].

Rocksteady Studios (2015). *Batman: Arkham Knight* [Video Game]. Warner Bros. Interactive Entertainment.

Santa Monica Studio (2005). *God of War* [Video Game].

Santa Monica Studio (2007). *God of War II* [Video Game].

Santa Monica Studio (2010). *God of War III* [Video Game].

Santa Monica Studio (2018). *God of War* [Video Game].

Santa Monica Studio (2022). *God of War: Ragnarök* [Video Game].

Sega (1991). *Sonic the Hedgehog* [Video Game].

Sega. (1992). *Sonic the Hedgehog 2* [Video Game].

Sega. (1994). *Sonic the Hedgehog 3* [Video Game].

Shiny Entertainment (2005). *The Matrix: Path of Neo* [Video Game]. Atari.

Square (1987). *Final Fantasy* [Video Game].

Square (1991). *Final Fantasy IV* [Video Game].

Square. (1992). *Final Fantasy V* [Video Game].

Square. (1995). *Chrono Trigger* [Video Game].

Square (1997). *Final Fantasy VII* [Video Game].

Square (2001). *Final Fantasy X* [Video Game].

Square Enix (2002). *Kingdom Hearts* [Video Game].

Square Enix (2005). *Kingdom Hearts II* [Video Game].

Square Enix (2007). *Crisis Core: Final Fantasy VII* [Video Game].

Square Enix (2009). *Final Fantasy XIII* [Video Game].

Square Enix (2010). *Kingdom Hearts Birth by Sleep* [Video Game].

Square Enix (2013). *Final Fantasy XIV: A Realm Reborn* [Video Game].

Square Enix (2016). *Final Fantasy XV* [Video Game].

Square Enix (2018). *Final Fantasy XV: Royal Edition* [Video Game].

Square Enix (2019). *Kingdom Hearts III* [Video Game].

Square Enix (2020). *Final Fantasy VII Remake* [Video Game].

Strategic Simulations, Inc. (1988). *Pool of Radiance* [Video Game].

Studio Wildcard (2017). *Ark: Survival Evolved* [Video Game].

Supergiant Games (2021). *Hades* [Video Game].

Supermassive Games (2015). *Until Dawn* [Video Game]. Sony Computer Entertainment.

Sumo Digital (2020). *Sackboy: A Big Adventure* [Video Game]. Sony Interactive Entertainment.

Team Silent (1999). *Silent Hill* [Video Game]. Konami.

Team Silent (2001). *Silent Hill 2* [Video Game]. Konami.

Telltale Games (2012). *The Walking Dead: A Telltale Game Series* [Video Game].

ThatGameCompany (2012). *Journey* [Video Game]. Santa Monica Studios.

Thunder Lotus Games (2020). *Spiritfarer* [Video Game].

Traveller's Tales (2005). *Lego Star Wars: The Video Game* [Video Game]. Eidos Interactive.

Traveller's Tales (2012). *Lego The Lord of the Rings* [Video Game]. Warner Bros. Interactive Entertainment.

Traveller's Tales (2022). *Lego Star Wars: The Skywalker Saga* [Video Game]. Warner Bros. Interactive Entertainment.

Ubisoft Montréal (2003). *Prince of Persia: The Sands of Time* [Video Game]. Ubisoft.

Ubisoft. (2007). *Assassin's Creed* [Video Game].

Ubisoft Montréal (2009). *Assassin's Creed II* [Video Game]. Ubisoft.

Valve (2007). *Portal* [Video Game].

Valve (2011). *Portal 2* [Video Game].

Valve (2013). *DotA 2* [Video Game].

Verant Interactive & 989 Studios (1999). *EverQuest* [Video Game]. Sony Online Entertainment.

Vigil Games (2010). *Darksiders* [Video Game]. THQ & Konami.

Vigil Games (2012). *Darksiders II* [Video Game]. THQ.

Visceral Games (2010). *Dante's Inferno* [Video Game]. Electronic Arts.

Visual Concepts (2022). *NBA 2K23* [Video Game]. 2K Sports.

Wardle, J. (2021). *Wordle* [Web Application]. The New York Times Company.

Zynga (2009). *FarmVille* [Video Game].

SCHOLARLY SOURCES

Aabom, H. (2014). Exploring the intrinsic nature of video game achievements. Aalborg University, Copenhagen, Denmark. 1, 1-114.

Agriogianis, T. (2018). The Roles, Mechanics, and Evolution of Boss Battles in Video Games.

Alighieri, D. (2015). *Dante's inferno*. Рипол Классик.

Alighieri, D. (2017). *The divine comedy.* Aegitas.

Allen, J. J., & Anderson, C. A. (2018). Satisfaction and frustration of basic psychological needs in the real world and in video games predict internet gaming disorder scores and well-being. *Computers in Human Behavior*, 84, 220-229.

Amalia, E. R., & Khoiriyati, S. (2018). Effective Learning Activities To Improve Early Childhood Cognitive Development. *Al-Athfal: Jurnal Pendidikan Anak*, 4(1), 103-111.

Andrade, M. J., & Pontes, H. (2017). A brief update on videogame play and flow experience: From addiction to healthy gaming. *Mental Health and Addiction Research, 2*(1), 1-3.

Ang, R. P., & Goh, D. (2008). Online video game therapy for mental health concerns: A review. *International Journal of Social Psychiatry, 54*(4), 370-382.

Antonio, M., & Weixi, K. (2022). The relationship between areas of life satisfaction, personality, and overall life satisfaction: An integrated account [article]. *Frontiers in Psychology*, 13.

Arnott, L. (2017). Mapping Metroid. *Games and Culture, 12*(1), 3-27.

Aytemiz, B., & Smith, A. M. (2020, September). A Diagnostic Taxonomy of Failure in Videogames. In *International Conference on the Foundations of Digital Games*, (pp. 1-11).

Babulal, G. M., Foster, E. R., & Wolf, T. J. (2016). Facilitating Transfer of Skills and Strategies in Occupational Therapy Practice: Practical Application of Transfer Principles. Asian *Journal of Occupational Therapy, 11*(1), 19-25.

Banks, J., & Bowman, N. D. (2013). *Close intimate playthings? Understanding player-avatar relationships as a function of attachment, agency, and intimacy* Internet Research, Denver, USA.

Banks, J., & Bowman, N. (2014). Avatars are (sometimes) people too: Linguistic indicators of parasocial and social ties in player-avatar relationships. *New Media & Society, 18.*

Barbour, K., Marshall, D., & Moore, C. (2014). Persona to persona studies. *M/C Journal: A Journal of Media and Culture, 17*(3), 1-6.

Barnet, J. (2019). Exploring the Relationship Between Religiousness and Video Game Addiction (Publication Number 28268685) [M.A., East Tennessee State University]. ProQuest Dissertations & Theses Global. Ann Arbor.

Barnett, J., & Coulson, M. (2010). Virtually real: A psychological perspective on massively multiplayer online games. *Review of General Psychology, 14*(2), 167-179.

Barr, M. (2020). The Force Is Strong with This One (but Not That One): What Makes a Successful Star Wars Video Game Adaptation? *Arts, 9*(4), 131.

Bartle, R. (1996). Hearts, clubs, diamonds, spades: Players who suit MUDs. *Journal of Online Environments, 1*(1).

Bartle, R. (2004). Designing Virtual Worlds. New Riders.

Barton, M. (2008). Dungeons and desktops: The history of computer role-playing games. A K Peters, Ltd.

Bateman, C., & Boon, R. (2006). 21st century game design. Course Technology.

Batty, C. (2010). The physical and emotional threads of the archetypal hero's journey: proposing common terminology and re-examining the narrative model. Journal of Screenwriting, 1(2), 291.

Bean, A. M. (2015). Video gamers' personas: A five factor study exploring personality elements of the video gamer. Pacifica Graduate Institute.

Bean, A. M., & Groth-Marnat, G. (2016). Video gamers and personality: A five-factor model to understand game playing style. *Psychology of Popular Media Culture, 5*(1), 27-38.

Bean, A. (2019). *The Psychology of Zelda*. Benbella Books, Inc.

Bean, A. (2020). *The Psychology of Final Fantasy: Surpassing the Limit Break*. Leyline Publishing, Inc.

Bean, A. (2022). *The Psychology of Pokémon: The Power to Catch 'em All*. Leyline Publishing, Inc.

Bean, A. M., Daniel jr., E. S., & Hays, S. A. (2020). Integrating Geek Culture into Therapeutic Practice: The Clinician's Guide to Geek Therapy. Leyline Publishing.

Billieux, J., Van der Linden, M., Achab, S., Khazaal, Y., Paraskevopoulos, L., Zullino, D., & Thorens, G. (2012). Why do you play World of Warcraft? An in-depth exploration of self-reported motivations to play online and in game behaviours in the virtual world of Azeroth. *Computers in Human Behavior, 29*(1), 103-109.

Bíró, G. I. (2014). Didactics 2.0: A Pedagogical Analysis of Gamification Theory from a Comparative Perspective with a Special View to the Components of Learning. *Procedia - Social and Behavioral Sciences, 141*, 148-151.

Blahuta, J. P., & Beaulieu, M. S. (2009). Final Fantasy and philosophy: The ultimate walkthrough.

Blasko, D. G. (1999). Only the tip of the iceberg: Who understands what about metaphor? *Journal of Pragmatics, 31*(12), 1675-1683.

Bosboom, J., Demaine, E. D., Hesterberg, A., Lynch, J., & Waingarten, E. (2016). Mario Kart is hard. In *Discrete and Computational Geometry and Graphs* (pp. 49-59). Springer International Publishing.

Breuer, J., Scharkow, M., & Quandt, T. (2013). Sore losers? A reexamination of the frustration–aggression hypothesis for colocated video game play. *Psychology of Popular Media Culture.*

Brockmyer, J. H., Fox, C. M., Curtiss, K. A., McBroom, E., Burkhart, K. M., & Pidruzny, J. N. (2009). The development of the Game Engagement Questionnaire: A measure of engagement in video game-playing. *Journal of Experimental Social Psychology, 45*(4), 624-634.

Broderick, P. C., & Blewitt, P. (2020). *The Life Span: Human Development for Helping Professionals* (Fifth ed.). Pearson Education, Inc.

Buchanan-Oliver, M., & Seo, Y. (2012). Play as co-created narrative in computer game consumption: The hero's journey in Warcraft III. *Journal of Consumer Behaviour* (6), 423-431.

Byrne, M. L. (2000). Heroes and Jungians [research-article]. *The San Francisco Jung Institute Library Journal, 18*(3), 13.

Byrne, U. (2005). Wheel of Life:Effective steps for stress management. *Business Information Review, 22*(2), 123-130. https://doi.org/10.1177/0266382105054770

Caci, B., Scrima, F., Tabacchi, M. E., & Cardaci, M. (2019). The Reciprocal Influences among Motivation, Personality Traits, and Game Habits for Playing Pokémon GO. *International Journal of Human–Computer Interaction, 35*(14), 1303-1311.

Campbell, J. (1949). The hero with a thousand faces. New World Library.

Carlsson, U. (2010). Children and Youth in the Digital Media Culture. University of Gothenburg.

Cassar, R. (2013). God of War: A Narrative Analysis. Eludamos. *Journal for Computer Game Culture, 7*(1), 81-99.

Ceranoglu, T. A. (2010). Video games in psychotherapy. *Review of General Psychology, 14*(2), 141-146.

Chen, V., & Duh, H. (2010). Socializing in an online gaming community: Social interaction in World of Warcraft, [in:] Virtual Communities: Concepts, Methodologies, Tools and Applications, Information Resources Management Association.

Coulson, M., Barnett, J., Ferguson, C. J., & Gould, R. L. (2012). Real feelings for virtual people: Emotional attachments and interpersonal attraction in video games. *Psychology of Popular Media Culture, 1*(3), 176-184.

Cowley, B., Charles, D., Black, M., & Hickey, R. (2008). Toward an understanding of flow in video games. *Computers in Entertainment, 6*(2), 20:21-20:27.

Cravens, G. (2014). *Evo Moment 37: One of the most famous moments in competitive gaming history.* Glenn Cravens.

Csikszentmihalyi, M. (1975). Beyond boredom and anxiety. Jossey-Bass Publishing.

Csikszentmihalyi, M. (2008). Flow: The psychology of optimal experience. Harper Perennial Modern Classics.

Curlango Rosas, C. M., Ibarra Esquer, J. E., Chávez Valenzuela, G. E., González Ramírez, M. L., Arredondo Acosta, L. E., & Rodríguez, M. D. (2014). Understanding Game Playing Preferences [research article]. *CLEI Electronic Journal*, (3), 10.

David Bowman, N., Keene, J., & Najera, C. J. (2021, May). Flow Encourages Task Focus, but Frustration Drives Task Switching. In *Proceedings of the 2021 CHI Conference on Human Factors in Computing Systems* (pp 1-8).

de Gortari, A. B. O., Aronsson, K., & Griffiths, M. (2011). Game Transfer Phenomena in video game playing: a qualitative interview study. *International Journal of Cyber Behavior, Psychology and Learning (IJCBPL), 1*(3), 15-33.

Delmas, G., Champagnat, R., & Augeraud, M. (2007). Bringing Interactivity into Campbell's Hero's Journey.

Dickey, M. D. (2005). Engaging by design: How engagement strategies in popular computer and video games can inform instructional design. *Educational Technology Research and Development, 53*(2), 67-83.

Dimock, G. E. (1919). *The Odyssey.* Harvard University Press.

Domahidi, E., Festl, R., & Quandt, T. (2014). To dwell among gamers: Investigating the relationship between social online game use and gaming-related friendships. *Computers in Human Behavior, 35,* 107-115.

Domsch, S. (2013). Storyplaying: Agency and Narrative in Video Games. De Gruyter.

Dowsett, A., & Jackson, M. (2019). The effect of violence and competition within video games on aggression. *Computers in Human Behavior, 99,* 22-27.

Eden, A., Maloney, E., & Bowman, N. D. (2010). Gender attribution in online video games. *Journal of Media Psychology: Theories, Methods, and Applications, 22*(3), 114-124.

Erikson, E. (1980). *Identity and the Life Cycle.* W. W. Norton and Company, Inc.

Evans, M. A., Norton, A., Chang, M., Deater-Deckard, K., & Balci, O. (2013). Youth and video games: Exploring effects on learning and engagement. *Zeitschrift für Psychologie, 221*(2), 98-106.

evo2kvids. (2015, August 27). *Official Evo Moment #37, Daigo vs Justin Evo 2004 in HD* [Video].

Farca, G., Lehner, A., & Navarro-Remesal, V. (2020). Regenerative Play and the Experience of the Sublime: Breath of the Wild. In Mythopoeic Narrative in The Legend of Zelda (pp. 205-221). Routledge.

Felix, S., & Jan-Noël, T. (2014). Video Game Characters. Theory and Analysis [article]. *Diegesis: Interdisziplinäres E-Journal für Erzählforschung, 3*(1).

Ferguson, C. J. (2010). Blazing angels or resident evil? Can violent video games be a force for good? *Review of General Psychology, 14*(2), 68-81.

Ferguson, C. J., & Olson, C. K. (2013). Friends, fun, frustration and fantasy: Child motivations for video game play. *Motivation and Emotion, 37*(1), 154-164.

Ferguson, C., Van Oostendorp, H., & Van Den Broek, E. L. (2019). The Development and Evaluation of the Storyline Scaffolding Tool. Presented at IEEE.

Fernandez-Luque, L., Tøllefsen, T., & Brox, E. (2011). Healthy Gaming – Video game design to promote health. *Applied Clinical Informatics, 2*(2), 128-142.

Ferreira, A. M. D., & da Rocha, L. G. S. (2018). *Bulbasaur, Charmander or Squirtle: An Application of Artificial Neural Networks for Pattern Recognition* Proceedings of SBGames - Computing Track - Short Papers, Brazil.

Field, S. (2005). *Screenplay: The Foundations of Screenwriting*. Bantam Dell.

Fogg, B. J. (2009, April). A behavior model for persuasive design. In *Proceedings of the 4th International Conference on Persuasive Technology* (pp 1-7).

Fortes, L. S., De Lima-Junior, D., Fiorese, L., Nascimento-Júnior, J. R. A., Mortatti, A. L., & Ferreira, M. E. C. (2020). The effect of smartphones and playing video games on decision-making in soccer players: A crossover and randomised study. *Journal of Sports Sciences, 38*(5), 552-558.

Frankl, V. (1959). Man's Search for Meaning. Beacon Press.

Freud, S. (1913). *The interpretation of dreams*. Macmillan.

Freud, S. (1952). A general introduction to psychoanalysis. Washington Square. (Original work published 1920)

Fuster, H., Chamarro, A., Carbonell, X., & Vallerand, R. J. (2014). Relationship between passion and motivation for gaming in players of massively multiplayer online role-playing games. *Cyberpsychology, Behavior, and Social Networking, 17*(5), 292-297.

Gabbiadini, A., Mari, S., Volpato, C., & Monaci, M. (2014). Identification processes in online groups: Identity motives in the virtual realm of MMORPGs. *Journal of Media Psychology: Theories, Methods, and Applications, 26*(3), 141-152.

Gackenbach, J., Darlington, M., Ferguson, M.-L., & Boyes, A. (2013). Video game play as nightmare protection: A replication and extension. *Dreaming, 23*(2), 97-111.

GameCentral. (2017). Why do so few people beat the games they play? – Reader's Feature.

Garland, J. L., & Chesbro, S. B. (2012, 2012 Spring-Summer). Culturally competent interviewing: applying Hill's three-stage model of helping skills to healthcare practice. *Journal of the National Society of Allied Health, 9*(10), 6+.

Gee, J. P. (2006). Are Video Games Good for Learning? Nordic *Journal of Digital Literacy, 1*(3), 172-183.

Ginsburg, K. R., and the Committee on, C., and the Committee on Psychosocial Aspects of, C., & Family, H. (2007). The Importance of Play in Promoting Healthy Child Development and Maintaining Strong Parent-Child Bonds. *Pediatrics, 119*(1), 182-191.

Glasser, W. (1976). *Positive Addiction*. Harper & Row, Publishers, Inc.

Glasser, W. (1999). *Choice Theory: A New Psychology of Personal Freedom*. HarperCollins Publishers.

Granic, I., Lobel, A., & Engels, R. C. M. E. (2014). The benefits of playing video games. *American Psychologist, 69*(1), 66-78.

Greitemeyer, T. (2013). Playing video games cooperatively increases empathic concern. *Social Psychology, 44*(6), 408-413.

Greitemeyer, T., & Osswald, S. (2010). Effects of prosocial video games on prosocial behavior. *Journal of Personality and Social Psychology, 98*(2), 211-221.

Greitemeyer, T., Osswald, S., & Brauer, M. (2010). Playing prosocial video games increases empathy and decreases schadenfreude. *Emotion, 10*(6), 796-802.

Guiley, R. (2009). *The encyclopedia of demons and demonology*. Infobase Publishing.

Guterman, J. T. (2006). *Mastering the Art of Solution Focused Counseling*. American Counseling Association.

Hamilton, E. (2017). Mythology (75th Anniversary Illustrated Edition): *Timeless Tales of Gods and Heroes*. Hachette UK.

Hamlen, K. R. (2013). Understanding children's choices and cognition in video game play: A synthesis of three studies. *Zeitschrift für Psychologie, 221*(2), 107-114.

Harris, B. (2014). *Console Wars: Sega Vs Nintendo-and the Battle that Defined a Generation*. Atlantic Books Ltd.

Harth, J. (2017). Empathy with Non-Player Characters? An Empirical approach to the Foundations of Human/Non-Human Relationships. *Journal For Virtual Worlds Research, 10*(2).

Hartmann, T., Jung, Y., & Vorderer, P. (2012). What determines video game use? The impact of users' habits, addictive tendencies, and intentions to play. *Journal of Media Psychology: Theories, Methods, and Applications, 24*(1), 19-30.

Henrich, S., & Worthington, R. (2021). Let Your Clients Fight Dragons: A Rapid Evidence Assessment regarding the Therapeutic Utility of 'Dungeons & Dragons'. *Journal of Creativity in Mental Health, 1*, 1-19.

Hilvert-Bruce, Z., Neill, J. T., Sjöblom, M., & Hamari, J. (2018). Social motivations of live-streaming viewer engagement on Twitch. *Computers in Human Behavior, 84*, 58-67.

Hitchens, M., & Drachen, A. (2009). The many faces of role-playing games. *International journal of role-playing, 1*(1), 3-21.

Hughes, J. (1988). Therapy is Fantasy: Roleplaying, Healing and the Construction of Symbolic Order. *RPG Research, 1*, 1-16.

Jerz, D. (2015). Cave Gave Game: Subterranean Space as Videogame Place. *Digital & Natural Ecologies*, 1-30.

Jin, S.-A. A. (2011). "My avatar behaves well and this feels right": Ideal and ought selves in video gaming. *Social Behavior and Personality, 39*(9), 1175-1182.

Johannes, N., Vuorre, M., & Przybylski, A. K. (2021). Video game play is positively correlated with well-being. *Royal Society Open Science, 8*(2), 202049.

Johnson, D., Jones, C., Scholes, L., & Carras, M. (2013). Videogames and wellbeing: A comprehensive review.

Johnson, J. A., Keiser, H. N., Skarin, E. M., & Ross, S. R. (2014). The Dispositional Flow Scale–2 as a Measure of Autotelic Personality: An Examination of Criterion-Related Validity. *Journal of Personality Assessment, 96*(4), 465-470.

Johnson, M. R., & Woodcock, J. (2017). Fighting games and Go. *Thesis Eleven, 138*(1), 26-45.

Johnson, M. R., & Woodcock, J. (2019). The impacts of live streaming and Twitch.tv on the video game industry. Media, Culture & Society, 41(5), 670-688.

Jones, C., Scholes, L., Johnson, D., Katsikitis, M., & Carras, M. (2014). Gaming well: links between videogames and flourishing mental health [Original Research]. *Frontiers in Psychology, 5*, 1-8.

Jones, K. (2014). An Exploration of Personality Development through Mythic Narratives. *Advanced Development, 14*, 42-58.

Jung, C. G. (1954). *The Development of Personality: Papers on Child Psychology, Education, and Related Subjects*. Princeton University Press.

Jung, C. G. (1960). Psychology and religion. Yale University Press.

Jung, C. G. (1971). Psychological types: The collected works of C.G. Jung (Vol. 6). Princeton University Press.

Juul, J. (2009). Fear of failing? the many meanings of difficulty in video games. The video game theory reader, 2(237-252).

Kang, H., & Kim, H. K. (2020). My avatar and the affirmed self: Psychological and persuasive implications of avatar customization. *Computers in Human Behavior, 112*, 106446.

Kato, P. M. (2010). Video games in health care: Closing the gap. *Review of General Psychology, 14*(2), 113-121. (Video Games: Old Fears and New Directions)

Kaufmann, D. A. (2016). Personality, motivation, and online gaming [Order No. 10246131, Available from ProQuest Dissertations & Theses Global (1860872558).

Kaufmann, D. A. (2018). Reflection: Benefits of gamification in online higher education. *Journal of Instructional Research, 7*, 125-132.

Kaufmann, D. A. (2019). Counselor development as the Hero's Journey: Reflections from a counselor educator. *Journal of Instructional Research, 8*, 17-32.

Kaufmann, D. (2020-2022). *The Gaming Persona* [Audio Podcast]. Dr. Gameology.

Kaufmann, D. (2021). Personality type and motivation to play MMO games. *Journal of Scholarly Engagement, 4*(1), 96-118.

Kaufmann, D. (2022). Learning to be the very best: The trainer's journey. In A. Bean (Ed.), *The Psychology of Pokémon: The Power to Catch 'em All*. Leyline Publishing.

Kaufmann, D., & Diez-Morel, S. (2022). Examining the flow experience in Final Fantasy XIV Online through the lens of player personality and motivation to play. DiGRA 2022, Kraków, Poland.

Kaufmann, D., & Ferguson-Lucas, T. (2020). Using frustration awareness to assist counseling students in succeeding with their online curriculum. *Journal of Instructional Research, 8*(2), 24-33.

King, D., Delfabbro, P., & Griffiths, M. (2009). Video game structural characteristics: A new psychological taxonomy. *International Journal of Mental Health and Addiction, 8*(1), 90-106.

Kiraly, O., Urban, R., Griffiths, M., Agoston, C., Nagygyorgy, K., Kokonyei, G., & Demetrovics, Z. (2015). The mediating effect of gaming motivation between psychiatric symptoms and problematic online gaming: An online survey. *Journal of Medical Internet Research, 17*(4), 1-15.

Klimmt, C., Blake, C., Hefner, D., Vorderer, P., & Roth, C. (2009). Player Performance, Satisfaction, and Video Game Enjoyment. In (pp. 1-12). Springer Berlin Heidelberg.

Korkeila, H., & Hamari, J. (2020). Avatar capital: The relationships between player orientation and their avatar's social, symbolic, economic and cultural capital. *Computers in Human Behavior, 102*, 14-21. https://doi.org/10.1016/j.chb.2019.07.036

Kowert, R., & Oldmeadow, J. A. (2013). (A)Social reputation: Exploring the relationship between online video game involvement and social competence. *Computers in Human Behavior, 29*(4), 1872-1878.

Kowert, R., & Quandt, T. (2021). *The Video Game Debate 2: Revisiting the Physical, Social, and Psychological Effects of Video Games.* Routledge.

Kreissl, J., Possler, D., & Klimmt, C. (2021). Engagement With the Gurus of Gaming Culture: Parasocial Relationships to Let's Players. *Games and Culture, 16*(8), 1021-1043.

Kübler-Ross, E., & Kessler, D. (2005). *On grief and grieving: Finding the meaning of grief through the five stages of loss.* Simon and Schuster.

Kübler-Ross, E. (2012). *The wheel of life.* Simon and Schuster.

Kwon, J.-H., Chung, C.-S., & Lee, J. (2011). The effects of escape from self and interpersonal relationship on the pathological use of internet games. *Community Mental Health Journal, 47*(1), 113-121.

Laato, S., & Rauti, S. (2021). Central Themes of the Pokémon Franchise and why they Appeal to Humans. Proceedings of the 54th Hawaii International Conference on System Sciences.

Laconi, S., Pires, S., & Chabrol, H. (2017). Internet Gaming Disorder, Motives, Game genres and Psychopathology. *Computers in Human Research, 75*, 652-659.

Ladkin, D., Spitler, C., & Craze, G. (2018). The journey of individuation: A Jungian alternative to the theory and practice of leading authentically. *Leadership, 14*(4), 415-434.

Lalot, F., Zerhouni, O., & Pinelli, M. (2017). "I Wanna Be the Very Best!" Agreeableness and Perseverance Predict Sustained Playing to Pokémon Go : A Longitudinal Study. *Games for Health Journal, 6.*

Lang, A., Bradley, S. D., Schneider, E. F., Kim, S. C., & Mayell, S. (2012). Killing is positive! Intra-game responses meet the necessary (but not sufficient) theoretical conditions for influencing aggressive behavior. *Journal of Media Psychology: Theories, Methods, and Applications, 24*(4), 154-165.

Lattimore, R., & Baskin, L. (1962). *The Iliad of Homer.* CUP Archive.

Lawson, G. (2005). The hero's journey as a developmental metaphor in counseling [Article]. *Journal of Humanistic Counseling, Education & Development, 44*(2), 134-144.

Lee, I. (2017). The Role of the Ego in Jungian Individuation and Yogacara Buddhism's Enlightenment. *Pastoral Psychology, 66*(2), 281-293.

Lee, I., & Yu, C.-Y. (2011). Leaving a Never-Ending Game: Quitting MMORPGs and Online Gaming Addiction.

Lemenager, T., Neissner, M., Sabo, T., Mann, K., & Kiefer, F. (2020). "Who am I" and "How should I be": A systematic review on self-concept and avatar identification in gaming disorder. *Current Addiction Reports, 7*(2), 166-193.

Leonardelli, G. J., Pickett, C. L., & Brewer, M. B. (2010). Optimal distinctiveness theory: A framework for social identity, social cognition, and intergroup relations. *Advances in Experimental Social Psychology, 43*, 63-113.

Liao, G.-Y., Huang, H.-C., & Teng, C.-I. (2016). When does frustration not reduce continuance intention of online gamers? The expectancy disconfirmation perspective [Article]. *Journal of Electronic Commerce Research, 17*(1), 65-79.

Lou, J.-K., Park, K., Cha, M., Park, J., Lei, C.-L., & Chen, K.-T. (2013). Gender swapping and user behaviors in online social games. Proceedings of the 22nd international conference on World Wide Web.

Lyons, E. J., Tate, D. F., Ward, D. S., Ribisl, K. M., Bowling, J. M., & Kalyanaraman, S. (2014). Engagement, enjoyment, and energy expenditure during active video game play. *Health Psychology, 33*(2), 174-181.

Maciejewski, P. K., Zhang, B., Block, S. D., & Prigerson, H. G. (2007). *An Empirical Examination of the Stage Theory of Grief*. JAMA, 297(7), 716-724.

Mancini, T., & Sibilla, F. (2017). Offline personality and avatar customisation. Discrepancy profiles and avatar identification in a sample of MMORPG players. *Computers in Human Behavior, 69*, 275-283.

Mancini, T., Imperato, C., & Sibilla, F. (2019). Does avatar's character and emotional bond expose to gaming addiction? Two studies on virtual self-discrepancy, avatar identification and gaming addiction in massively multiplayer online role-playing game players. *Computers in Human Behavior, 92,* 297-305.

Maree, J. G. (2021). The psychosocial development theory of Erik Erikson: critical overview. *Early Child Development and Care,* 1-15.

Markey, P., & Ferguson, C. (2017). Moral Combat: Why the War on Violent Video Games is Wrong. BenBella Books, Inc.

Markey, P. M., Markey, C. N., & French, J. E. (2014). Violent video games and real-world violence: Rhetoric versus data. *Psychology of Popular Media Culture, 4*(4), 277.

Marks-Tarlow, T. (2017). I Am an Avatar of Myself: Fantasy, Trauma, and Self-Deception. *American Journal of Play, 9*(2), 169-201.

Marks-Tarlow, T. (2017). Awakening clinical intuition: Creativity and play. Play and Creativity in Psychotherapy (Norton Series on Interpersonal Neurobiology).

Marlowe, C. (2005). *Doctor Faustus.*

Marmor, J. (2018). *Modern Psychoanalysis.* Routledge.

Maslow, A. H. (1958). A Dynamic Theory of Human Motivation. In Understanding human motivation. (pp. 26-47). Howard Allen Publishers.

Mattheiss, E., Hochleitner, C., Busch, M., Orji, R., & Tscheligi, M. (2017). *Deconstructing Pokémon Go – An Empirical Study on Player Personality Characteristics.*

Mazurek, M. O., Engelhardt, C. R., & Clark, K. E. (2015). Video games from the perspective of adults with autism spectrum disorder. *Computers in Human Behavior, 51,* 122-130.

McBride Steinberg, B. (2014). Embracing the journey. *California English, 20*(1), 16-18.

McCullough, H. (2019). "Hey! Listen!": Video Game Dialogue, Integrative Complexity and the Perception of Quality. *Press Start, 5*(1), 94-107.

McGonigal, J. (2011). Reality is broken: Why games make us better and how they can change the world. Penguin Group.

Moore, C., Barbour, K., & Marshall, P. D. (2019). Persona studies: An introduction. John Wiley & Sons.

Moran, J. (2021). The Hero's Journey in Player Experiences. [Swinburne University of Technology].

Morse, W. C. (2020). Recreation as a Social-Ecological Complex Adaptive System. *Sustainability, 12*(3), 753.

Moyles, J. R., Stoll, L., & Fink, D. (1989). Just playing?: The role and status of play in early childhood education. Open University Press.

Mullen, C. A., & Schunk, D. H. (2012). Operationalizing phases of mentoring relationships. *The SAGE handbook of mentoring and coaching in education*, 89-104.

Murdock, N. L. (2017). Theories of Counseling & Psychotherapy: A Case Approach (Fourth ed.). Pearson Education, Inc.

Navarro, J. L., & Tudge, J. R. H. (2022). Technologizing Bronfenbrenner: Neo-ecological Theory. *Current Psychology, 1*, 1-17.

Newzoo. (2021). Newzoo's Gamer Segmentation: An overview of the nine unique personas.

Newzoo. (2021). Newzoo Global Games Market Report 2021.

Nicholls, F. S., & Cook, M. (2022). *The Dark Souls of Archaeology: Recording Elden Ring* FDG 2022,

Nilsson, H., & Kazemi, A. (2016). Reconciling and Thematizing Definitions of Mindfulness: The Big Five of Mindfulness. *Review of General Psychology, 20*(2), 183-193.

Nordby, K., Løkken, R. A., & Pfuhl, G. (2019). Playing a video game is more than mere procrastination. *BMC Psychology, 7*(1).

Olson, C. K. (2010). Children's motivations for video game play in the context of normal development. *Review of General Psychology, 14*(2), 180-187.

Oswald, C. A., Prorock, C., & Murphy, S. M. (2014). The perceived meaning of the video game experience: An exploratory study. *Psychology of Popular Media Culture, 3*(2), 110-126.

Pallavicini, F., Ferrari, A., & Mantovani, F. (2018). Video Games for Well-Being: A Systematic Review on the Application of Computer Games for Cognitive and Emotional Training in the Adult Population [Systematic Review]. *Frontiers in Psychology, 9.* 1-16.

Paraskeva, F., Mysirlaki, S., & Papagianni, A. (2010). Multiplayer online games as educational tools: Facing new challenges in learning. *Computers & Education, 54*(2), 498-505.

Pearson, C. S. (1991). *Awakening the Heroes Within: Twelve Archetypes to Help Us Find Ourselves and Transform Our World.* HarperOne.

Perry, R., Drachen, A., Kearney, A., Kriglstein, S., Nacke, L. E., Sifa, R., Wallner, G., & Johnson, D. (2018). Online-only friends, real-life friends or strangers? Differential associations with passion and social capital in video game play. *Computers in Human Behavior, 79*, 202-210.

Petter, S., Barber, C. S., & Barber, D. (2020). Gaming the system: The effects of social capital as a resource for virtual team members. *Information & Management, 57*(6), 103239.

Pieracci, M. (1990). The mythopoesis of psychotherapy. *The Humanistic Psychologist, 18*(2), 208-224.

Plante, C., Gentile, D., Groves, C., Modlin, A., & Blanco-Herrera, J. (2018). Video Games as Coping Mechanisms in the Etiology of Video Game Addiction. Psychology of Popular *Media Culture, 8.* 385-394.

Poels, Y., Annema, J. H., Verstraete, M., Zaman, B., & De Grooff, D. (2012). Are you a gamer? A qualititive study on the parameters for categorizing casual and hardcore gamers. *IADIS International Journal on WWW/INTERNET* (1), 1-16.

Przybylski, A. K., Rigby, C. S., & Ryan, R. M. (2010). A Motivational Model of Video Game Engagement. *Review of General Psychology, 14*(2), 154-166.

Psaila, R. (2015). *The Super Smash Bros Series, from casual to competitive play.*

Ratan, R., Beyea, D., Li, B. J., & Graciano, L. (2020). Avatar characteristics induce users' behavioral conformity with small-to-medium effect sizes: a meta-analysis of the proteus effect. *Media Psychology, 23*(5), 651-675.

Reinecke, L. (2009). Games and recovery: The use of video and computer games to recuperate from stress and strain. *Journal of Media Psychology: Theories, Methods, and Applications, 21*(3), 126-142.

Riva, E. F. M., Riva, G., Talò, C., Boffi, M., Rainisio, N., Pola, L., Diana, B., Villani, D., Argenton, L., & Inghilleri, P. (2017). Measuring Dispositional Flow: Validity and reliability of the Dispositional Flow State Scale 2, Italian version. *PLoS ONE, 12*(9), e0182201.

Rogers, B., Chicas, H., Kelly, J., Kubin, E., Christian, M., Kachanoff, F., Berger, J., Puryear, C., McAdams, D., & Gray, K. (2023). Seeing Your Life Story as a Hero's Journey Increases Meaning in Life. *Journal of Personality and Social Psychology.*

Rogers, C. R. (2007). The necessary and sufficient conditions of therapeutic personality change. *Psychotherapy: Theory, Research, Practice, Training, 44*(3), 240-248. (The Necessary and Sufficient Conditions at the Half Century Mark)

Rønnestad, M. H., & Skovholt, T. M. (2003). The journey of the counselor and therapist: Research findings and perspectives on professional development. *Journal of Career Development, 30*(1), 5-44.

Rooney, J. (2019). A Link to Your Mental Health: The Science Behind "Zelda Therapy". Medium.com.

Ross, T. L., & Weaver, A. J. (2012). Shall we play a game? How the behavior of others influences strategy selection in a multiplayer game. *Journal of Media Psychology: Theories, Methods, and Applications, 24*(3), 102-112.

Rosselet, J. G., & Stauffer, S. D. (2013). Using group role-playing games with gifted children and adolescents: A psychosocial intervention model. *International Journal of Play Therapy, 22*(4), 173-192. https://doi.org/10.1037/a0034557

Rubin, L. C. (2007). Using Superheroes in Counseling and Play Therapy. Springer Publishing Company.

Ryan, R., Rigby, C., & Przybylski, A. (2006). The motivational pull of video games: A self-determination theory approach. *Motivation and Emotion, 30*, 344-360.

Sagie, A., & Elizur, D. (1996). The Structure of Personal Values: A Conical Representation of Multiple Life Areas. *Journal of Organizational Behavior, 17*, 573-586.

Salen, K., & Zimmerman, E. (2004). Rule of play: Game design fundamentals. MIT Press.

Sapach, S. C. (2017). Gotta Catch Em' All: The Compelling Act of Creature Collection in Pokemon, Ni No Kuni, Shin Megami Tensei, and World of Warcraft. *Loading... The Journal of the Canadian Game Studies Association, 10*(16), 53-74.

Schrader, P. G., & McCreery, M. (2008). The acquisition of skill and expertise in massively multiplayer online games. *Educational Technology Research and Development, 56*(5), 557-574.

Sedgwick, D. (2015). On integrating Jungian and other theories [Article]. *Journal of Analytical Psychology, 60*(4), 540-558.

Seligman, M. E. P., & Csikszentmihalyi, M. (2014). Positive Psychology: An Introduction. In M. Csikszentmihalyi (Ed.), Flow and the Foundations of Positive Psychology: The Collected Works of Mihaly Csikszentmihalyi (pp. 279-298). Springer Netherlands.

Shoshani, A., Braverman, S., & Meirow, G. (2021). Video games and close relations: Attachment and empathy as predictors of children's and adolescents' video game social play and socio-emotional functioning. *Computers in Human Behavior, 114*, 1-12.

Sjöblom, M., & Hamari, J. (2017). Why do people watch others play video games? An empirical study on the motivations of Twitch users [Article]. *Computers in Human Behavior, 75*, 985-996. https://doi.org/10.1016/j.chb.2016.10.019

Skolnik, M. R., & Conway, S. (2019). Tusslers, Beatdowns, and Brothers: A Sociohistorical Overview of Video Game Arcades and the Street Fighter Community. *Games and Culture, 14*(7-8), 742-762.

Slobodskaya, H. R. (2021). Personality development from early childhood through adolescence. *Personality and Individual Differences, 172,* 110596.

Smith, M. M., Sherry, S. B., Vidovic, V., Saklofske, D. H., Stoeber, J., & Benoit, A. (2019). Perfectionism and the Five-Factor Model of Personality: A Meta-Analytic Review. *Personality and Social Psychology Review, 23*(4), 367-390.

Smythe, J. (2007). Beyond self-selection in video game play: An experimental examination of the consequences of massively multiplayer online role-playing game play. *Cyber Psychology and Behavior, 10*(5), 717-721.

Snodgrass, J. G., Lacy, M. G., Dengah Ii, H. J. F., Batchelder, G., Eisenhower, S., & Thompson, R. S. (2016). Culture and the Jitters: Guild Affiliation and Online Gaming Eustress/Distress. *Ethos, 44*(1), 50-78.

Song, W., & Fox, J. (2016). Playing for Love in a Romantic Video Game: Avatar Identification, Parasocial Relationships, and Chinese Women's Romantic Beliefs. *Mass Communication and Society, 19*(2), 197-215.

Spence, I., & Feng, J. (2010). Video games and spatial cognition. *Review of General Psychology, 14*(2), 92-104. (Video Games: Old Fears and New Directions)

Staines, D., Consalvo, M., Stangeby, A., & Pedraça, S. (2019). State of play: Video games and moral engagement. *Journal of Gaming & Virtual Worlds, 11*(3), 271-288.

Statista. (2022). *Number of sent and received e-mails per day worldwide from 2017 to 2025 (in billions).* Retrieved November 2022 from

Stavropoulos, V., Pontes, H. M., Gomez, R., Schivinski, B., & Griffiths, M. (2020). Proteus effect profiles: how do they relate with disordered gaming behaviours? *Psychiatric Quarterly, 91*(3), 615-628.

Stein, M. (1998). Jung's map of the soul: An Introduction. Open Court.

Steinkuehler, C., & Williams, D. (2006). Where everybody knows your (screen) name: Online games as "third places". *Journal of Computer☐Mediated Communication, 11,* 885-909.

Tabacchi, M. E., Caci, B., Cardaci, M., & Perticone, V. (2017). Early usage of Pokémon Go and its personality correlates. *Computers in Human Behavior*, 72, 163-169.

Tamborini, R., & Skalski, P. (2012). The role of presence in the experience of electronic games. In Playing video games (pp. 263-281). Routledge.

Taylor, J., & Taylor, J. (2009). A Content Analysis of Interviews with Players of Massively Multiplayer Online Role-Play Games (MMORPGs): Motivating Factors and the Impact on Relationships. In (pp. 613-621). Springer Berlin Heidelberg.

Teng, C.-I. (2009). Online game player personality and real-life need fulfillment. International *Journal of Cyber Society and Education,* 2(2), 39-50.

Teng, C.-I., & Han-Chung, H. (2012). More Than Flow: Revisiting the Theory of Four Channels of Flow [Article]. *International Journal of Computer Games Technology*, 1-9.

Throuvala, M. A., Janikian, M., Griffiths, M. D., Rennoldson, M., & Kuss, D. J. (2019). The role of family and personality traits in Internet gaming disorder: A mediation model combining cognitive and attachment perspectives. *Journal of Behavioral Addictions, 8*(1), 48-62.

Tolkien, J. R. R. (1937). *The hobbit or there and back again.* Houghton Mifflin Company.

Tolkien, J. R. R. (1954). *The Fellowship of the Ring.* Allen & Unwin.

Tolkien, J. R. R. (1954). *The Two Towers.* George Allen & Unwin.

Tolkien, J. R. R. (1955). *The Return of the King.* George Allen & Unwin.

Toronto, E. (2009). Time out of mind: Dissociation of the mind. *Psychoanalytic Psychology, 26*(2), 117-133.

Trepte, S., & Reinecke, L. (2010). Avatar creation and video game enjoyment: Effects of life-satisfaction, game competitiveness, and identification with the avatar. *Journal of Media Psychology: Theories, Methods, and Applications, 22*(4), 171-184.

Trepte, S., Reinecke, L., & Juechems, K. (2012). The social side of gaming: How playing online computer games creates online and offline social support. *Computers in Human Behavior, 28*(3), 832-839.

Utz, S. (2000). Social information processing in MUDs: The development of friendships in virtual worlds. *Journal of Online Behavior, 1*(1), 1-27.

Utz, S. (2003). Social identification and interpersonal attraction in MUDs. *Swiss Journal of Psychology, 6*(2), 91-101.

Utz, S., Jonas, K. J., & Tonkens, E. (2012). Effects of passion for massively multiplayer online role-playing games on interpersonal relationships. *Journal of Media Psychology: Theories, Methods, and Applications, 24*(2), 77-86.

Vahlo, J., & Hamari, J. (2019). Five-Factor Inventory of Intrinsic Motivations to Gameplay (IMG) 52nd Hawaii International Conference on System Sciences.

Van Looy, J., Courtois, C., & De Vocht, M. (2010). Player identification in online games: Validation of a Scale for Measuring Identification in MMOGs. *Media Psychology*, 197-221.

Velez, J. A., & Ewoldsen, D. R. (2013). Helping behaviors during video game play. *Journal of Media Psychology: Theories, Methods, and Applications, 25*(4), 190-200.

Virvou, M., Katsionis, G., & Manos, K. (2005). Combining Software Games with Education: Evaluation of its Educational Effectiveness. *Educational Technology & Society, 8*(2), 54-65.

Vogler, C. (2007). *The writer's journey*. Michael Wiese Productions Studio City, CA.

Wallach, O. (2020, November 23). 50 Years of Gaming History, by Revenue Stream (1970-2020). Visual Capitalist.

Warlick, C. A., Nelson, J., Krieshok, T. S., & Frey, B. B. (2018). A call for hope: The mutually beneficial integration of positive psychology and dialectical behavior therapy. *Translational Issues in Psychological Science, 4*(3), 314-322.

Whitebread, D., Basilio, M., Kuvalja, M., & Verma, M. (2012). The importance of play. University of Cambridge, Toy Industries of Europe. The importance of play.

Wilkinson, P. (2009). *Myths and legends: An illustrated guide to their origins and meanings*. Penguin.

Williams, D., Yee, N., & Caplan, S. E. (2008). Who plays, how much, and why? Debunking the stereotypical gamer profile. *Journal of Computer-Mediated Communication, 13*, 993-1018.

Wolfe, M. J. (2010). Theorizing Navigable Space in Video Games. In S. Gunzel, M. Liebe, & D. Mersch (Eds.), Logic and Structure of the Computer Game (pp. 36-62). Potsdam University Press.

Wulf, T., Bowman, N. D., Velez, J. A., & Breuer, J. (2020). Once Upon a Game: Exploring Video Game Nostalgia and Its Impact on Well-Being. *Psychology of Popular Media, 9*(1), 83-95.

Xu, Y. (2015). Effective gamification design: A literature review. The SIJ Transactions on Computer Science Engineering & its Applications (CSEA). *The Standard International Journals (The SIJ), 3*(4), 47-54.

Yang, C.-c. (2017). Motives Matter: Motives for Playing Pokémon Go and Implications for Well-Being. *Cyberpsychology, Behavior, and Social Networking, 20*, 2017.

Yee, N. (2006). The labor of fun: How video games blur the boundaries of work and play. *Games and Culture - Game Cult, 1*, 68-71.

Yee, N. (2006). The demographics, motivations, and derived experiences of users of massively multi-user online graphical environments. *PRESENCE: Teleoperators and Virtual Environments, 15*, 309-329.

Yee, N. (2006). Motivations for play in online games. *CyberPsychology and Behavior, 9*(6), 772-775.

Yee, N. (2006). The psychology of MMORPGs: Emotional investment, motivations, relationship formation, and problematic usage. In R. Schroeder & A. Axelsson (Eds.), Avatars at work and play: Collaboration and interaction in shared virtual environments (pp. 187-207). Springer-Verlag.

Yee, N., Ducheneaut, N., & Nelson, L. (2012, May 5-10, 2012). Online gaming motivations scale: Development and validation CHI'12, Austin, TX.

Young, M. E., & Cole, J. J. (2012). Human sensitivity to the magnitude and probability of a continuous causal relation in a video game. *Journal of Experimental Psychology: Animal Behavior Processes, 38*(1), 11-22.

Zarzycki, A. (2016). Epic video games: Narrative spaces and engaged lives. *International Journal of Architectural Computing, 14*(3), 201-211.

READY TO JOURNEY INTO THE

Checkpoints & Autosaves
By the time you reach the last page, you will have a guide to finding common ground with your child that will help you as a parent foster a better relationship, and maybe a new favorite hobby.

Final Fantasy
The Psychology of Final Fantasy guides gamers on a real-world quest of self-discovery so that they can surpass their own limit break.

Dungeons & Dragons
The Psychology of Dungeons & Dragons, is relevant to players, game masters, and even game designers. It applies decades of established and cutting-edge research to help readers understand how playing the game drives behaviors, shapes play, impacts relationships, and changes players once they put away the dice.

Bluey
Through expert commentary, character studies, and thematic explorations, "The Psychology of Bluey" reveals how the show's nuanced portrayal of everyday life can teach us about patience, understanding, and the joy found in life's simplest moments.

My Hero Academia
The Psychology of My Hero Academia" offers a distinctive and contemplative exploration, catering to devoted fans of the series and those intrigued by the psychological impact of storytelling.

Geek Therapy Card Deck
The Geek Therapy Card Deck helps people find balance, reduce stress, bring awareness into their lives, and be mindful in the moment allowing them to manage distress, regulate their emotions and understand life relationships using Geek Cultural Artifacts and insights found within.

GEEK PSYCHOLOGY SERIES?

Meme Life
This book seeks to explain how memes influence societies and cultures.

Pokémon
The Psychology of Pokémon guides gamers on a real-world quest of self-discovery to unravel the mysteries of the Pokémon series.

Elden Ring
Few games have loomed as large in popular video game culture in recent years as Elden Ring, a devastatingly difficult sword-and-sorcery RPG that became a bestseller when it launched on PC, PlayStation, and Xbox consoles back in February 2022.

Gamers Journey
In video games, we are asked to travel through breathtaking virtual creations, all the while collecting a limitless experience which we are fortunate enough to see, hear, and move through as we feel the unleashed joy of our play. This book will bring you through that journey yourself.

The Witcher
Uncover the secrets behind the complex motivations and behaviors of Geralt of Rivia, Yennefer of Vengerberg, and other iconic characters in this captivating exploration of the acclaimed fantasy series.

The Last of Us
In "The Psychology of The Last of Us," delve deep into the hauntingly profound narrative and characters of the groundbreaking video game that captured the hearts and minds of players worldwide.

Visit our website for the full collection of Geek Psychology Series: **shop.geektherapeutics.com**